BEING TORAH

A Teacher's Guide

Ruthy Levy, Debi Mahrer Rowe, and Melanie Berman

With Chapter Overviews by Joel Lurie Grishaver

ISBN 1-891662-67-8

©2005 Torah Aura Productions

Torah Aura Productions
4423 Fruitland Avenue
Los Angeles, California 90058
Manufactured in the United States of America

TABLE OF CONTENTS

THE *BEING TORAH* CURRICULUM

The New *Being Torah*

Being Torah, **The Student Commentary**, and this **Teacher's Guide** have all been recreated for the religious school universe as it exists twenty years later. When we first created **Being Torah**, religious schools classes met, for the most part, three days a week. Computers had not yet influenced the way we communicate and the way we learn. "No Child Left Behind" had not yet influenced the way schools were shaped and the styles of learning we emphasized. When we started reconsidering

Being Torah for a twentieth anniversary edition we took these changes and others into consideration. Among the things we did:

- Employ full color in both the educational and the graphic designs.

- Shorten the learning process by both eliminating some content and facilitating access to the big ideas in the text.

- Prioritize the material and see to it that the deep insights into the process and the nature of Torah could be reached in a more direct (and less time-consuming) process.

This Teacher's Guide was reworked to fit with the new book and student commentary. Originally the Teacher's Guide was written to work with the original Student Commentary; now the guide has been recreated to work with the new Student Commentary. Material that is no longer part of "the new process" has been moved to the end of the lessons as "additional activities."

An Introduction

Being Torah is a revolutionary tool. Teachers all over North America have had an exciting way of introducing their students to the adventure of exploring the biblical text. Over twenty years they've shared wonderful stories with us.

In St. Paul, Minnesota, a teacher passed out copies of **Being Torah** to her class and gave them a few minutes to flip through its pages. She began her introduction, "Over the course of this year, you're going to learn to love this book." She heard some whispering and stopped her presentation. One student raised his hand and explained, "We already love it."

In Los Angeles, California, one third-grade student managed to lose four copies of **Being Torah** between the time school began and winter vacation. The school principal was irate and sold him a new book, each time with a stronger warning. The morning after the first night of Hanukkah, the school principal received a phone call from this student's mother. A wonderful story unfolded. The night before, both parents and both siblings had been given copies of **Being Torah** as gifts. The "lost" books had been cleverly purchased—the student's only notion of how to procure the perfect gift.

Outside of Washington, D.C., a. substitute teacher was called at the last minute and rushed into class, unsure of the lesson that was to unfold. She didn't have to worry. The students gathered around her desk and showed her the wonderful new text they'd been using. After only a few weeks of study they showed her how to teach a **Being Torah** lesson.

Being Torah is more than a well-written and beautifully designed textbook. It is a process. It is an opportunity for transforming the Jewish classroom back to a setting where a learning community evolves and where each student finds his/her own sense of value and importance. In a review in *Pedagogic Reporter*, Arthur Kurzweil helped us to understand the real impact of what we had accomplished.

"**Being Torah**," he wrote, "will surely be called 'radical' by some, and it is, in the original sense of the word radical, going back to the root. For **Being Torah** does not teach about Torah, it teaches Torah. It invites the student: to jump in, to get involved, to study, to be Torah…The most remarkable feature of **Being Torah** is that the hero is not a biblical character, not an ancient sage, not a faceless commentator. Rather, the hero of **Being Torah** is the young person who has been given the opportunity to study Torah and to be Torah."

What is *Being Torah*?

Being Torah is a third- to fourth-grade Bible text that uses real biblical texts (in careful translation) to teach the stories in the Torah. It is designed to introduce students to the process of close reading and show them how the Torah conveys its message both in its stories and in the way its stories are told.

So why is it called *Being Torah*?

The Maggid of Mezerich used to teach his students to do more than just learn the words in the Torah; he told them to BE TORAH. **Being Torah** is a book obsessed with evoking a student's personal sense of ownership of Torah. This is done through the design—Torah is visualized through student images, through the commentaries that conjure participation in the text, and through the study process created by the exercises that lead students to discover for themselves the text's workings. In each and every sense, this book strives to go beyond mere knowledge of Torah into a participation in living Torah.

That sounds nice, but what am I supposed to teach?

For each text, there are three things to accomplish.

- First, there is mastery of the plot (in Hebrew this is called *p'shat*, the plain meaning of the text). For each story, we want students to know the characters, places and dramatic happenings.

  With the "plot" will come quests for meaning. Students will wonder about some actions. They will have positive or negative feelings about certain characters. And they will have questions. These elements will naturally lead to a search for the meaning and application of this story.

- Second, **Being Torah** allows you to look at how the story was told. For each text, students should have a sense of the way the Torah told the story, how the Torah taught its lesson. These narrative elements echo the story's message.

- Third, for each story/text, students should have a sense that they have learned at least one lesson or value they can "live" in their own experience.

Sounds good, but I don't understand this "narrative echoes" business.

Learning Torah means relearning how to slow down and move our lips when we read. To work its magic, the Torah needs to be heard, and its words need to echo and linger in our ears. The essence of **Being Torah** is the way it introduces the art of close reading. This is slow, careful reading of the text. It involves the gathering of clues, the tracing of allusions, the asking of questions and the projecting of meaning. While the text is highly inventive, it uses five basic patterns to convey its messages. The narrative process is rooted in theme and variation. Once we can recognize these elements, it becomes easy to follow the prompts and look for meaning.

MISSING INFORMATION: The Torah has a precise style of storytelling. When you read a biblical story, just about all you will find are two elements. There is the description of significant action, and there is a transcript of important dialogue. We look at events from the outside. We are forced to complete the picture. When a line of dialogue is spoken, we have to imagine the subtext; it is up to us to fill in the way it was spoken. When a person reacts to a situation, we will often be told what he or she does, while being left to project the reason or rightness of that action. As with radio drama, the burden of completion is on the audience. The Torah only records the big moments. What happens in between is often totally omitted. These holes and gaps are another way the text invites both our extrapolation and our invention.

THEME-WORD: Torah was originally an oral experience; it was created to impact a listener. To this end, the text uses the nature of the Hebrew language to maximal efficiency. Hebrew is a language that is built out of word stems (a.k.a. roots). The same two- or three-letter meaning cluster can reconstitute itself as a verb (in a number of active and passive tenses), as a number of adverbs, as a number of nouns, and as a number of adjectives. Almost every word in Hebrew can be torn down to isolate its word stem, and every word stem can manifest itself as a great number of word forms. The Torah uses this modular construction effectively.

In almost every biblical story you can find one or two word stems that are used repeatedly. Often the form or precise meaning of the word will change, but its core three-letter sound will be heard over and over. Sometimes this is complemented by the presence of sound-alike combinations. While these are often lost to the casual reader, and are repeatedly ploughed under the surface by the act of translation, they stand out clearly to one focused on hearing the text. Martin Buber and Franz Rosenzweig were the first to specifically identify this process. They labeled these repeating word stems "leading words"; for our purposes, we have relabeled them "theme-words," because they serve as a statement of the text's basic theme or purpose.

NUMBER-WORD: In the biblical universe, numbers are very important indicators. Even the casual observer knows that the numbers 7, 10 and 40 are important to the Torah. In its very careful embedding of clues within the narrative, the Torah sometimes uses the number of appearances of a word or element as a prompt. Often theme-words are found 5, 7, 10, or 12 times within a single story. Sometimes these number clues are used to establish parallels. Noah is the tenth in a family line, and so is Abram. Other times they are there to point out connections. In the story of Cain and Abel, each of their names is used a factor of 7 times; so is the theme-word "brother." While the midrash makes some use of these number patterns, the discovery of their true importance was made by Umberto Cassuto, an Italian Jew who did his scholarship in the early twentieth century.

TEXT REPETITION: As we have already noted, the Torah is very careful in its use of words. Nothing seems extra or unnecessary. Almost every construction seems purposeful and able to release some prompt toward an insight or meaning. This is often contradicted by the frequent appearance of repetitions in the text. Lists will reappear. A character will reflect upon a speech, foreshadowing its words; give the speech, repeating those words; and then report on its delivery, stating it a third time under the scrutiny of close reading. Almost every instance of a repetition reveals itself as a hidden message. When you look closely at such

Narrative Echo Posters can be found on pages 140–144. They are designed to be photocopied and used in the classroom.

a passage, something has usually been changed. There may be small additions or careful editing. The change in the text is usually the key to finding a major insight. Every time the Torah repeats material, it is putting up a flag, instructing us to note carefully the way that material is presented this time.

ECHOES: It is a mistake to think of the Torah as a collection of independent texts and stories. While you can isolate individual segments or sequences, everything is interconnected. The Torah intentionally evolves the meaning of certain words through expanding their context each time they are repeated. The word "keeper" is a perfect example. In sequence, people are told (1) to be keepers of the garden, (2) to be their brother's keeper, (3) to be the keeper of a covenant and the keepers of Shabbat, and (4) that God is Israel's keeper. Other times, a phrase or two is repeated just to link two stories, two ideas or two characters. These echoes are the Torah's way of saying, "Apply what we learned there to this situation," or "Compare these two moments." Every echo we can perceive is a clue that the Torah has revealed a nuance from which it wants us to draw meaning.

I'm impressed, but I'm no Bible scholar. I can't find these things.

Relax. You don't have to. We've built a whole series of support devices for the teacher. **Being Torah** is a curriculum that clusters three books, each of which enables your teaching process.

Being Torah: The Textbook. The textbook has been specifically constructed to prompt the discovery of these elements. In each chapter we have included one or two insights into the textual message of this story. We have prompted this by printing the key words in various colors.

Being Torah: The Student Commentary. To accompany **Being Torah**, we've developed an interactive student workbook. It guides the students through the text, helping them to identify and collect clues. Then it helps them to write their own comments about the text and collect others from their classmates.

For the teacher, **The Student Commentary** provides more than structured activities. It is built as a complete lesson for each chapter of the text. Most lessons include the set induction, the investigation, and a place where students can draw their own conclusions to guide these activities; each page has its own A-B-C organizational outline.

Being Torah: The Teacher's Guide. This volume is designed to provide you with complete resources for your teaching. On a chapter-by-chapter basis you will find both a detailing of the needed background content and helpful pedagogic supports.

O.K. You've told me a lot, but what if I need help? I'm not sure I can do all this on my own.

Fear not. Torah Aura Productions is here to help you through the process. If you would like help preparing a specific text, give us a call or drop us a note. If you would like to let us know what is wonderful or what is a pain about **Being Torah**, please give us a call. Don't worry about bugging us—we want you to be a success, and we want **Being Torah** to be a helpful tool.

How do I contact Torah Aura?

Inside California, call 323-585-7312; elsewhere call toll-free 1-800-BE TORAH. Or you can write to us at TORAH AURA PRODUCTIONS, 4423 Fruitland Avenue, Los Angeles, California. 90058. **Misrad@TorahAura.com** will also reach us.

HUGE IDEAS

Being Torah was constructed around these four ideas:

1 Every student should learn how to become a biblical commentator.

The most powerful way of making the Torah significant in the lives of our students is inviting them to see it as a series of questions to which they have found their own answers. Sometimes the process of finding answers is a process of choosing between established answers. Other times it involves truly creative efforts.

2 The Torah communicates through using established patterns.

Prior to the Torah, most religious literature was epic poetry. Torah was the first prose. It retains a lot of poetic tools that we will introduce in **Being Torah**. For example, Torah often wraps a story around a single word-core. Martin Buber noted this pattern and called such words "leading words." We follow his work and that of Rabbi Umberto Cassuto, who specialized in finding and commenting on literary patterns in the Torah. In **Being Torah** we train students to recognize the ways the Torah communicates.

3 Torah study is a dialogue that takes place in _hevruta_ and in community.

The traditional way of studying Torah is in dyads, using the conversation between partners. These partnerships are then expanded into a learning community. **Being Torah** is written to facilitate the growth of Torah communities. It helps to link students to each other.

4 Torah study takes place in a tradition.

Jews have thousands of years of experience studying the Torah. These traditions contain both questions and answers. Often there are many different answers to the same question. **Being Torah** is designed to have students begin to study Torah within the tradition. While we do not often quote Rashi or specific midrashim, we build a context, especially through the questions we reveal, for future Torah study.

THE *BEING TORAH* TEACHER'S GUIDE
Debi's Prologue

Teaching Torah is one of my favorite activities. Even when I was a child, Bible stories were special to me. The people in them lived vividly in my imagination. I "met" the prophets as a camper at a Jewish educational summer camp. Their ideals and values elevated me to a new level of awareness. As a university and graduate student I became fascinated with the intricate weavings of the words of the text. I still get goose bumps when I study and/or teach certain passages.

Our goal is for you to get equally excited—or re-excited—through your explorations and explanations of the text. A rabbi once wrote of Torah: "Let us drink and taste it, breathe and speak it, hear and see it." For us, the time of collaboration and engagement that went into the creation of this guide was dedicated to helping you to create that spirit in your classroom.

Practical Considerations

CHAPTER ORGANIZATION

NOTICE how each lesson is organized. For each chapter in **Being Torah**, this teachers' guide contains five sections: **ABSTRACT, OVERVIEW, TEACHING TOOLS, ACTIVITIES** and **ADDITIONAL LESSON SEEDS**.

The **ABSTRACT** is a quick, brief summary of the salient text elements in the chapter. Each abstract is a compact capsule of an entire lesson. Each of the major elements of the text is listed and referenced by a number, which will later correspond to the appropriate **OBJECTIVE** and still later to the correlative exercise in the Student Commentary.

The **OVERVIEW** is an introduction to the content of the Torah text you and your students are about to study. All important aspects of the text will be introduced: the story, the literary devices (**TEXT CUES**), and other information related to the text. We've taken great care to help you come to your own understanding of its meaning by including this basic "crash course" for each chapter.

In the **TEACHING TOOLS** section you will find all the significant elements of the chapter, those you'll need to plan your own (from-scratch) lessons. This includes three sections: **OBJECTIVES, SLIDE-IN VOCABULARY** and **KEY HEBREW VOCABULARY**. The **OBJECTIVES** delineate those behaviors that will demonstrate the skills and knowledge the students should have at the end of the unit. The **SLIDE-IN VOCABULARY** includes those words in the **Being Torah** text we thought might be difficult for some students. We've included simple definitions that can be slide into your presentation (without pausing for formal explanations). **KEY HEBREW VOCABULARY** lists words and phrases central to the chapter that can be added to your students' Hebrew vocabulary (even without a "reading knowledge") to build a working Judaic vocabulary. You need not know Hebrew yourself in order to help your students learn these words and phrases.

The **ACTIVITIES** section delineates step-by-step lesson plans: successful blueprints to guide you through each chapter from the first reading through the final making of meaning. Each **OBJECTIVE** is developed, weaving together the reading of the **Being Torah** chapter, the appropriate Student Commentary activities and additional activities.

ADDITIONAL LESSON SEEDS take you beyond the text and the Student Commentary. You may be directed to elements of the textbook not covered in the Student Commentary; creative lesson strategies may be suggested; further readings (or filmstrips or videos or records) may be presented. You will have the chance to pick and choose that which will be most appropriate for your students.

These lessons have been built around a specific vision of the Jewish classroom. They are designed to facilitate classroom community and transform each instructional group into a Torah circle.

LESSON STRUCTURE

Ordinary lessons are like meetings; they have beginnings, middles, and ends. Text lessons are more like conversations; they have a tendency to wander and grow with the relationship that evolves. **Being Torah** has been designed as a fusion. While it is possible to work your way through its texts verse by verse, just as in traditional text lessons, we have prepared the Student Commentary and this teacher's guide to provide a structured lesson pattern to these texts. While these structured lessons will never reveal all of the text's secrets, they do allow major features to become clear in an easily instructible manner.

Each lesson has been crafted to revolve around a five-step process.

1. SET INDUCTION: The **Being Torah** process begins with SET INDUCTION, the process of engagement. Here questions are asked, elements of the students' own experiences are brought to the classroom, and the students acquire the necessary mind-set to approach the text. Exploration is motivated.

2. READING THE TEXT: The translation and graphic design of **Being Torah** were constructed to reveal the text's inner structure, to help the reader identify theme-words and perceive echoing phrases, etc. In each chapter we have designed a process of reading the text out loud that helps to further prompt the elements that will lead to

its core meanings. You will find directions for this first encounter with the text. This first reading is designed to both raise issues and identify clues. It is only the beginning of the lesson.

3. FINDING THE CLUES: The material in the Student Commentary centers around specific questions in the text—questions the Torah itself urges us to ask. Individually, in pairs or small clusters, students explore the text (for a second time) and gather clues from which to work out their own solutions.

4. MAKING MEANING: Each chapter's exercise in the Student Commentary provides students with their own opportunity to decide on the solution that best suits their understanding of the text. With all of the clues amassed, students take time to write their own solutions/comments. Students are not simply retracing old understandings but making the text meaningful on their own terms.

5. NETWORKING COMMENTS: Students now have the opportunity to share these solutions with their classmates. Saul Wachs has taught us that real Jewish learning takes place when each student values the opinions of his/her peers as well as the teacher. We have institutionalized this process by building active listening to the comments of others into the commentary process.

The best way to clearly explain this five-part lesson is to quickly take you on a visit to a **Being Torah** classroom. Here, a lesson from chapter 7, "Abram: Leaving Home," is taking place.

Each of the twelve students has arrived carrying a suitcase, knapsack, or paper bag. Jane, the teacher, begins: "I want to know everything you know about a guy named Abram." Hands are quickly raised; information is volunteered. Jane writes each and every item on the board. Soon the board is covered with: "The first Jew," "Had camels and tents," "Smashed idols?" "Married to Sarah," etc.

This listing has taken three or four minutes.

Next Jane reviews the homework assignment. The students have been asked to bring from home three things they would take with them if they had to leave home forever. She has the students get ready to share their objects. The class goes through a minute of chaos and joking, and then groups' attention is quickly refocused. Jane goes around the circle. Each of the kids opens his or her bag and reveals the hidden treasures. There are lots of laughs: teddy bears, salamis, a tape recorder. There are also lots of poignant touches: the family candlesticks, a photo album, a most important book, etc. This portion of the lesson runs about twenty minutes, about ten minutes longer than Jane had anticipated. But because it was a warm, fun, sharing moment, she didn't rush the activity. Instead, she just shifted her lesson plan.

The plan had been to move from the students' objects to a fantasy list of what Abram and Sarai might have brought with them. Instead, Jane made a quick transition. In three sentences Jane moves into the text. "Last week we watched Terah take the family from Ur to Haran. This week, the family is on the move again. Just as you pretended to do, they are going to have to leave home. Let's open up **Being Torah** to page 56, and we'll get to see him leave home and become the first Jew."

Jane has just finished SET INDUCTION. Not only has the class been motivated to engage the text, they have also been focused into the text. They are ready to begin reading the Torah with an ear to understanding why Abram went on this pilgrimage.

Quickly Jane divides the class into three groups. She assigns one group to read the words printed in blue (Abram), another group to read the words printed in red (land), and the third group to read the words printed in green (seven lines of blessings). As the teacher, she serves as narrator and master of ceremonies. The class reads the two-page text; the blue word "Abram," the red word "land" and the green words of blessings ring out from the two groups. Before Jane has a chance to ask her regular question, "What did you hear in the text?" three hands go up. All three of them know that the word "land" is used seven times in this story. These are the best students in the class, but their insight is no miracle. After finding seven "goods" in "Beginnings," seven "covenants" in "After the Flood" and seven "brothers" in "Cain and Abel," a few of them have internalized the lesson.

READING THE TEXT took only a couple of minutes, but it has focused the rest of the lesson. Based on what was heard and perceived in this quick reading, the rest of the lesson will unfold. All of this was a simple response to the word-patterns encoded in the **Being Torah** text.

Jane writes "land" and "seven". She then asks, "What else did you hear?" Quickly, the class contributes "Adonai," "Abram," "bless," and "see"— all the prompted words. Jane carefully edits the list, writing only "bless," "Abram" and "land" on the board. She divides the class in half, asking each half to count instances of one of these words. The Abram group comes up with the word being used seven times in the text. The bless group reports five usages. Jane redirects the whole class to look at the text one more time and count not the number of times the word "bless" is used, but the number of blessings given. Within seconds every hand in the room is raised. The textbook is encoded with the blessings numbered one through seven. On board are now listed three words: land, Abram, and bless, each with the number seven. Jane then asks, "What do you think it means?" A number of answers are suggested: "Abram belongs on the land." "The land is blessed." etc.

This has been the FINDING THE CLUES section of the lesson. Here Jane has led the class to gather information about one aspect of this text, carefully editing out other valuable insights that won't lead toward the completion of this lesson's objectives. In the course of this step Jane has also prepared the class for the next step, MAKING MEANING. This whole section took only six or seven minutes.

Next Jane directs the class to open their Student Commentaries to page 23 and complete the exercise. She asks students to work with a partner. They spend about eight minutes filling in the blanks and then writing their comments. Jane circulates throughout the room, stopping to encourage and assist.

The MAKING MEANING section of this lesson is easy. Rather than breaking new ground, the written exercises in the workbook allow students to record and collate material that was already introduced and explored as a class in the previous step. At the same time, the writing of comments allows students to individualize their own reactions to this material and to develop a sense of ownership. The rehearsal of possible comments at the end of the FINDING THE CLUES stage of the lesson allowed Jane to model possible solutions without imposing any single sense of meaning.

Jane gathers the class once more. She has students share their comments. She records each and every one, along with the name of its author, on the blackboard. Then she asks students to copy one comment from one of their classmates into their Student Commentary in the section labeled "_____'s Comment." After ten or eleven weeks of class the students have the routine down. This is done quickly. Jane then reviews the lesson. Asking one last time, "So what did we learn?" she accepts a number of different comments (forgetting the one about Danny Kaufman's teddy bear, which he brought in his suitcase). She then wraps up the lesson by writing "Abram = Land = Blessing" on the board, adding, "When Abram and his family are in the Land of Israel, there is blessing." The lesson ends with some compliments, a joke, and a wish to have a good week.

In this last part of the lesson Jane has the class share their insights, each of which is affirmed. She also insures by her insistence that every student add one of his/her classmate's insights to his/her commentary that Torah is a community experience. In a **Being Torah** classroom, every student is a commentator and a teacher. Finally, in reviewing the lesson, she shapes the conclusions, making sure that the lesson's major insight has been clearly expressed and restated.

Debi's Postscript

The guidance offered here is really only a starting point. In the adventure of learning Torah together with your students, you will be the ultimate guide. Upon completion of one section of study, a student commented to me: "You know, this is easy, but it's hard." She knew that our process was in one sense easy; we explored small sections and developed concrete understandings. However, we stretched far and dug deep within our minds and hearts to do so. Her statement became a bemused rallying cry for our class. It is also our best encouragement for you. Your task will indeed be easy—teaching the delight of Torah study. The text, Student Commentary and this guide are all aids to ease the accomplishment of this task, but it will also be a challenge. Nothing truly worthwhile comes easy. Enjoy your adventure. It will be easy, hard and definitely rewarding.

Debi Rowe
Ruthy Levy
Melanie Berrnan
Sivan, 5746

AN APPENDIX OF POSSIBILITIES

Rather than projecting specific activities for each chapter, trying to anticipate the style and tone of individual classroom development, we've collected the list here, knowing that teachers can selectively employ them in their instructional process. Obviously this list is not exhaustive, merely suggestive. The best guide will clearly be your natural skill and ability. And, too, you are the best judge of your students, their needs and abilities.

Don't panic if you don't know how to do all the activities listed. Check with your principal or various school specialists for assistance.

ARTS AND CRAFTS

Bulletin board display

Class mural or frieze

"Stained-glass" pictures using tissue paper

Shoe-box diorama or shadowbox

Maps

Backdrop scenery for class decoration or for a dramatic production

Cartoons

Mobiles

Pictures: drawn, colored, pasted, cut

Graffiti

Collage

Montage

Soap carvings

Potato carvings

Finger paint, foot paint

Calligraphy

Seed/bean paintings & boxes

Modeling: clay, play dough, plaster of paris, papier-mâché

Sculpture: metal, wire, toothpicks

Mosaics: ceramic, paper, etc.

Prints: sponge, linoleum, potato, Styrofoam

Decoupage

Wall hangings

Weaving, embroidery, string art

Paper cuts

Masks

DRAMATICS

Paper bag dramatics— 4 or 5 objects in a bag that must be used in a skit

Charades

Puppet shows—from finger puppets to marionettes

Writing and/or reciting poetry

Pantomimes

Listen to and/or perform dramatic reading

Debate

Make a slide show with narration

GAMES—STUDENT-MADE AND/OR TEACHER-MADE

Guessing games

Rebuses

Mazes

Jigsaw puzzles

Concentration

Lotto

Crossword puzzles

Word searches

Scrambled words

Create-a-game

Who would have said (or who said)

Quiz show: College Bowl, Jeopardy, Hollywood Squares

Decode the message

MUSIC

Singing as a group

Listening to musical settings of biblical stories

Making up lyrics to familiar melodies

Using instrumental music for mood setting

MISCELLANEOUS

Surveys (Gallup poll)

Values clarification exercises

Make-up quizzes

Riddles

Sequence a story (or several stories) by hanging pictures on clothesline

Kinesthetic letters for Hebrew/ English vocabulary: sandpaper, cardboard, yarn, cutouts

Family trees

Interview: God, Torah, or story characters

Create a "family album" using illustrations or photographs

BIBLIOGRAPHY

TORAH STUDY

Alter, Robert. *The Art of Biblical Narrative* (New York: Basic Books, 1981).

Alter applies the principles of literary analysis as he explores the text. The examples he cites will be familiar to you.

Cassuto, Umberto. *A Commentary on the Book of Genesis* (Jerusalem: The Magnes Press, 1978). This work can be a bit tedious because of its meticulous attention to detail, but this is also its fascination and brilliance. Cassuto cross-references the full spectrum of Jewish commentary and ancient near-Eastern texts and plumbs the depths of the biblical text to make meaning.

Fox, Everest. *In the Beginning, A New English Rendition of the Book of Genesis* (New York: Schocken Books, 1983).

—*Now These are The Names, A New English Rendition of the Book of Exodus* (New York: Schocken Books, 1986).

In these translations with commentary and notes, Fox helps us hear the biblical text, its meter and sound, literary devices, echoing the original Hebrew as much as possible. Language notes are fairly extensive, historical notes briefer. Fox's work was a significant influence in the translations of *Being Torah*.

Ginzberg, Louis. *Legends of the Bible* (Philadelphia: Jewish Publication Society, 1966).

—*Legends of the Jews* (Philadelphia: Jewish Publication Society, 1909).

Leibowitz, Nehama. *Studies in Bereshit* (Jerusalem: World Zionist Organization, 1974).

—*Studies in Shemot* (Jerusalem: World Zionist Organization, 1976).

Plant, W. Gunter. *The Torah, A Modern Commentary* (New York: Union of American Hebrew Congregations, 1981).

A full Torah text, translation and commentary. Includes linear notes as well as essays and excerpts from Jewish and non–Jewish scholarship.

Silberman, Dr. A.M. and Rev. M. Rosenbaum, Translators. *Pentateuch with Targum Onkelos, Haphtaroth and Rashi's Commentary,* Genesis and Exodus volumes (Jerusalem: The Silbermann Family, 5733).

TORAH TEACHING

Good-is, Karen Lipschutz. *The Learning Center Book of Bible People* (Denver: Alternatives in Religious Education, 1981).

Grishaver, Joel. *Bible People, Books I & II* (Denver: Alternatives in Religious Education, 1980, 1981).

Grishaver, Joel. *Bible Places Ditto Pak* (Denver: Alternatives in Religious Education, 1983).

Klepper, Jeff, and Jeff Salkin. *Bible People Songs* (Denver: Alternatives in Religious Education, 1981).

Loeb, Sorel Goldberg, and Barbara Binder Kadden. *Teaching Torah: Insights and Activities* (Denver: Alternatives in Religious Education, 1997).

Simon, Solomon, and Morrison David Bial. *The Rabbis' Bible, Volume I* (West Orange, N.J.: Behrman House, 1966) and accompanying *Teacher's Resource Book.*

INTRODUCTION—Being Torah

Being Torah, pages 6-7
Student Commentary, page 3

ABSTRACT
WHAT DOES IT MEAN TO "BE TORAH"?

By reading the story of the Maggid of Mezerich students begin a discussion of the difference between knowing Torah and being Torah.

OVERVIEW

The idea of **Being Torah** is rooted in this Talmudic story (that you will not want to share in class):

Rabbi Kahana once went in and hid under Rav's bed. He heard him chatting [with his wife] and joking and doing what he required. Rabbi Kahana said to him:

Being Torah Student Commentary page 3

INTRODUCTION
Being Torah

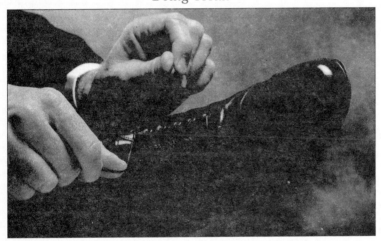

The **Maggid** was a teacher who taught, "**Don't just say words of Torah—Be Torah.**" His students used to watch him closely. They watched the way he prayed, the way he learned, the way he taught, the way he always tried to do *mitzvot*, the way he treated other people, the way he listened, and even the way he tied his shoes. They believed that they could learn some Torah from everything he did. His students constantly tried to "Be Torah" in everything they did.

Choose someone else's comment and write it here.

My Comment: If I could watch one person to learn how to "Be Torah," I would watch _____. One time when this person did something that I think is really "Being Torah" was _____ _____.

_____'s Comment:

_____ told the story of when _____ did something that was "Being Torah." That person _____ _____ _____ _____.

3

"One would think that you had never tasted this dish before!" He said to him: "Kahana, are you here? Go out, because it is rude." He replied: "It is a matter of Torah, and I must learn it." (*Brakhot* 62a)

From this story emerged the notion that Torah makes an impact on even the ordinary details of your life. This "tying shoes" Hasidic version continues an idea that we should study the life of Torah scholars to see the way they "live Torah," and that we should "be Torah" in our own lives.

TEACHING TOOLS
OBJECTIVES

1.1 Through studying the story of the Maggid of Mezerich students will express their own ideas of what it means to "be Torah" and pick an idea of their classmates' that they find compelling.

ACTIVITIES

What is the meaning of "Being Torah"?

1. READ page 6 of the **Being Torah** textbook. DISCUSS the idea of "Being Torah." Have students express their own understandings of what it means to "be Torah."

2. BREAK the class into *hevruta* pairs (dyads) and have them READ the three comments on page 7 of the **Being Torah** text. ASSIGN them to PICK the commentary they like best. DISCUSS the choices and the reasons for the choices.

3. Have the class OPEN the Student Commentary to page 3. Introduce it by saying, "Here we are going to learn more about the teachings of the Maggid and more about picking the commentaries that speak to us."

4. READ the text. Assign students to WRITE their own commentaries.

5. Have students share their commentaries. Write the name of the student and a summary of the comment on the blackboard. Assign students to pick the comment from the board that speaks to them the most and copy it into their student commentary.

6. CONCLUDE: Studying Torah is not only forming our own opinions but learning from our fellow students.

CHAPTER 1—
BEGINNINGS

Being Torah, pages 8-17
Student Commentary, pages 4-6

ABSTRACT
WHAT IS THE MESSAGE OF "BEGINNINGS"?

Follow the **THEME-WORD** "creation." It is a book-end word used in the first and last sentences of the story.

Count the number of times the **NUMBER-WORD** "good" is used. Answer: 7.

Combine these two prompted words, and they teach: All creation is good.

OVERVIEW

The real focus of this story of cosmic genesis is not "how things first got made." Ultimately what is revealed is the essence of the world in which we live.

Logically enough, the Torah opens with a story about the "Beginnings" of the world. It starts with a simple two-part message: (1) The world that we live in is the product of God's acts of creation. (2) God's creations are good. This first biblical account is more than just a story about "how things were created"; its real significance is as a description of the present reality—of "the way things are."

The Torah uses words very carefully. By their presence and by their absence, the message of the text emerges. In a story about creation, one expects to see the word "created" appear frequently. One would expect the text to read "God created this and God created that, then God created this other thing." In Beginnings the word "created" is used very sparingly, and specifically it appears only four times. In all other cases in this chapter, the verb "made" is employed.

The word "created" works like a set of bookends for this story. The story begins "BEGINNINGS: GOD CREATED THE HEAVENS AND THE EARTH." It ends, "EVERYTHING HAD BEEN CREATED." From this pair of sentences we learn that all contained between, everything on heaven and earth, everything there is, was created by God. It is also used on the sixth day. The Torah tells us, "God created people, both man and woman." People are the epitome of creation; singling them out by the use of "created" makes sense.

In addition (and causing something of a problem), the word "created" is also used on the fifth day: "AND GOD CREATED THE GREAT SEA-SERPENTS." By using "created" here, the Torah is emphasizing the fact that all living things were created by God (especially monster animals that you might consider to be other gods).

The other focal word clue in this story is the word "good." It is used seven times, though not once on each of the seven days of creation, as one might expect. This is a classic use of a theme-word whose constant repetition points us toward the story's central message. Joining these two theme-words, we learn that "creation is good."

Throughout **Being Torah** we have worked hard to present the Torah in language elementary students will understand, yet leave the text of our English "renditions" a good replica of the original Hebrew text. This story, because it is the first, contains a major exception, because we wanted to emphasize the connection between "hearing" the text and beginning to decode it. Thus we have made a major change here. In the actual biblical text God sees that it is good. Here, in order to enable choral reading (and begin this hearing/reading connection), God says "GOOD."

The Torah uses pattern and exception as one of its vehicles for prompting us to absorb a story's full meaning. In the case of the creation of people, a rich fabric of exceptions and clues points to the unique role of humanity within God's master plan. As we have seen before, one of the rare uses of the word "created" is reserved for people, in a sense equating their creation with the whole process of creation. Likewise, the word "good" is augmented after the addition of people. The sequence concludes: "God saw everything God had made. God said, 'Very good'." When God creates people, we are told something not revealed for the other acts of creation—part of God's thinking. "God said: 'Let Us make people in Our image. Let them rule over the fish and the birds, over the beasts and the creeping things." To complete our understanding of the uniqueness of people's role, the Torah restates the blessing given to the animals with an important addition. The fish and birds were told: "Be fruitful, and become many, and fill the waters and the sky." When the blessing was given to people, God added: "And master it." The literary breaks and exceptions that surround their creation reveal an image of humanity's best possible nature. People are the climax, the epitome of creation—the final act that gives meaning to the rest. Woman's and man's creation in God's image provides them with a leadership role, a responsibility for the administration of that which has been created. People have the potential and the responsibility to be "very good."

TEACHING TOOLS

OBJECTIVES

1.1 The learner will trace the THEME-WORD "created" and the NUMBER-WORD "good" to extract the central message of "Beginnings": Creation is good.

1.2 Through close reading of the text the learner will uncover three clues to use in answering the question "How was the creation of people different than that of God's other creations?" These clues will be used to write the learner's own comment (not in Student Commentary).

1.2b After listening to the comments created by classmates, the learner will write in his/her own words one Torah lesson learned from a member of his/her Torah community.

1.3 Through writing an entry in Adam's or Eve's diary, the learners will explore a sense of wonder and awe over the experience of creation.

Being Torah Student Commentary page 4

CHAPTER 1: BEGINNINGS
What is the message of "Beginnings"?

To uncover the "big" message of this story we are going to have to find a **theme-word** and a **number-word**.

Theme-Word: In every Torah story there are one or two ideas that are most important. The central idea in a story is called the "theme." The Torah has different ways of showing us a story's theme. One way it does this is by using a **theme-word**. This is a key word that is used over and over again. Another way of doing this is by using a **theme-word** at the beginning and ending of a story.

Number-Word: One special kind of **theme-word** is a **number-word**. Sometimes the Torah uses a word a special number of times in a story. Often we find a word used 5, 7, 10, or 12 times. Each of these numbers has a Jewish meaning. When we find a word used one of these numbers of times we know that the Torah wants us to see that this word teaches something important.

4

SLIDE-IN VOCABULARY

Image—very much like someone else
To master—to have control

KEY HEBREW VOCABULARY

b'reshit—beginnings (also Genesis)
tov—good
tzelem elohim—God's image

ACTIVITIES
WHAT IS THE MESSAGE OF "BEGINNINGS"?
Student Commentary, pages 4-5

Two words stand out as significant in this story—the **THEME-WORD** "**created**," which is used like bookends in the first and last sentences of this story, and the **NUMBER-WORD** "**good**," which is used seven times. By drawing our attention to these two themes, the Torah leads us to a simple conclusion. With the linking of these two themes we learn that all creation is good. This exercise will allow the student to discover this.

Being Torah Student Commentary page 5

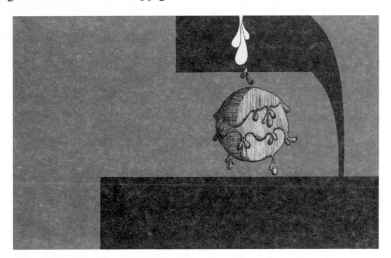

Find a Theme-Word

There is a word that you would expect to be used a lot in this story. Instead the Torah holds back and only uses it a few times. This word is used as this story's bookends. It is used at the beginning and at the end.
This word is_____*create*_____.
Hint: This word is in red.

Find a Number-Word

Count the number of times the word "good" is used in this story. It is used __*7*__ times.
Hint: This word is in blue.

This is the same number as the _____*days of the week*_____.

> **My Comment:** Two words teach us about the theme (central message) of this story.
> They are _____*create*_____ and _____*good*_____.
> Together they teach us that *creation was good, everything that God created was good*

5

1. **SET INDUCTION:** REVIEW what it means to "Be Torah." ASK: "What do you expect to learn when you study a story from the Torah?" ACCEPT all answers. WRITE on the blackboard the comment made by each student and the student's name.

INTRODUCE the lesson as the first time they will study the actual words found in the Torah. POINT OUT that this is a very special moment. SAY the *brakhah* "*She-he-he'yanu.*" EXPLAIN that this is the *brakhah* that is said anytime a Jew does something for the first time. Have the class JOIN in saying this *brakhah*.
Barukh atah Adonai, Eloheinu melekh ha-olam she-he-he'yanu, v'kiy'manu, v'hi-gi-anu laz-man ha-zeh.

2. READING THE TEXT: As NOTED above, this particular translation has been structured for oral reading. It was designed to have the teacher read the part of the biblical narrator while the children voice God's part. In this way the NUMBER-WORD "good" will stand out.

OPEN **Being Torah** to page 8. ASSIGN the class as a whole to read the parts said by God. The teacher should be the primary reader. Afterwards ASK: "What did you hear?" The ANSWER will be: "**good**." INTRODUCE the idea of a theme-word.

3. FINDING THE CLUES: TEACH or REVIEW the concepts of THEME-WORD and NUMBER-WORD. Page 4 in the Student Commentary can be used as a reference. Have students WORK in small GROUPS (or perhaps alone) to complete page 5 on their own. OPTION: Because this is the first of these exercises, you may want to work this one through as a class, helping students understand the method. MONITOR their work.

4. MAKING MEANING: The last part of page 5 in the Student Commentary asks students to combine the two clues they have found and extrapolate a conclusion.

This is the first act of "making meaning" in the text. While this may come automatically as part of completing the page, you may need to help them work it through. DISCUSS this meaning out loud before ASKING students to WRITE their answers.

5. NETWORKING COMMENTS: In future lessons we will expect different students to have found different explanations of the clues. That probably will not be the case this first time. Normally, "networking" will be a chance to share these insights.

ADAM'S OR EVE'S DIARY
Student Commentary, page 6

This exercise is the first of a series of **Being Torah** pieces in the Student Commentary that let students put themselves into biblical situations. Our concern here is to have students reach to feel the wonder of creation (as if seeing through the eyes of the first people on the first day). The idea for this particular

---

Being Torah Student Commentary page 6

Adam or Eve's Diary

Dear Diary,

It is really great to be alive. God created us on what is called "The Sixth Day." People were the last things created. Everything else came first: _____, _____, comets, stars, _____, squash, _____, blueberries, peas, _____, _____, trout, sharks, _____, _____, vultures, eagles, _____, moose, groundhogs, _____, _____, and even _____.
But God did something special for us. Every time God created something, God would see it and say "_____." When God finished creating people, out came the words "_____ _____."

Almost as soon as we opened our eyes and looked around, it began getting dark. The sun went away, and everything was black. I was very scared, and so was Eve/Adam (*circle one*). We held each other tight. I was afraid that creation was ending. I thought that God had made the world just to see what it was like, and now it was falling apart. When the stars came out I felt better. When the moon came out I knew everything was going to be okay. God had created a good world. We said our prayers and fell asleep.

The next morning we had our chance to explore the world God created. Let me tell you what we found. _____
_____
_____

When it came time for the sun to set today, I wasn't scared at all. Eve/Adam even thought the sunset was beautiful. I think God did a good job.

Until next time—

Love, _____(Adam/Eve)

6

---

fantasy is drown from a Midrash, Ecclesiastes Rabbah 728, and focused by Danny Siegel's poem "Stroll."

1. SET INDUCTION: If possible, find a copy of Danny Siegel's collection of poetry, *And God Braided Eve's Hair*. The poem "Stroll" is found on pages 78–79. Have students CLOSE their eyes and IMAGINE what it would be like to take a walk in the Garden of Eden. What would it be like to be the first man and woman alive on the first day before the first Shabbat? READ the poem.

2. FOCUS: PLAY with the poem's images. ASK: "What was the best thing you saw in your mind while I read the poem?" SHARE images and explore what it was like to see the world for the first time. What was Adam's favorite creation? What was Eve's?

3. OPEN the Student Commentary to page 6. CHECK for understanding of the concept of a diary. EXPLAIN that this exercise asks them to pretend they are either Adam or Eve and to write an imaginary diary page about their first day.

4. READ the exercise aloud. To get the juices going, allow students to CALL OUT and SUGGEST various answers for every blank. MAKE SURE this is FUN! Write some of these suggestions on the board so that the students will have a handy reference for spelling.

5. CREATING THE FANTASY: DIRECT students to decide if they want to be Adam or Eve for this exercise, and have them FILL IN the signature of the diary first. TELL students to complete the rest of the exercise.

6. NETWORKING COMMENTS: Have students SHARE their versions of this diary.

ADDITIONAL LESSON SEEDS
EXTRA LESSON: How Are People Different from Animals? (Not in Student Commentary)

Compare God's comment after each act of creation up to the creation of people with God's comment after their creation. Answer: For all other acts of creation, "good"; after people, "very good." This is a **TEXT REPETITION**.

Compare the blessing God gives to the animals, fish and birds with the blessing God gives to people. Answer: This, too, is a **TEXT REPETITION**. The same blessing is repeated with "and master it" being added for people.

No description is given for the form used for any created life except for people. Find the form used for people. Answer: "God created people in God's image."

When we put these three things together we can conclude: People were created to be special, with the potential to be very good, because they were "created in God's image."

MIDRASH T'MUNAH

Pages 8-9: The large black area is the Hebrew letter Bet, the first letter in the Hebrew word *B'reshit* (translated in the text as "beginnings"), which is the first word of the Torah. Pages 16–17: The Hebrew letters on these two pages spell Shabbat, meaning "Sabbath."

COMMENTS, *Being Torah* page 18

The Torah's comment here about the difference between "truth" and "history" is very important. It gives you a chance to look at the meaning of the Torah being "true".

CHAPTER 2—THE GARDEN

Being Torah, pages 19-28
Student Commentary,
pages 7-8

ABSTRACT
HOW DOES THE STORY OF THE GARDEN TEACH A NEW MESSAGE ABOUT CREATION?

Compare the opening sentence of each of the first two stories in the Torah. We find a TEXT REPETITION. Both use "creation" and "heavens and earth." The second story adds "family history."

Compare the focus of the two stories. The first story talks about the order of cosmic history. The second story tells of Adam's family history.

Draw a conclusion: The two stories show creation from two different angles. The second story focuses on human experience.

EATING FROM THE TREE

When we look at the process of eating from the tree we learn that a TEXT REPETITION reveals a secret. First God says, "**You may not eat from it** (the tree in the middle of the garden)." When the snake asks, "Did God really say that **you may not eat** from any of the trees in the garden?" Eve answers, "God said, 'The tree in the middle of the Garden, **you may not eat from it** and **you may not touch it.'**"

When Adam and Eve do eat from the tree, the Torah teaches that (1) "**she took a fruit**, and (2) **she ate from it.**"

When Eve adds to the TEXT REPETITION by saying "**and you may not touch it**," she sets herself up to be fooled by the snake.

OVERVIEW

The story of the Garden is really a story of evolution that looks at trials and tribulations through which people evolve with maturity and independence.

The story of the Garden presents a second story of creation. Through close reading we can easily find how the Torah separates the differing focus of these two tales. The first sentence of each story provides the clue.

Story 1—"Beginnings: God created the heavens and the earth."

Story 2—"This is the family history of the heavens and the earth."

The first tale is a cosmic tale. While people are important to that story, their importance is in their relationship to the rest of created order. This second story has a human focus. Here the heavens and the earth and the rest of creation are viewed in terms of their importance to humanity.

The central issue in this story is maturity. Unlike many Christian readings, sin is not an important element here. In this story we are exploring the evolution of people. We move from embryonic stages to human relationships, from dependence to independence, from innocence to experience, from being like children to becoming parents.

At some level, everyone who studies this passage has a problem with what seems to be its message. It seems very clear that the Torah (and God) feels that it is bad that Adam and Eve disobeyed God's word. We intuitively think that "knowing good from evil" is a good thing. Given the choice between being totally cared for in the Garden and the intellectual freedom and self-reliance of the post–Garden experience, it is human nature to opt for the latter. And the nature of human nature may indeed be the ultimate message of this story.

Hidden in the theme-word of this story is a wonderful insight—human behavior and global ecology are directly connected. The word "soil," out of which the HUMAN was made, also forms the root of ADAM's name. It is people's essence. At the end of the story God tells Adam: "The ground will be cursed because of you. You will have to sweat and work for your bread until you return to the soil from which you were taken." It is ADAM's behavior that changes the relationship between people and the environment. His corrupt behavior makes it more difficult to grow crops. For the Torah, the ethical and natural order are directly related. We will see this same theme recur with Cain and with Noah.

It is worth noting that the Torah inverts the word pair "dust" and "soil" at the end of the story. Biblical scholars call this a chiasmus; we've labeled it an "x-pattern." This is another device the Torah uses to focus our attention on particular keyword ideas.

The story ends with trade-offs. People will die, but death is a force that gives people's life meaning. Birth will cause pain, but parenthood will provide joy and purpose. People must work for food, but work invites invention, industry and satisfaction. The Garden has been lost, but in its place is an open environment that can be designed and fashioned. The relationship with God has been strained, but *t'shuvah* (rapprochement) is now possible.

TEACHING TOOLS
OBJECTIVES

By comparing the first sentence of Beginnings and The Garden, the learner will identify the differing focuses of these two accounts of creation.

Being Torah Student Commentary page 7

CHAPTER 2: THE GARDEN
The Garden Teaches a New Message About Creation

Text Repetition: When the Torah repeats a piece of text, it usually does it with a change. When the Torah says something twice, the second time we see the message there is usually a change. Something is either added or taken away. When we find the change we have a clue to the meaning the Torah is trying to teach us.

In Chapter 1 we learned that God created a good universe.
In the story of the The Garden we get a different message about the beginning.

Find the Change: The Torah begins (Being Torah page 9)

Beginnings:
God created the **heavens** and the **earth**.

The story of The Garden begins: (Being Torah page 19)

This is the **family-history** of the heavens and the earth from their creation.

The thing that these two "beginnings" share is talking about:

The ___**heavens**___ and the ___**earth**___ .

What was added to the second version was: ___**family history**___ .

My Comment: I think that the Torah added ___**family history**___ to the second story to teach us this difference between the two stories. **Beginnings** teaches us about the creation of the universe. **The Garden** will teach us about **the first biblical family, the beginnings of a family that will eventually become the Jewish people, our family history** .

7

By tracing the repetitions of "not eating" from the tree in the middle of the Garden the learner can see how the snake fooled Eve and then Adam.

SLIDE-IN VOCABULARY
knowledge of good from evil—telling right from wrong
commanded—ordered

KEY HEBREW VOCABULARY
dam—blood
adam—human (ADAM)
adamah—soil
etz hayim—tree of life
etz lada'at tov v'rah—tree of the knowledge of good from evil

ACTIVITIES

The Garden consists of one chapter broken into three subsections. This is a compromise. While the whole story constitutes a single literary unit, our awareness of the attention span of the youngest readers using **Being Torah** has led us to break the story into three short segments.

HOW DOES THE STORY OF THE GARDEN TEACH A NEW MESSAGE ABOUT CREATION?
Student Commentary, page 9

The first story of creation tells the story of the creation of the heavens and the earth. This story repeats that idea, with a change. Here we are told the story of the "family history of the heavens and the earth." The phrase "family history" has been added. "Beginnings" tells us about the cosmic order; "The Garden" introduces the genesis of people.

1. SET INDUCTION: REVIEW the idea of TEXT REPETITION with your students. MAKE SURE they can state the concept in their own words.

    EXPLAIN that in this second chapter we will also be reading about creation. ASK: "What will you look for if you know this whole story is a TEXT REPETITION?" ESTABLISH that they will need to check for changes, specifically additions or subtractions.

    ASK: "Why are there two stories about creation?" ESTABLISH: "If the Torah repeats something, there is something to learn from the repetition. Each story must have something special to teach."

3. READING THE TEXT: The story of the Garden is not a theme-word–centered text. Little can be gained from a specific collective reading. We suggest that you use the opportunity to read it very slowly in small sections, getting a chance to dwell on some of the word pictures that evolve. Depending on the oral reading skills of your class, this may be a good opportunity to allow students to read short sections.

    OPEN **Being Torah** to page 19 and read through page 22.

3 FINDING THE CLUES: This is the second story you've

worked on. Students should be developing skill at working in groups and solving problems. DIVIDE the class into groups of 3 or 4 students. DIRECT students to complete the exercise on page 7 of the Student Commentary and then SHARE answers.

4 MAKING MEANING: DISCUSS the differences in the two stories. ESTABLISH that the first story details the creation of everything on earth, with people being created last. This story skips most of the details except for the creation of people. ASK: "What new messages about Creation does The Garden teach?" SOME ANSWERS include: "People help God with creation," "It is not good for people to be alone," "People are supposed to be keepers."

YOU MAY WANT TO SHARE this midrash.

The rabbis taught: "When God made Adam, God collected dust from the four corners of the earth: white sand, rich black soil, red and yellow clay."

WORK TOGETHER in groups to figure out the message of this midrash.

Being Torah Student Commentary page 8

Eating from the Tree

Find the Change: First God gives a rule about eating from the Tree of Knowledge. Then Eve retells this rule to the snake. In the retelling there is a change.

When God put the Human in the garden, God said:

"You may eat from every other tree in the garden
except from the Tree of the Knowledge of good from evil.
You may not eat from it.
Once you eat from it, you must die."

The snake asked the woman:

"Did God really say that you may not eat
from any of the trees in the Garden?

The woman answered the snake:

"We may eat the fruit from any of the other trees
in the garden, but God said,
'The fruit from the tree in the middle of the Garden
you may not eat it and **you may not touch it**,
or you will die.'"

1. God ordered: *Not to eat from the center tree* .
2. The snake asked: *Can't you eat from any tree?* .
3. Eve's change was: *We can't eat and we can't touch the fruit from the center tree.*

My Comment: Eve made a mistake. The Torah teaches that she "(1) **took a fruit** and (2) **ate it.**" Eve's change to God's commandment was adding ___ *we can't touch the fruit.* .

When nothing happened after she broke the made-up part of the commandment, Eve went on to *eat it and give it to Adam to eat.* .

The lesson we can learn is _____
_____ .

8

BEFORE going on, READ pages 24 and 25 of **Being Torah**. The work in the Student Commentary does not focus on the details of this section. CHECK for understanding of the story sequence so far.

EATING FROM THE TREE
Student Commentary, page 8

1. OPEN to page 8 in the Student Commentary. We will not be using the textbook for this piece of learning.

2. Review the idea that with TEXT REPETITION we look for the changes—things that were added and things that were taken away.

3. Break the class into two groups and a single student. Have the single student read the black lines, one group read the red lines and the other group read the green lines. PERFORM the text and then go to the questions at the bottom.

    1. God ordered: "Not to eat from the center tree."

    2. The snake asked: "Can't you eat from any tree?"

    3. Eve's change was: "We can't eat and we can't touch the fruit from the center tree."

4. Have students WRITE their own comments. SHARE comments, RECORDING each on the board. You may want students to vocalize which other comments they really like.

ADDITIONAL INSIGHT: WHERE DO PEOPLE COME FROM?

Abstract

Trace the THEME-WORD "soil." You will find: (a) God made Adam from the "soil"; (b) as a punishment Adam and Eve find the "soil cursed"; and (c) when people die, "they return to the soil."

The Hebrew word for soil is ADAMAH. Find the root words. Answer: ADAM, the first man's name and the Hebrew word for people; DAM, the Hebrew word that means blood.

Draw a conclusion: People are connected to the soil. Their relationship with the environment is tied to their behavior.

Objective

Through close reading of the text and the manipulation of the ADAMA CARDS, students will explain the relationship between the Hebrew words for "blood," "soil" and "human".

Activities

The Hebrew THEME-WORD ADAMA (soil/HUMAN/ADAM) teaches one of this story's essential lessons, a lesson we will relearn regularly throughout the Torah. People are connected to the soil. People's behavior affects their relationship to the soil. The culmination of this relationship comes in the giving of the land of

This is the family history of the heavens and the earth
from their creation.
On the day when Adonai God made earth and heaven,
there were no bushes and there were no plants growing,
because Adonai God had not yet made rain.
There was no Human to till the soil.

The Garden (Genesis 2:4b-25)

Adonai God formed Adam from the dust of the soil
and breathed into his nose the breath of life.
Adam came alive.

19

Israel to the people of the covenant.

1. SET INDUCTION: Have students OPEN **Being Torah** to pages 19–22. ASK: "Pick the one word you think is most important in this story." WRITE the list of words on the blackboard. Expect God, GOOD and TREE to be among the choices. If ADAM, HUMAN and soil don't make the list, then try a second round of suggestions. ASK: "What is the connection between soil and people?" ANSWER: "Adonai God formed ADAM from the dust of the soil."

2. READING THE TEXT: DIRECT students to the last part of this story, pages 24–25 in **Being Torah**. ASK them to watch how the same words, dust and soil that were important at the beginning of this story (pages 19–21) are used here at the end. READ the last part of the story. ASSIGN one student to read God's words, another to read

the part of ADAM. Have the rest of the class serve as a chorus and read the words in bold.

3 ESTABLISH (1) that people are connected to the soil (because they are made from the dust of the soil), and (2) that people's behavior affects the earth. People can make land that should be able to feed many people turn into a desert, and vice versa. DISCUSS how people can make the earth a better or worse place.

5 NETWORKING COMMENTS: SHARE comments and have students write down comments from a classmate. ENABLE this process by recording comments on the board and allowing students to copy. SHARE the restatement of the comments, too. This is a place to REINFORCE the value of the class being a "TORAH COMMUNITY" learning from one another.

COMMENTARIES

The first comment allows one to explore the Garden of Eden as a mythic setting. As we've done with the diary in the previous chapter, it is possible to visit this garden in our imagination. Art projects (creating the trees), drama (with guided tours), etc. are suggested.

The second comment about "the battle of the sexes" triggers an issue that is often raised here. The exercise "People" on page 13 of *Bible People, Vol. I.* (Joel Lurie Grishaver, A.R. E., Denver, 1980) would be a good way of exploring this value question.

The third comment about growing up is reminiscent of the chapter entitled "The First Parent Had Trouble Too," in Bill Cosby's book *Fatherhood*. This would make a good text to read and enjoy with your students. This story provides you with a chance to talk and explore the difference between kids and grownups.

MIDRASH *T'MUNAH*

The art on pages 20 and 23 of **Being Torah** is an expression of Hebrew words as ideas. The word ADAM shows Adam being created from the dust of the soil. The words *Etz Hayyim* are indeed a living tree. You may want to give your students a chance to play with Hebrew letters, making a person out of ADAM and a tree out of *Etz Hayyim*.

CHAPTER 3—CAIN AND ABEL

Being Torah, pages 26–28
Student Commentary, pages 9-10

ABSTRACT
WHAT IS THE BIG MESSAGE OF THIS STORY?

Find the THEME-WORD in this story. Answer: "brother"

Count how many times it is used. Answer: 7 (which also wakes it a NUMBER-WORD)

Count how many times Cain's name is used. Answer: 14 (two 7s)

Count how many times Abel's name is used. Answer: 7

Draw a conclusion: Brotherhood is "good." The "keeping" of a brother-sister is a basic human obligation.

OVERVIEW

This is a story about the dark side of human nature, directing us to the pain and hurt we can cause both to others and to ourselves when we lose control.

For our purposes, the story of Cain and Abel presents an ideal training ground for developing biblical "attack" skills. Almost the entire repertoire of tools and patterns with which we are trying to equip our students is directly applicable here.

The story of Cain and Abel is a perfect biblical mystery. The text tells us exactly what happened but doesn't begin to fully explain why.

> Cain and Abel are both born; only Cain's name is explained.
>
> Cain and Abel both make gift-offerings to God, but God accepts only Abel's offering.
>
> God warns Cain to "master" his anger but doesn't command him not to hurt or kill.
>
> Cain kills Abel after a conversation that isn't recorded.
>
> God asks Cain where Abel is when God already knows that answer.

By and large, this is the Torah's teaching style. It shows us a set of snapshot-like action clips and asks us to make sense of them. The Torah draws us into its process by enticing us to complete the lesson.

Snapshot # 1—The Births

> ADAM knew his wife EVE.
> She became pregnant and gave birth to CAIN.
> She said: CAIN means I got a man with God's help.
> Later on she gave birth to ABEL, his brother.

The name CAIN is the clue to a basic biblical message. Every child is the result of three partners: the father, the mother, and God. Eve's statement affirms this:

Chapter 3 *Cain and Abel* Genesis 4.1–26

Adam knew his wife Eve.
She became pregnant and gave birth to Cain.
She said: "Cain means I got a man with God's help."
Later on she gave birth to Abel, his brother.

Abel became a shepherd. Cain farmed the soil.

When time passed,
Cain brought the fruit of the soil as a gift-offering for Adonai.
Also Abel brought the best firstborn of his flock.

Adonai accepted Abel and his gift,
but Cain and his gift Adonai didn't accept.

29

"I got a man with God's help." We will see this over and over again. Many of the key figures in the Bible, including Isaac, Jacob, Joseph, Samson, and Samuel, have mothers who have great difficulty in getting pregnant. Each of these births echoes this basic vision that God is a partner in the birth of each child.

The theme-word "brother" dangles out of place at the end of this section. Our expectation would be for Eve to correlate Abel's birth back to God or to Adam, her husband. Instead, the Torah only references Abel's birth to his brother. This seems to be a clear marker showing us that the relationship between brothers is to be the story's central focus.

Snapshot #2

When time passed,
CAIN brought the fruit of the soil
as a gift-offering for Adonai.
Also ABEL brought the best firstborn of his flock.
The LORD accepted ABEL and his gift,
but CAIN and his gift Adonai didn't accept.
CAIN grew angry.
His face fell.

The two brothers bring burnt offerings. Our first impression is that their actions are parallel and that God acts capriciously in accepting one and rejecting the other. At once an inner voice cries out, "That is unfair. How could God do that?" This reaction is exactly what the Torah wanted to evoke. We want an explanation; we need an explanation, so we go back and closely reread the text. Suddenly a clue and an explanation emerge.

CAIN brought the fruit of the soil…
ABEL brought the best firstborn of his flock.

One word stands out and breaks the parallel. One word reveals a substantive difference. We learn that Abel offered the best of what he produced. By contrast we learn that Cain only brought "some fruits." Suddenly, God's action is understandable—God wants our best.

Snapshot #3

While we now understand God's reaction, Cain doesn't. He is angry. God talks to him.

"Why are you angry? Why has your face fallen?
When you are good, aren't you lifted up?
But when you don't do good, sin haunts your door, ready to tempt you.
But you can master it."

At first the dialogue seems cryptic. If God is going to talk to Cain, our first expectation is that the dialogue should be more obvious and more direct. Again our expectation isn't fulfilled; the speech demands a careful, close rereading.

Instead of saying, "I know that you are angry because I rejected your offering," God asks a question: "Why are you angry?" This question triggers an echo. Back a chapter, God asks a similar question. God asks Adam and Eve, "Where are you?" Then God asks, "Who told you that you were naked? Did you eat from the forbidden tree?" The echo connects these passages. By assembling all of these questions, we find a pattern. God uses questions to teach.

The second question, "When you are good, aren't you lifted up?" also has to be coaxed to reveal its content. God's message has two levels. The question is rhetorical. The message is simple—doing good is rewarded. The application immediately goes back to the sacrifice. Through a question, God is trying to lead Cain to the understanding "If you had brought your best as a gift offering, you would have been rewarded."

God then drops out of the question mode. God makes a statement—"Your sins will haunt you." It is a warning—a direct warning.

Finally, God ends with a pep talk. "YOU can master it (the 'sin' your emotions are driving you to commit)." The word "master" is programmed to trigger a reaction. It is a clear echo of God's blessing to Adam and Eve upon their creation "to fill the earth and master it." We learn (by connection) that mastering the world involves mastering the self. It must be noted here that this [ECHO] has been overstated in the **Being Torah** translation. In the actual text, the connection is conceptual. In Beginnings, the Hebrew is *kiv-shuhah,* which means "master" in terms of conquering or subduing. Here God employs *timshol bo,* "master it" in the sense of limit or control. We have used "master" to replace both words.

Snapshot #4

CAIN said something to his brother ABEL.
When they were in the field,
CAIN rose up upon his brother ABEL
and killed him.

Cain is guilty. Before the murder there is a fragment of conversation Cain speaks to his brother. The sentence is truncated. The murder takes place without explanation. We are left to extrapolate.

Again the word "brother" stands out as a signpost. In the midst of Cain's cry of anger, in the middle of the murder, the Torah uses the word "brother." In contrast to the violence of the story, the narrative underlines the relationship that should have been.

Snapshot #5

Adonai said to CAIN:
"Where is your brother ABEL?'
He said: "I don't know.
Am I my brother's keeper?"
God said: "What have you done?
The voice of your brother's bloods
shouts to me from the soil.
From now on, you are cursed from the soil
because the soil opened its mouth
to take your brother's bloods from your hand."

Again God starts with a question. The echo is renewed. The word "brother" is again underscored—the sin is given a chance to haunt.

Cain asks, "Am I my brother's keeper?" For the reader, an alarm goes off. Cain has made a connection to the brother relationship. The word "keeper" also echoes, recalling God's definition of human responsibility (to the Garden) "to work it and to keep it." Through Cain's denial of these connections we learn of their ultimate importance. Through the story we have been trained to answer, "Yes, people are responsible to keep brothers and sisters."

Finally, God brings the final message. "The voice of your brother's bloods shouts to me from the soil." Another echo sounds. We learned in the story of the Garden that Adam was made from the dust of the soil. From conception people are connected to the earth. At the end of that story, God tells Adam and Eve: "Because you ate from the forbidden tree, the soil will be cursed because of you." Human actions have ecological implications.

Hindsight

Woven into the text of this story are three words used a specific number of times. The theme-word "brother" is used 7 times, further emphasizing its importance. Cain's name is used 14 times (a factor of 7), and Abel's name is also used 7 times. Together they underline the connection that should have existed.

TEACHING TOOLS

OBJECTIVES

The students will identify the THEME-WORD "brother" as one key to discovering the main message of this story.

The students will express some of the feelings of living with the consequences of a wrongful act by creating an entry in Cain's diary.

SLIDE-IN VOCABULARY

gift-offering—a thank-you present

haunts—what a ghost does

Chapter 3 **Cain and Abel** Genesis 4.1–26

Adam knew his wife Eve.
She became pregnant and gave birth to Cain.
She said: "Cain means I got a man with God's help."
Later on she gave birth to Abel, his brother.

Abel became a shepherd. Cain farmed the soil.

When time passed,
Cain brought the fruit of the soil as a gift-offering for Adonai.
Also Abel brought the best firstborn of his flock.

Adonai accepted Abel and his gift,
but Cain and his gift Adonai didn't accept.

29

HEBREW VOCABULARY

shomer aḥi—brother's keeper
yetzer ha-tov—urge to do good
yetzer ha-ra—urge to do bad

ACTIVITIES

This story is the first time that we will see all of the Torah's literary devices fully employed. This is a text where active listening can be a major vehicle for motivating close reading.

WHAT IS THE "BIG MESSAGE" OF THIS STORY?
Student Commentary, page 9

The story of Cain and Abel is a story about sibling rivalry; it dwells on the consequences of anger and conflict. To contrast the violence and to direct us toward its message, the Torah embeds the THEME-WORD "brother" seven times in the text. It also uses Cain's name 14 times (two sevens) and Abel's name seven times. This connection of the two brothers and the state of brotherhood is one key to meaning. The centrality of the ideal brother–sister relationship stands in marked contrast to the violence that emerges. When Cain asks, "Am I my brother's keeper?" we know with surety that the answer is yes.

1. **SET INDUCTION:** ASK How is studying Torah like being a detective? ACCEPT all answers. ESTABLISH that Torah study is a process of finding hidden clues and then figuring out what really happened. POINT OUT that in studying the story of Cain and Abel, we are going to have to be detectives figuring out a murder mystery. When we read this story, we know that Cain killed Abel. Our job is to figure out why.

2. **READING THE TEXT:** In reading this story, ASSIGN one group to read the words in **red**. ASSIGN a second group to read the words printed in **blue**. ASSIGN a third group to read the words printed in **green.** As teacher, READ the remainder of the text. READ the whole text. Then ASK: "What did you hear?" ANSWERS will include CAIN, ABEL and brother. ASK: "What do you think is the most important word in this story?" EXPECT answers like "God" and "murder." (In none of our test classrooms did the word we most expected—"keeper"—emerge).

3. **FINDING THE CLUES:** TURN to page 9 in the Student Commentary. DIVIDE the class into Torah circles (three/four students in a group). EXPLAIN to them that as a group they will work together, listening to each other and solving problems. By asking them to write the comments and ideas of other members we are developing listening skills, skills of cooperation, and a reinforced understanding that there is more than one right answer to issues in the text. We are fostering cooperative individuality.

EDITOR'S NOTE: When the term Torah circle was first introduced in the Student Commentary, it was intended to represent an ideological comment about the class. We saw it as a way of defining the class as a Torah circle or a Torah community. In developing the teacher's resources, Ruthy immediately understood it as a pedagogic methodology. Both understandings are helpful. Have the groups COUNT the number of times that "brother" is used. ANSWER: 7. ASK: "What is the THEME-WORD of this story?" ANSWER: "brother." (You may have to review the concept of a theme-word.) THEN SAY: "Because it is used seven times, it is also a NUMBER-WORD. The Torah really wants us to

---

Being Torah Student Commentary page 9

CHAPTER 3: CAIN AND ABEL
What is the Big Message of This Story?

A Number-Word Pattern

Count the number of times that Cain's name is used. _____ **14**

Count the number of times that Abel's name is used. _____ **7**

Count the number of times that the word brother is used. _____ **7**

My Comment: The pattern I see is ____ *all three things, Cain, Abel and* *brother are used a multiple of 7 times* .

I think the connection between these words and the word "**good**" in the story **Beginnings** is *they are all used 7 times* _____ _____ .

By connecting these names and words with the number _**7**_ I think that the Torah is trying to teach *that they are* *connected. Being a brother is good.* _____ .

_____ Choose someone else's comment and write it here.

_____'s **Comment:**
_____ thinks that the Torah connected all these words with the number _____ in order to teach the lesson that _____
_____
_____
_____
_____ .

9

know that this word is important:" Direct students to work in SMALL GROUPS to COMPLETE both exercises on page 9 of the Student Commentary.

4. NETWORKING COMMENTS: After the students have FINISHED their work, each circle should report to the class the results of their mutual efforts. The reporting should stress, "My Torah circle found…, counted…," etc. The report should include differing opinions. This is a methodology you will wish to employ periodically.

CAIN'S DIARY
Student Commentary, page 10

This diary entry focuses on Cain's feelings after the murder. It deals with guilt and loneliness. It provides lots of room for fantasy. The teacher may find that David Max Eichhorn's book *Cain: Son of the Serpent* (Rossel Books, Chappaqua, NY 1985) will be a wonderful resource. It is a weaving of the entire midrashic

tradition on Cain, doing for this story what S. Spiegel and *The Last Trial* do for the binding of Isaac.

1. **SET INDUCTION:** READ to students the big-type sections in chapter 16 of *Cain, Son of the Serpent*. This is a fictionalized version of the midrashim about his wandering. EXPLAIN that this is just what one author thought Cain's wandering might have been like.

2. **MAKING MEANING:** INTRODUCE this diary page as a chance for students to make up their own versions of what Cain's life might have been like after the murder. Students should work individually on this task.

3. **NETWORKING COMMENTS:** SHARE the finished exercises as a whole class, or within Torah circles.

4. **EXTENSION:** This material suggests a number of creative activities, such as interviewing Cain, designing an original "sign" that God put on his head, holding a murder trial, etc.

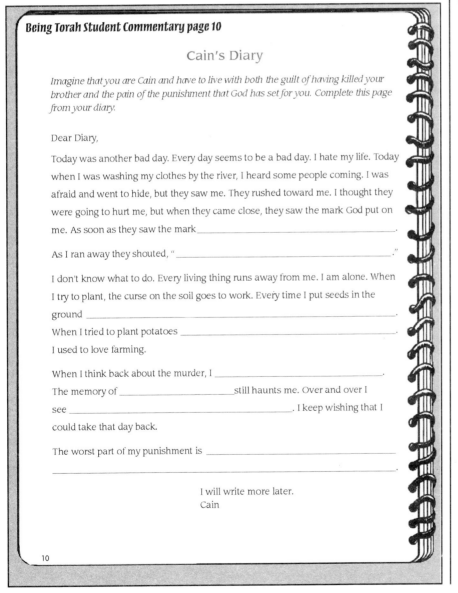

Being Torah Student Commentary page 10

Cain's Diary

Imagine that you are Cain and have to live with both the guilt of having killed your brother and the pain of the punishment that God has set for you. Complete this page from your diary.

Dear Diary,

Today was another bad day. Every day seems to be a bad day. I hate my life. Today when I was washing my clothes by the river, I heard some people coming. I was afraid and went to hide, but they saw me. They rushed toward me. I thought they were going to hurt me, but when they came close, they saw the mark God put on me. As soon as they saw the mark _____.

As I ran away they shouted, " _____."

I don't know what to do. Every living thing runs away from me. I am alone. When I try to plant, the curse on the soil goes to work. Every time I put seeds in the ground _____.

When I tried to plant potatoes _____.

I used to love farming.

When I think back about the murder, I _____.

The memory of _____ still haunts me. Over and over I see _____. I keep wishing that I could take that day back.

The worst part of my punishment is _____

_____

I will write more later.
Cain

10

ADDITIONAL INSIGHT THE "KEEPER" [ECHO]

Compare how the word "keeper" is used in both the story of the Garden and the story of Cain and Abel. In the Garden, God puts people on the earth to "work" it and to "keep" it. In this story we learn (from Cain's question) that people must "keep" their brothers/sisters. Draw a conclusion from this [ECHO]: People are supposed to be keepers. Keeping is a prime human task.

Objectives

Students will trace the "keeper" from the Garden to Cain and Abel.

The "Keeper" [ECHO]

Student Commentary, page 10

In this section we discover the next of the text's literary devices, [ECHO], a word or phrase that bounces from story to story, conjuring the images of all the previous times we have heard it adding new layers to our understanding with each iteration. Specifically, we hear an [ECHO] of the word "keep" from the Garden. Now we are keepers not only of our environment, but of people as well.

1. **SET INDUCTION:** If possible, TAKE YOUR STUDENTS to a place where a true [ECHO] can be heard. If not, try to find a recording of sounds echoing. ASK students what they heard. How does an echo sound? Are things the same? Do they change? ESTABLISH that words in the Torah do the same thing. We can hear them over and over again, always reminding us. In this section we are going to listen for an [ECHO].

2. **FINDING THE CLUES:** Have students put one finger in page 20 of **Being Torah**.

   Read the middle paragraph.

   Adonai God put the Human in the Garden of Eden,
   to work it and to keep it.

   Then turn to page 31 and read the text.

   Adonai said to Cain:
   "Where is your brother Abel?"
   He said, "I don't know. Am I my brother's keeper?"

3. **MAKING MEANING:** POINT OUT the connection between the two verses. Ask "What is the answer to Cain's question?" ESTABLISH that people are supposed to be each other's keepers. ASK: "How do we know that answer is correct?" EXPECT: "Just because" and a lot of floundering. ESTABLISH: "God ordered us to be keepers back in the Garden."

4. NETWORKING COMMENTS: AS A CLASS, share responses. As a class, or in small groups, students can now GENERATE A LIST of many things they can do as keepers. FOCUS THEIR work by directing their attention to the various settings in which they find themselves: school, home, religious school, scout troops, etc.

ADDITIONAL LESSON SEEDS

COMMENTARIES

David's comment raises the question of God's fairness. It suggests a discussion of "Is God fair?" It is a big question, but one that is very important. Harold Kushner's book *When Bad Things Happen to Good People* will be a valuable resource.

Philip's comment focuses on controlling anger. This is a good chance to share feelings. *Pirke Avot 4.1* will provide a good discussion trigger. Rabbi Tarfon teaches "Who is strong? One who can conquer/master his/her own evil impulses."

MIDRASH *T'MUNAH*

Page 32: When you look at Cain, you see that he is all alone. This is the loneliness that he himself called the real suffering in his punishment.

CHAPTER 4— AND INTRODUCING NOAH

Being Torah, pages 34–37
Student Commentary, pages 11–13

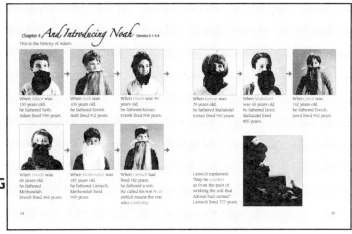

ABSTRACT

WHY DOES THE TORAH SPEND TIME LISTING THE NAMES OF PEOPLE AND THE NUMBERS OF YEARS THEY LIVED?

Count the number of generations from Adam to Noah. Answer: 10

Count the number of times God speaks to create in the story "Beginnings." Answer: 10

Explain this NUMBER-WORD connection: A 10 is a prompt that something is a new creation. The Noah story is the story of a second creation.

WHAT IS A "COMFORTER"?

Find the meanings of the names Adam, Eve, and Noah. Adam's name means "soil"; Eve's name means "life-giver"; Noah's name means "comforter."

What do these three names teach us about names in the Bible? Answer: Biblical names teach lessons; they explain something important about the person. In the Bible, people live up to their names.

Explain the name "Noah." God was angry at people because they weren't doing what was right. God cursed the soil. Noah's father wanted the soil to be uncursed. He hoped his son would make God comfortable with people again.

GOD WALKING

Find the [ECHO] of the word "walking" between the Garden and the Flood. In the Garden, "God walks in the Garden." In the Flood, "Noah walks with God."

Draw a conclusion: Walking is a metaphor for God coming close to people. When the Torah says "Noah walked with God," it suggests both a coming close and a following of God's prescribed way.

DID THE FLOOD DO ANY GOOD?

Find the THEME-WORD in the last three paragraphs of the Noah story (10, 11, and 12). Answer: "covenant." Count how many times it is used. Answer: 7 times.

Compare the blessings God gave Adam and Eve in "Beginnings" with the blessing that God gives to Noah. This is a TEXT REPETITION [-]. The blessing is exactly the same, except "and mastered" has been removed.

Draw a conclusion: The flood is a new beginning. The idea of people being masters has been replaced with a covenant (and partnership) between God and people.

OVERVIEW

The Noah story introduces the idea of a covenant between God and humanity. It is the story of the recreation of the world, a recreation directed toward changing people's original mission of mastery into a covenantal partnership.

On one level, the Torah is the record of God's three attempts to shape the course of human development. The first attempt was the original creation. Given the behavior of Adam and Eve, Cain and the generation of the flood, it wasn't a success. The story of Noah is the story of a readjustment. It is the story of a second creation. God destroys all that has evolved and starts again from the beginning. Just like Adam and Eve, Noah and family are a single unit responsible for repopulating the earth. This is God's second attempt to direct history. As we close-read this story we can uncover and collect a series of clues that reveal the essence of this new beginning.

This second creation was also less than fully successful. When Creation needs a third beginning, no new destruction will be forthcoming. The slate can never again be wiped clean. A third recreation is not possible. As a culmination of the Noah story, God promised that never again would the earth be destroyed. God can't destroy and rebuild. Another solution must be found. God's third attempt at improving human behavior involves the new tool first introduced with Noah. This time the covenant is to be upgraded and given a more substantial role.

God's unique relationship with Abram is begun through a deal made with one family. God intends to reshape and re-evolve all of creation. This will be the story of the Jewish people.

What There Is to Learn from a Genealogy

Chapter five of Genesis is the kind of chapter most people are prone to skip. It doesn't tell a story. Instead it lists the names of fathers and their sons in succession. It doesn't seem important until we realize that Noah is the tenth generation.

As we have seen before, the number ten is important in the Torah's cosmology. God speaks ten times in creating the world. God brings ten plagues on Egypt. God gives ten commandments at Mt. Sinai. Ten is two hands' worth of fingers. Ten presents a sense of being a whole. It can be an end, the complete total, and it can be a beginning. Here Noah is both the last of his line and the first of a new line. The insight that

the ten generations that lead up to Noah have meaning, that they are a prompt to recognize a new beginning, takes on a greater validity when we find that ten generations also introduce Abram in a parallel genealogy.

What There Is to Learn from a Name

In mechanical succession, we meet nine successive generations. For each we learn their name, their age when their son was born, the number of years remaining in their lives, and the total number of years they lived. When we get to Noah the action slows, the text pauses, and we are told:

He called his son NOAH (which means the one who comforts).
LAMECH explained:
May he comfort us from the pain of working the soil which Adonai had cursed.

When the Torah provides us with the explanation of a name, it is usually a clue to the nature or essence of that person. Names are important. In the Torah they often define a person's life-course. Noah's name directs him to be the comforter. Since Adam and Eve violated God's command, people have been estranged from the soil, It has been hard to grow food. Lamech dedicates his son to the task of restoring humanity's original relationship with God.

The Torah then moves away from Noah's family, but an echo remains. The theme-word "comfortable" resonates. We are shown the evil that people are doing. The Torah tells us:

Adonai was uncomfortable about having made people.
Adonai said:
"I created them: people, beasts, crawling things and sky birds.
I'm uncomfortable that I made them."
But NOAH found favor in Adonai's eyes.

Destruction and Recreation

Just like "Beginnings", the story of Noah is filled with both patterns and exceptions. Beneath the text's surface details is a chiasmatic skeleton that provides structure and meaning to the whole account. The text's numbering of days provides us with our first glimpse of the hidden anatomy. Noah's family spends 7 days in the ark before the flood. It rains for 40 days and nights. The water rises for 150 days. This is the first half of a three-element x pattern. The water then recedes for 150 days. Forty days later Noah sends out a raven, and then the dove, which returned. 7 days later the dove was again sent out. We have a pyramid.

$$150 \cdots 150$$
$$40 \cdots\cdots 40$$
$$7 \cdots\cdots\cdots 7$$

The two halves are even and equal. The time spent destroying the earth is matched by the process of reconstruction.

The Noah story is told in twelve paragraphs. Six are spent in describing the preparation and the coming of the flood. Six are spent removing the flood and renewing creation. As with the number of days, the halves are equal. Justice and mercy are balanced. When we look closely at these twelve paragraphs, a much more elaborate version of our matched pyramid emerges.

```
              6 • • • • • 7
          5 • • • • • • • • 8
       4 • • • • • • • • • • 9
    3 • • • • • • • • • • • • • 10
2 • • • • • • • • • • • • • • 11
1 • • • • • • • • • • • • • • • 12
```

In the first paragraph we are told "The earth was being destroyed while God watched." In the last paragraph God tells us: "Never again will waters become a flood to destroy all life." In the second paragraph, God promises: "I will make my covenant with you." In the eleventh paragraph that covenant is given: "As for me, I now make my covenant with you." Section by section, word-echoes connect the six paragraphs of destruction with the six paragraphs of recreation.

Seven

To make meaning out of the flood, it must be more than an act of punishment. For the second creation to have meaning, something must have changed. Close reading reveals that God did more than just remix the elements and start over as before. Here, our close-reading reveals two clues.

Adam and Eve and Noah and his family were in parallel positions—both were responsible for populating the earth. The Torah emphasizes this connection by restating to Noah and family the blessing given to the first people. As is the Torah's way, a subtle change in that blessing reveals the essence of this story. Adam and Eve were blessed: "Be fruitful and become many, and fill the earth, and master it." When the blessing is repeated to Noah and family, God says: "Be fruitful, and become many, and fill the earth." The notion of mastery has disappeared.

The second clue is found in the use of the theme-word "covenant." That word first appeared in the second paragraph of this story. It appeared as a promise of a future covenant to be given. That covenant is indeed given in the matching eleventh paragraph. Once stated, the word then manifests itself as a theme-word, regularly punctuating the last two paragraphs of the Noah story. A count reveals that "covenant" is used seven times. Six paragraphs of recreation culminate in a sevenfold statement of a covenant. This is the essence of the new creation. God promises never to destroy the world again, and people in turn abandon a quest for world mastery, joining themselves to a partnership with God.

TEACHING TOOLS
OBJECTIVES

The learner will count the number of generations from Adam to Noah, discover that there are ten, and then relate this prompt to a new generation.

The learner will use the Noah naming formula (which defines him as a "comforter") as an opportunity to explore the importance of names/naming in the Torah.

This exploration will take the form of finding and comparing Noah's naming with the naming of Adam and Eve.

The learner will research her/his own name to find its meaning, its general significance, its family history, and its message.

The learner will explore the image of "God walking" by finding two places where the Torah talks about God walking.

The learner will create his/her own vision of a walk with God.

The learner will use collected clues: (1) the THEME-WORD NUMBER-WORD COVENANT (used 7 times) and (2) the TEXT REPETITION[-] restatement of the Divine blessing to "be fruitful" (without "and master it") to establish that God restarted the world with a different basis: the covenant.

SLIDE-IN VOCABULARY

covenant—a contract or deal
righteous—does what is right

HEBREW VOCABULARY

brit—covenant
ish tzadik—a righteous person

ACTIVITIES

This story is long and demanding. It is our expectation that two to three class sessions will be needed to complete it. We assume that classes will need to read this material twice—once on a section-by-section basis, and one whole reading to catch the structure of the story. We've used this model for organizing this material.

JOEY'S QUESTION
Student Commentary, page 15

This seemingly simple exercise touches the core of our chapter—the idea that the flood provides a new beginning for creation. By guiding the students to look for similarities and find the number ten in both stories, we allow the students to discover the bond between the story of the flood and the story of the creation.

1. **SET INDUCTION/READING THE TEXT:** In this lesson, the first reading of the text will serve as the inducing of the learning set. BRING a costume beard to class (just like the ones used on pages 38–39 of **Being Torah**). SAY: "In order to perform this text, we need ten students." PICK ten readers and LINE them up in front of the board. REFER to the ten readers as often as possible.

DIRECT the first student to read the paragraph beginning "When ADAM was…" the next student the box beginning "When SETH was…"

and so on. Follow the arrows across the two-page spread, moving down to ENOCH after JARED.

GIVE the first student (ADAM) the beard. TELL him/her to WEAR it during his/her reading and then PASS it on to the next reader. The last reader, NOAH, will have nothing to say. He should receive the beard and then have no part.

Before SITTING DOWN, ASK each of the ten readers to WRITE the name of his/her person on the board.

After performing the text, ASK: "What can we learn from this passage?" EXPECT a number of silly answers about age. ENJOY them. (If you used the beard, you've provoked them). REDIRECT: "What does the Torah want us to learn from the list of names? There is an important 'secret message' here. Who can find it?" ALLOW several minutes for exploration. ACCEPT all "incorrect" answers with phrases like "Good insight, but we're looking for something else." "Nice idea, but there is something else to find," etc.

Being Torah Student Commentary page 11

CHAPTER 4: AND INTRODUCING NOAH

Why does the Torah Spend Time Listing the Names of People and the Number of Years They Lived?

When Joey read this story he had a problem with it. Read his comment.

I don't know why the Torah wastes space listing the names of people and then doesn't tell us anything about them. Also, I don't believe that anyone could live 976 years. My grandfather is 81, and he is very old, even if he still walks 2 miles every morning. I don't know...

Joey

Unlock the Number Pattern

Open up *Being Torah* to pages 34-35 and count the number of generations from Adam to Noah.

There are _____**10**_____ generations between Adam and Noah.

What else in the Torah uses this same number? **Ten Commandments, ten plagues**

My Comment: I think the Torah tells us the story of Adam's family-history to teach us **to let us know that Noah, the tenth generation, will be the new beginning for the family**

Choose someone else's comment and write it here.

_____'s Comment:

_____ thinks that the Torah tells us the story of Adam's family-history to teach us _____

11

If no one is close, you may offer this CLUE (a math problem). It must be done out loud without paper or pencil.

A man is taking a bus from Boston to Miami. He gets on in Boston with 11 other people. In New York City 5 people get off and 22 people and a dog get on. In Philadelphia, 3 more people get on and 1 woman and her dog get off. In Baltimore, 15 people get off and a baseball team with 9 players gets on. In Washington, 11 people get off and 3 FBI agents get on. In Atlanta, 4 people, the 3 FBI agents, and a man they've arrested get off. A family of 7 gets on. At last the bus gets to Florida. How many stops did it make?

POINT OUT: "Our Torah lesson is like this math problem. There are lots of names and numbers that distract us. The answer is in the number of stops." EXPECT hands to go up. ESTABLISH that there are ten names in this chain from ADAM to NOAH.

2. **FINDING THE CLUES:** Break students into small _hevruta_ groups. Have them COMPLETE page 11 in the Student Commentary. ALLOW working time. GO OVER answers.

3. **MAKING MEANING:** REVIEW the idea that the number ten is connected to creation. ASK students to write their own comments.

4. **NETWORKING COMMENTS:** ASK as many students as possible (preferably the whole class) to READ and SHARE their comments. USE the board, etc., to record each of these comments. HAVE STUDENTS write their favorite comment in their own words.

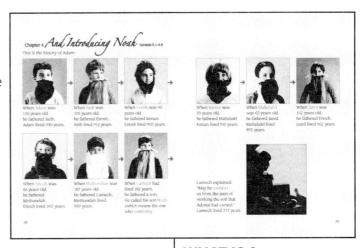

WHAT IS A "COMFORTER"?
Student Commentary, page 11

Noah's name means "comfort." It dedicates his life to giving comfort. This exercise combines class discussion, sharing of experiences, and text inquiry. We learn about the importance of names in the Bible and how our own experience provides a context for biblical inquiry. Our names and our experience of being comforted help us understand this story.

1. **SET INDUCTION:** Have students tell the meaning of their name and the story behind it. Work with what students know. Class discussion about the history of the students' names is a favorite activity. Here we are looking for the connection between the reason a name was given and the effect that name has upon the person. ASK: "How does a name help to shape who a person is?" (FOR FUN you can play a recording of Johnny Cash's song "A Boy Named Sue.") ACCEPT all answers.

2. **READING THE TEXT:** Beginning on page 34 of **Being Torah**, ASK the class to read the colored word(s). READ the part of narrator yourself. Start at "When LAMECH had lived…" and read through page 35.

3. **FINDING THE CLUES:** ASK "What did you hear?" ACCEPT all answers. If necessary ASK: "What is the theme-word of this story?" ANSWER: "comfort." ASK: "What does this teach?" ACCEPT a few suggestions, then direct students to the exercise in the student commentary.

4. **MAKING MEANING:** BREAK the class into _hevruta_ groups. Have them complete parts A and B in the Student Commentary. You can find the meaning of ADAM'S name on page 24 of **Being Torah**. The meaning of EVE's name is revealed on page 28. Because of the specific nature of part C, this is a good individual activity. When everyone has COMPLETED parts A, B, and C, GO OVER this material. Then DIRECT students to WRITE their own comments.

5. **NETWORKING COMMENTS:** Have students READ their comments. WRITE them on the board (etc.) and have students COPY one of their fellow students' comments into their Student Commentary. The idea of comforting God is a good basis for a role play. You may want to have some fun, staging a phone call between Noah and God, trying to make God comfortable with people. The scene where Noah and his father rehearse the phone call could also be fun.

Being Torah Student Commentary page 12

What is a "Comforter"?

In the Torah we can learn a lot from people's names.

Adam's name means _"earthling"_ and teaches us that people **come from the earth** _____

_____.

Eve's name means _"life-giver"_ and teaches us that people _____

_____.

In this story we learned that **Noah**'s name means **comfort** _____.

Noah's father chose the name Noah because he wanted **comfort** _____ from working the _____ **soil** _____ (_Being Torah_, page 35). It was cursed when _____ **Cain** _____ killed his brother Abel.

Choose someone else's comment and write it here.

My Comment: If I were **Noah** and my name meant _"the one who comforts"_ and it was my job to make God comfortable with people, the first thing I would do is _____ **follow God's rules, be the best person I could be.** _____.

_____'s **Comment:** If _____ were Noah his/her first step to make God comfortable with people would be _____

_____.

12

THE FLOOD—GOD WALKING
Student Commentary, pages 18–19

The rabbinic principle of *de bra Torah b'lashon b'nai adam*—"the Torah speaks in human terms"—inspires this exercise. We want the students to ask the questions "How can God walk?" and "What does it mean that Noah walked with God?" and answer these questions themselves.

I. **SET INDUCTION:** Assume that your students already know a lot about the Noah story. There are more Noah books, games, stuffed animals, puzzles and toy sets than all other biblical material lumped together. People like Noah; it is the zoo story. ASK students to BRING whatever "Noah-bilia" they have to class. BRING all the storybooks you can find, too.

Being Torah Student Commentary page 13

THE FLOOD
God Walking

Echoes: Another way the Torah points out lessons it wants us to learn is by making connections between two stories by using the same words in both stories. When we hear words that remind us of the words in an earlier story, we are hearing an echo of the first story in the second.

Find the Echo:

In the story **The Garden** we are told:

> They heard the sound of Adonai God walking around in the Garden at the windy time of day.

In the story **The Flood** we are told:

> Noah was a righteous person.
> He was the best in his generation.
> Noah walked with God.

When we bring these two sentences together we learn that God does a lot of **walking**

My Comment: God isn't just invisible. God doesn't have any shape or form. God doesn't have any legs (or other body parts). God doesn't "walk" the way that people do. When the Torah talks about God "walking" I think it wants us to understand that _____

God is with us, God is everywhere .

When the Torah says that **"Noah walked with God"** I think it is telling us that Noah _____

Noah walked the "walk" by walking on the righteous path .

13

READ one or two of these storybooks together. Make an OUTLINE of the Noah story on the board. (Even if you don't have any storybooks in class, your students should be able to help you outline the basic story.)

ESTABLISH that today we are going to read the real words the Torah uses to tell this story in **Being Torah**. DIRECT students by saying, "We are going to look for some of the messages hidden in these words. We are going to USE the close-reading tools we have been building." ASK students to list these tools. REVIEW: THEME-WORD, NUMBER-WORD, [ECHO] and TEXT REPETITION.

2. **COMPARING TEXTS:** READ the two texts on page 13 of the **Being Torah Student Commentary.** Have students alone or with a partner work through the questions. Go over these questions.

When we bring these two sentences together, we learn that God does a lot of walking.

My comment: God isn't just invisible. God doesn't have any shape or form. God doesn't have any legs (or other body parts). God doesn't "walk" the way that people do. When the Torah talks about God "walking," I think it wants us to understand that…

When the Torah says that "God walks" it is telling us that this is a moment when God is close to us.

DISCUSS the idea of "God walking." You may want to INTRODUCE the "big word" anthropomorphism (meaning: making something human that isn't human). Walt Disney drawing hands on a broom and having it carry buckets of water in *Fantasia* is an example of anthropomorphism. The same is true of the phrase "walking with God."

You may also want to INTRODUCE the rabbinic phrase *de'bra Torah b'lashon b'nai Adam*, "the Torah speaks to us in human terms." You will want to spend some time discussing the idea that while God is nothing like a person, most of the words we use make God seem like a person, since that is the closest description we know how to use.

4. **MAKING MEANING:** Have students write their comments on page 13 of the Student Commentary. SHARE comments from page 13 first. It is important to es-tablish here that the phrase "Noah walked with God" directs us that he was a faithful or righteous person. It suggests that his ways and God's ways were in one direction. That is not the exact intent of God walking in the Garden story. The individual comments here can indeed be quite open-ended.

5. **NETWORKING COMMENTS:** As a group, READ through the exercise on page 19 of the Student Commentary. Have students SUGGEST some possible fill-ins for the blanks. Then have students WRITE their own "walks with God." SHARE these. You may choose to have the children illustrate their comments in class or as closure homework.

This exercise seems especially well designed for creative activities. Imagine an Albert Brooks film showing the places a person has walked with God and what they did and/or talked about. The students may have seen some of the *Oh God* movies. DISCUSS what connection they may have to the Noah texts.

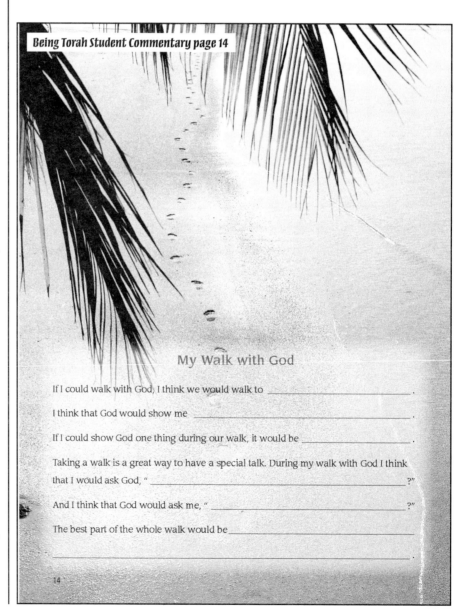

Being Torah Student Commentary page 14

My Walk with God

If I could walk with God, I think we would walk to _____ .

I think that God would show me _____ .

If I could show God one thing during our walk, it would be _____ .

Taking a walk is a great way to have a special talk. During my walk with God I think that I would ask God, " _____ ?"

And I think that God would ask me, " _____ ?"

The best part of the whole walk would be _____

_____

14

AFTER THE FLOOD

Student Commentary, pages 16–18

The last three paragraphs of this story (pages 47–48) form a closing unit that presents the final message of this epic. Here the sevenfold use of "covenant" and the restated blessing that omits "mastery" set the direction for this second creation.

1. **SET INDUCTION:** REVIEW the plot of the Noah story. If you still have the toys and books available, use them to go over the basic events.

2. **READING THE TEXT:** OPEN **Being Torah** to page 45 and quickly work your way through sections 7, 8, and 9. This lesson will focus on the last three sec-

tions, 10, 11, and 12. When you reach page 47 (section 10) ASSIGN a third of the class to read the parts in green letters. ASSIGN the remainder of the class to read the parts in red type. READ the part of narrator yourself.

3. **FINDING THE CLUES:** DISCUSS "When you listen to this text, what things stand out?" IDENTIFY "covenant" as a THEME-WORD. COUNT and establish that it is used seven times, which also makes it a NUMBER-WORD.

MAKE SURE that students understand the idea "covenant." TALK about the two sides to this deal. MAKE LISTS on the blackboard of agreements they know of and the obligations of each side of the partnership.

4. **MAKING MEANING:** The resolution of this lesson requires two distinct conclusions. First, students must recognize that the covenant is a new factor added to a renewed creation. Second, they must recognize that the idea of "mastering" has been taken out. Our field tests tell

---

Being Torah Student Commentary page 16

AFTER THE FLOOD

What Did God Not Repeat in the Noah Story?

Find What Was Taken Away

When the world was empty except for Adam and Eve, God said to them:

"Be fruitful,
and become many
and fill the earth
and **master** it."

When the world was empty except for Noah and his family, God said to them:

"Be fruitful,
and become many
and fill the earth."

The thing that God took away when creation was restarted was: **and master it**
.

What Did God Add to Creation after the Flood?

Count the Number Word

The word covenant is used for the first time in the Torah in the last two paragraphs of the Noah story (sections 11 and 12, pages 47 and 48).

Count how many times it is used ____**7 times**____.

My Comment: The thing that was taken away from Noah and his family was **master it**.

The thing that was given for the first time to Noah and his family was **a covenant**.

When you put these two things together you learn that one message of the Noah story is:

We are now in a covenant (2-part promise)

with God. We agree to fill and take care of the

earth. God promises not to make another

16 **flood to destroy the earth.**

Choose someone else's comment and write it here.

_____ 's Comment:

_____ thought that the thing taken away and the thing added in the Noah story taught: _____

_____

_____

_____

_____

us that students can indeed isolate and understand each of these insights. Finding and correlating both is somewhat difficult. Therefore we have divided them into two different exercises. This first insight has been achieved in part three and is reinforced on page 16 of the Student Commentary. Have students COMPLETE this page and then GO OVER the material as a class. REVIEW once more the meaning of a covenant.

WORK THROUGH the two blessings together. ESTABLISH that the second blessing (Noah's blessing) is a TEXT REPETITION [-]. The idea of people being masters has been taken out of creation. PUT the two ideas together. God has added "covenant" and taken out "mastering." ASK: How is the second creation different? ANSWER: This time instead of being the bosses, people are God's partners. ALLOW the students time to write their comments.

5. **NETWORKING COMMENTS:** Have students share their comments, network them, and record a comment in their books. Then spend a few minutes on the covenant God made. Make a LIST of things God will do for people and a LIST of things God expects people to do.

THE NOAH PATTERN, PARTS 1 AND 2
Pages 17–18

1. **SET INDUCTION:** EXPLAIN that sometimes the Torah buries a pattern in the biblical text.

2. **FINDING THE CLUES:** Turn to page 17 in the **Student Commentary.** Work through the pattern found in the texts on the page. POINT OUT that while we could find the same pattern in **Being Torah** or in the Bible, the workbook makes it easier to see the pattern.

The pattern is 7 days, 40 days, 150 days, 150 days, 40 days, and 7 days.

Have students TURN to page 18 in the **Student Commentary**. WORK THOUGH the twelve sections of the Noah story (each section represents a paragraph) together. FIND the words that the first and the last paragraphs have in common. Then the second and the next to last, etc. Here is what you will find.

Being Torah Student Commentary page x

The Noah Pattern Part 1

The Noah story was written with a hidden pattern. Find the secret pattern in this chart.

A Number Pattern

7 days from now I will make it rain upon the earth.

The rain fell on the earth 40 days and 40 nights.

The water swelled for 150 days.

After 150 days there was less water.

After 40 days Noah opened the window and sent out a raven.

He waited another 7 days and again sent the dove from the ark.

The pattern of these numbers is:

| 7 | 40 | 150 | 150 | 40 | 7 |

like a pyramid

17

1/12 destroy

2/11 as for me...I will make my covenant with you

3/10 living things on the face of the earth

4/9 Noah, with his sons and his wife and his sons' wives, came into/went out of

5/8 Adonai shut him in/Go out of the ark

6/7 all the high mountains were covered

POINT OUT that the twelve paragraphs on this page of the **Student Commentary** follow the same pattern as the previous page. HELP students DISCOVER that what is destroyed (or taken away) in the first six paragraphs is put back or recreated in the last six paragraphs.

3. **MAKING MEANING:** Have students fill in, then share their interpretations of this pattern.

ADDITIONAL LESSON SEEDS
COMMENTARIES, Page 43

Rachel's comment allows you to play with the image of the ark and the animals. More children's books have been created around the theme of Noah's ark than perhaps any other story. Collecting many of these and comparing their vision of the story is fun. Some classes have also had a good time filling their rooms with two of every stuffed animal. We have heard of a class that even made a rock video of songs about Noah.

David's comment focuses on the notion of being the "only righteous person." It anticipates a discussion in the Midrash (glossed by Rashi) about how righteous the only righteous person in a generation would be on an absolute scale. This provides a good opportunity to talk about peer pressure.

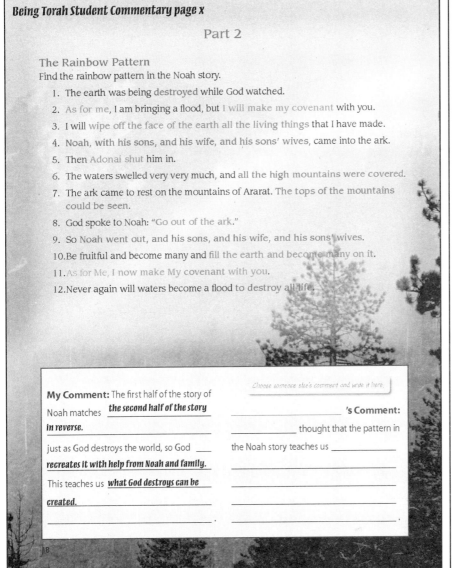

Being Torah Student Commentary page x

Part 2

The Rainbow Pattern
Find the rainbow pattern in the Noah story.

1. The earth was being destroyed while God watched.
2. As for me, I am bringing a flood, but I will make my covenant with you.
3. I will wipe off the face of the earth all the living things that I have made.
4. Noah, with his sons, and his wife, and his sons' wives, came into the ark.
5. Then Adonai shut him in.
6. The waters swelled very very much, and all the high mountains were covered.
7. The ark came to rest on the mountains of Ararat. The tops of the mountains could be seen.
8. God spoke to Noah: "Go out of the ark."
9. So Noah went out, and his sons, and his wife, and his sons' wives.
10. Be fruitful and become many and fill the earth and become many on it.
11. As for Me, I now make My covenant with you.
12. Never again will waters become a flood to destroy all life.

My Comment: The first half of the story of Noah matches *the second half of the story in reverse.*

just as God destroys the world, so God *recreates it with help from Noah and family.*

This teaches us *what God destroys can be created.*

Choose someone else's comment and write it here.

_____ 's Comment:

_____ thought that the pattern in the Noah story teaches us _____

Harrison notices the line "Adonai shut him in." He uses it to talk about the partnership between God and people. It is a good theme to explore.

COMMENTARIES, Page 49

Shawna picks up on the words "God remembers." She uses them to talk about her feelings of both security and insecurity with God. These conversations are important. We provide our students with little chance to talk about God, particularly to voice their anxieties and uncertainties. For some background, see the CAJE Symposium on *When Bad Things Happen to Good People*, August 1986.

MIDRASH *T'MUNAH*

Page 36: The child here is playing with "Masters of the Universe." Talk about how these toys match the image of "the world being filled with violence."

Page 39: The Hebrew here says: Noah *Ish Tzadik*, Noah was a righteous person.

CHAPTER 5—THE TOWER OF BABEL

Being Torah, pages 50–51
Student Commentary, pages 19–21

ABSTRACT
WHAT DID THEY DO WRONG?

Find the reason that God destroyed the tower. Answer: The text is not specific. While a number of answers are suggested, none is specifically stated. This is a case of **missing information**. This is a place where we must make midrash.

OVERVIEW

The story of the Tower of Babel presents us with a perfect example of Divine justice that is given "measure for measure." There is, however, no clear explanation of the crime.

Just like the story the Flood, the account of the Tower of Babel is built (like a pyramid) out of a series of X-patterns. It is told in nine verses that are divided into two paragraphs—one for human action and one for Divine response.

In the first paragraph we learn:

(1) All the earth had one language.

(2) People traveled to the east and settled there.

(3) People said to their neighbors, "OKAY, let us make bricks.

(4) Let us build a city and a tower."

In the second paragraph, as God intervenes to prevent the building of the tower, all of these elements are repeated in reverse order.

(5) Adonai came down to see the city and the tower.

(6) (The LORD said:) "OKAY, let us babble their language so that people will not understand their neighbors' language."

(7) So Adonai scattered them from there.

(8) Adonai babbled the language of all the earth.

Each of the steps taken in creating the city is systematically undone in reverse order by God. The text, however, goes further in describing this ironic undoing. In the first paragraph, people express a specific desire: "Let us make a name for ourselves to keep us from being scattered over the face of all the earth." In the second paragraph, God's punishment is a direct negation of that desire: "Adonai scattered them over the face of all the earth."

The structure of this story and the careful recasting of the human actions and the Divine response are clear indications of the way God enacts judgment. God's punishment here is a direct application of the acts that are being punished—what the rabbis called *midah k'neged midah*, "a measure for a measure." This much we can uncover and understand.

וְנַעֲשֶׂה־לָּנוּ שֵׁם

What is unclear and what is difficult to understand is the wrongdoing that motivated God to intervene. A number of verses suggest a direction, but none of them offer comfortable explanations. The most common understanding comes from the statement "Let us build a city and a tower with a top in the sky." Those who root themselves in this verse hold that it is wrong for people to try to reach heaven (and try to be like God). Others use the next verse, "Let us make a name for ourselves," equating "name" with pride and arrogance. A third possibility comes in God's comment, "From now on, they will be able to do whatever they feel like doing." The words seem to imply that people could get too powerful for God.

At the beginning of this story there seems to be a basic unity to people's actions. God's disruption of this peace seems inappropriate. A fear of people reaching heaven, developing pride or becoming "too powerful" doesn't seem to justify the interaction. Therefore, the commentators looked for other solutions.

Cassuto, an important commentator who worked in the early twentieth century, finds his solution in the people's wish "to keep from being scattered over the face of the earth." He sees this as a direct violation of the commandment given to both Adam and Noah, "Fill the earth." While this explanation is consistent with prominent text clues, it is hard to see God destroying human unity in the name of better demographics.

Two Talmudic rabbis reach beyond the story revealed in the Torah. Building on the notions of "reaching heaven" and "making a name," Rabbi Shila suggests that people intended to cut a hole in the sky and cause a flood, just as God had done in Noah's age. Similarly, Jeremiah ben Eleazer concludes that people wanted to reach heaven and fight a war with God. For them, the division of humanity must have resulted from a kind of self-destructive tendency toward violence, making the separation an act of mercy as well as punishment.

In *Pirke D'Rabbi Eleazer*, Rabbi Pinchas suggests the explanation later popularized by Rashi. He also roots himself in the phrase "make a name." For him, the problem was not the building of the tower, but the way it was built. He teaches, "The tower grew so high that it took a year to walk up the steps to the top of the construction. If a person fell off, no one cared. If one of the bricks fell, people cried all day."

Chapters 5 and 6 of **Being Torah** provide us with an opportunity to introduce the tool of midrash. The actual term "midrash" will not he introduced in this lesson; that will happen in chapter 6. In this chapter we are doing a kind of "midrash readiness," showing that the actual text sometimes calls for the making of midrash. Here we are concerned with making explicit the reality that some answers can't be found by close reading of the biblical text, and that **missing information** really does exist. We also introduce the notion that the rabbis (of the Talmud and Midrash) engaged in the same kind of process that we do. They struggled to close-read the Torah and to make meaning from its questions just as we do.

We begin with a simple story. People again do wrong, and God makes another change in their lives. The text quickly reveals that it is built out of a series of ironic x-patterns. God frustrates each of humanity's actions and prevents them from reaching their goal. It is a good example of a biblical punishment fitting the crime. At the end of our first reading, we are unclear about that crime. When God finds something wrong with the construction in the valley of Shinar, God acts. No explanation is given to the builders. There is no warning, and there is no interactive teaching moment—things just change radically. The biblical narrator reveals little more. The Torah has left us with an incomplete understanding. We learn that the building of the tower was somehow wrong and that we are supposed to learn from its prevention. Then we are abandoned. The text in essence says, "That's all I'm telling—now you make sense out of it."

TEACHING TOOLS

OBJECTIVES

The learner will attempt to choose one verse from the story that shows why God punished the people of Babel, realize that no such sentence exists, and then synthesize an original explanation.

Each learner will draw a picture describing her/his concept of what the people did wrong.

SLIDE-IN VOCABULARY

scattered—caused to spread

KEY HEBREW VOCABULARY

la'asot shem—to make a name

ACTIVITIES

WHAT DID THEY DO WRONG?
Student Commentary, pages 19–21

The Torah's narrative style is predicated on leaving holes. Its tendency is to tell its story by describing the major actions and presenting key pieces of dialogue. It often tells little or nothing of what motivated these actions and words. That is its way of actively involving the reader by forcing him/her to come to his/her own understanding of these events. Such is the case in the story of the Tower of Babel. The Torah leaves us with no clear explanation of why God punished the people.

1. **SET INDUCTION:** READ page 19 in the **Student Commentary** with your class. This exercise tells the story of how Mrs. Henderly's class made meaning of this story. Their experience will serve as a model to your students. Here, by reading the first page, students will have their first reading of the text fo-

ונעשה־לנו שם

Being Torah Student Commentary page x

CHAPTER 5: THE TOWER OF BABEL
What Did They Do Wrong?

When Mrs. Mahrer's class was learning the story of THE TOWER OF BABEL they had a big argument about the meaning of the story. It all started over the question:

What did they do wrong?

Mrs. Mahrer broke her class into four groups. She asked each group to write down the sentence from the story that showed what the people who lived in the Land of Shinar did wrong.

Before you look at the next part of this workbook, open your *Being Torah* to page 50 and write down the number of the sentence that shows why God punished the people.

I picked sentence number _____

The words that were the clue were _____

19

---

cused. They will be directed to look for the reason God destroyed the tower.

MAKE SURE that the students understand that focus. ASK: "What are we looking for?" ACCEPT answers such as "A sentence telling us what sin/crime the people did" or "A sentence telling why God punished them." You will NOT have them fill out part A on the bottom of page 22 until after they have read the text.

2 **READING THE TEXT:** OPEN **Being Torah** to page 50. ASSIGN the parts of the narrator and God, and form a chorus to read the part of "the people." REHEARSE the text to make sure that everyone knows his or her part. Then PERFORM it a couple of times—TAKE the time to make sure it sounds good. SPEND the time needed to enjoy this reading.

3 **FINDING THE CLUES:** Next, direct students to complete the questions on the bottom of page 19 of the **Student Commentary**. Have students SHARE both the

sentences they chose and the words they selected as their clues. ACCEPT all answers. Make NO COMMENT about any answer being right or wrong. ASK no questions except those that help students clarify their positions. WRITE each person's NAME, the NUMBER of the sentence chosen, and a couple of words that describe each one's THEORY on the blackboard; where more than one person has the same theory, ADD THAT NAME to the same item on the blackboard.

TURN to page 20 in the **Student Commentary**. DIVIDE the reading aloud of Ms. Headerly's class among your students. ASK one student to read each group. Have him/her EXPLAIN, in his/her own words, that group's theory about the punishment. COMPARE this process to that of learning Torah from the comments made by other students in your own class. COMMENT: "The circle of Torah study is bigger than just this classroom. We can learn something from every person who struggles with the meaning of the text."

COMPARE the groups in Mrs. Mahrer's class with your own results. ADD their opinions (in the proper place) to your chart on the blackboard.

SURVEY your class. ASK students to raise their hands in support of the four differ-

ent groups in Ms. Mahrer's class. GROUP your students accordingly and give them time to WRITE their conclusions and reasoning as a group.

4 **NETWORKING COMMENTS:** SPEND a few minutes SHARING the results of your group work.

TURN to page 21 in the **Student Commentary**. SELECT a student to read the first paragraph. Then REVIEW the idea of **Missing Information** with your class. READ the next paragraph and EXPAND on Mrs. Mahrer's comment. EMPHASIZE that the Torah makes us work to fill in its holes.

READ the THREE RABBINIC opinions one at a time. STOP after every paragraph and have the students EXPLAIN IT in their own words.

COMPARE the rabbis' reasons for the punishment with your own. ADD these rabbis to your list on the blackboard.

5. **MAKING MEANING:** ASK students to draw their pictures of the wrongdoings of the people of Shinar. FIND artwork depicting the tower and share it

Sachi and David were Group 1. They picked the sentence: "OKAY, LET US BUILD A CITY AND A TOWER WITH ITS TOP IN THE SKY." They explained: "They wanted to get up to heaven and wanted to reach God. God didn't want people to reach heaven, so they were stopped."

Paulina, Sacha and Owen were Group 2. They also picked the sentence: "OKAY, LET US BUILD A CITY AND A TOWER WITH ITS TOP IN THE SKY." Paulina gave their reason: "God didn't want lots of people living in the same place." Owen added: "God said, 'Be fruitful and become many and fill the earth.'" Sacha interrupted: "You can't fill the earth if everyone lives in one place."

Shawna and Joey were Group 3. They picked a different sentence: "LET US MAKE A NAME FOR OURSELVES." Joey said: "'They only wanted to be famous, and no one cared about anyone else,'" Shawna added: "It was like a giant game of King of the Hill on this tower. Everyone wanted to be on top. Everyone wanted to have the most important name."

Angelica, Rachel and Harrison made up Group 4. They didn't pick a verse. Rachel said: "Nothing they told about in the Torah seemed bad enough to punish." Harrison said: "I liked what Joey said about 'making a name.'" Angelica told him to be quiet and that he couldn't steal Joey's idea. Mrs. Mahrer then said, "I really like what Harrison did, finding something he could believe in another student's idea. We are here to learn Torah from each other."

The argument went round and round. Which group do you think was right? Why?

_____

_____

_____

with the class. TALK about the students' drawings and the artists' views of the scene.

ADDITIONAL LESSON SEEDS

COMMENTARIES

Rachel talks about God as a parent. Expand that metaphor. What kind of parental activity is this story? Is it like taking a dangerous toy away from an infant? Losing one's temper? Dividing troublemakers? etc.

Paulina's comment focuses on the loss of unity. Work as a class or a group to devise a plan for bringing people back to having the same language and having one purpose.

וְנַעֲשֶׂה־לָּנוּ שֵׁם

Being Torah Student Commentary page 21

Mrs. Mahrer then wrote the words "Missing Information" on the blackboard.

Missing Information: Sometimes reading the Torah is like watching a television show where you leave for a couple of minutes and then have to come back and figure out what happened while you weren't watching. Often there are "holes" or MISSING INFORMATION in the story. When we find that a story has MISSING INFORMATION we have to use the information in the Torah to try to figure out what happened in the part of the story we weren't told.

She said, "'The right answer isn't in the Torah. This is one of those questions that the Torah makes us figure out for ourselves. Everyone who has studied this text had to work out his or her own answer."

In the Talmud, a rabbi named Shila said: "They were building the tower so that once it was finished they could climb up it with axes and cut a hole in the sky and make it rain. They wanted to be like God and make a flood."

A rabbi named Jeremiah, son of Eleazar, said: "They wanted to build a tower so that they could climb up it and then fight a war with God. This is why God scattered them."

A few years later, in a book of explanations of the Torah called Pirke d'Rabbi Eliezer, a rabbi named Pinchas had another idea. "The problem wasn't that they wanted to build a tower; the problem was the way they built the tower. They cared more about the building than the people working on it. The tower grew so tall that it took a year to walk up the steps to the top of the construction. If a person fell off, no one cared. If one of the bricks fell, people cried all day, because it would take a whole year to replace it. They made workers live their whole life on the tower. They were born, worked and died on it."

Mrs. Mahrer then had her class pick one of the ideas of what people did wrong and draw a picture. Do the same thing in this box.

21

CHAPTER 6—AND INTRODUCING ABRAM

Being Torah, pages 60–62
Student Commentary, page 22

ABSTRACT
ANOTHER GENEALOGY?

Count the number of generations from Adam to Noah. Answer: 10

Count the number of generations from Shem (Noah's son) to Abram. Answer: 10

Draw a conclusion: Like Noah, Abram represents another new beginning.

OVERVIEW

Just like the genealogy at the beginning of the Noah saga, the ten generations listed here provide an understanding that Abram (through his unique relationship with God) will bring humanity to a new phase of development.

As with the first genealogy we encounter in the Noah story "And Introducing Noah," careful close reading of the genealogy in this chapter allows us to discover an important insight in a passage that might normally be viewed as a historical relic. In that story we learned that NOAH was a child of the tenth generation of humankind. That clued us that Noah represented a new beginning. In this genealogy we find that Abram is the twentieth generation, and that he, too, represents a new beginning.

Our hope for this chapter is that some students will be able to generalize the insights learned from the genealogy of Noah and independently apply them to this second genealogy.

TEACHING TOOLS

OBJECTIVES

Through discovering that the genealogy from Noah to Abram represents another ten generations, students will identify Abram as another "new beginning."

ACTIVITIES

The ideal teaching moment offered by this story would be if one or more students generalized the lesson learned in Chapter 4, "And Introducing Noah," and started to count the generations here to see if they added up to ten. Our design in reading this story is to try to facilitate that leap of insight (without over-prompting it).

ANOTHER GENEALOGY
Student Commentary, page 22

In the Torah the number ten often signifies a new beginning. So far we have seen the ten statements of creation and the ten generations leading to Noah. This chapter narrows the focus of the Torah from humanity to one family's history. This is where God again tries a new beginning to history through choosing a people—the Jewish people.

1. **SET INDUCTION:** INTRODUCE this story as another genealogy, just like the one we had between ADAM and NOAH. REVIEW why that genealogy was important. ESTABLISH that NOAH was the tenth generation and a new beginning.

2. **READING THE TEXT:** BEFORE CLASS, take 5 x 7 cards and write the name of each of the generations on a card. RESIST the temptation to give everyone a part; only make signs for the names printed in bold type. PASS OUT the name cards. GIVE each one to a student. MAKE sure that each student knows how to pronounce his/her card's name.

   PERFORM the first paragraph. Have each person with a card stand up and say the name at the appropriate places. Don't be afraid to have fun with this. Try a rehearsal (or be prepared for several attempts before it works perfectly).

3. **FINDING THE CLUES:** After the performance, ASK: "What kind of lesson can you find in this piece of text?" WAIT for the answer. Don't be afraid to ask the

question two or three times. If no answer seems ready to emerge, then ASK: "How many people are in this genealogy?" RE-PERFORM the list (with the standing and sitting).

Once you've established that we have ten generations, ASK: "What other tens have we found?" ESTABLISH: Ten Commandments, ten sayings in Creation, and ten generations from Adam to Noah, etc. ASK: "What can you learn from the use of the number 10?" ACCEPT all answers. POINT OUT that 10 is often a number of new beginnings.

4. MAKING MEANING: READ with students the instructions on page 22 of the **Student Commentary**, and have students COMPLETE the work. Even though the prompts point the students to a logical conclusion for their comments, variety is still acceptable.

5. **NETWORKING COMMENTS:** USE your regular procedure for sharing and networking comments.

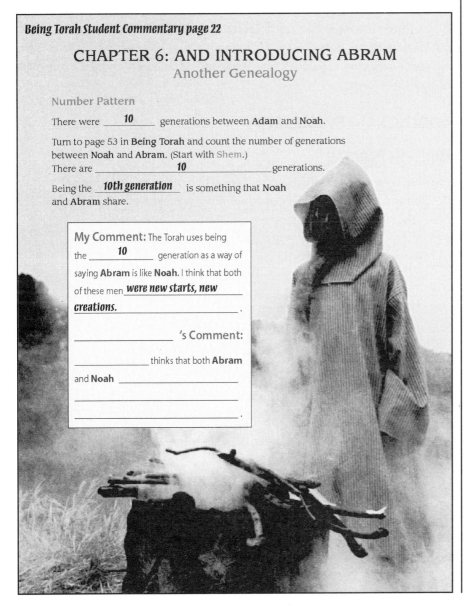

Being Torah Student Commentary page 22

CHAPTER 6: AND INTRODUCING ABRAM
Another Genealogy

Number Pattern

There were _____10_____ generations between **Adam** and **Noah**.

Turn to page 53 in **Being Torah** and count the number of generations between **Noah** and **Abram**. (Start with Shem.)
There are _____10_____ generations.

Being the ___10th generation___ is something that **Noah** and **Abram** share.

My Comment: The Torah uses being
the _____10_____ generation as a way of
saying **Abram** is like **Noah**. I think that both
of these men *were new starts, new*
creations. .

_____ 's Comment:

_____ thinks that both **Abram**
and **Noah** _____
_____
_____ .

Additional Lesson

In introducing Abram, the Torah leaves tantalizing gaps in its quick review of his early years. These gaps have become the impetus for some of the most famous and significant stories from the midrash.

The remainder of this chapter presents a very sketchy early history of Abram: (1) ABRAM is LOT's uncle; (2) LOT is an orphan; (3) ABRAM is married to SARAI, who is barren; (4) ABRAM's father, TERAH, took the family on a trip to Canaan. They only got as far as Haran. For some reason (unexplained in the text) they settled there; (5) TERAH died there.

Many questions are raised. We want to know details. Where the text is absolutely silent, we have only two choices: our own imagination or the collective imagination of our tradition. Both of these amount to midrash.

In writing **Being Torah** we were very careful to divide between Torah and midrash. We consciously wanted to avoid midrashic readings of the text until students had built a foundation of literal discoveries and could then understand the relationship of the two literatures. Our intent had been to present the Torah as a vast collection of mysteries and puzzles rather than a set of fairy tales. Too often the genius of midrashic invention has been reduced to children's stories. That process not only reduces their value, but also threatens to undermine the evolution of an adult relationship with the actual Torah text.

Our experiences with test classes in our laboratory schools have changed this view. We found that many students have an expectation of finding "the idol story." It was an interesting insight. We often believe that our students have no previous biblical experience, yet somehow the idol story is one learned and retained by almost every Jewish child.

Our research suggests that the first four chapters of **Being Torah** provide a substantial background in the way the Torah communicates, one that can be used to root the process of midrash as a response to the Torah's clues and messages. To establish this connection, chapters 5 and 6 of the **Student Commentary** provide a staged introduction. In the last chapter we used the ethical dilemma of God's unexplained actions in the story of the Tower as an opportunity for "midrashic readiness." We introduced two concepts: (1) that the Torah's storytelling style forces us to invent stories that fill in missing pieces and (2) that there is a long Jewish tradition of creating and sharing these fill-in explanations. In this chapter we will build upon this foundation, using the common knowledge of the "idol story." Here we will introduce the term "midrash" and define it as a series of comments written by the rabbis to fill in the same places with **Missing Information** that we also find in the Torah.

Midrash is a literature of explanations of the meanings of the biblical text. The classic collections were compiled by the rabbis at the same time as the Talmud, though the process of making midrash has continued to this day. While we principally know midrash as a collection of extra stories created around the biblical text, it is important to realize and to teach that these stories are a response to the Torah's text and not independent creations. This means that (1) the rabbis read the biblical text closely, just as we do; (2) they found the same kinds of clues in the text that we find; (3) they created stories or explanations built out of the facts and plot of the biblical text that "filled in the holes" or "made meaning" out of the clues that were left in the text; and (4) these midrashim were designed to do more than just fix problems in the Torah. They were designed to teach a major moral lesson from the clue that prompted their creation.

In the case of Abram and the idols, **Missing Information** about Abram's childhood and the incomplete move prompted the creation of a whole fabric of tales of boy Abram, the self-created "monotheistic advocate." These stories are all designed to teach us that worshiping things people make is a stupid behavior.

Our purpose here is twofold. Our first is to solve for our students the question of the missing "Bible" story. Our second concern is to provide an understanding of midrash that shows it as a process of study and commentary and not a collection of additional Torah.

ADDITIONAL LESSON SEEDS

MIDRASH *T'MUNAH*

Page 64: Note a subtle reminder of our "new beginning." A dove (from Noah?) sits atop the road signs, helping us remember the previous "new beginning" to which the students will be directed.

CHAPTER 7—ABRAM: LEAVING HOME

Being Torah, pages 56–57
Student Commentary, pages 23–24

ABSTRACT
A MATH CONNECTION

Count how many times Abram's name is used. Answer: 7

Count how many times the THEME-WORD "land" is used. Answer: 7

Count how many (lines of) blessing God gives Abram. Answer: 7

Draw a conclusion: Abram = Land blessing. When Abram is on the Land, there is a state of blessing.

HOW TO BE A BLESSING

Count how many times the THEME-WORD "bless" is used. Answer: 5

Count how many times God blesses Abram. Answer: 5 (See the following stories: Leaving Home, Lot Leaves, A Covenant, Abram Becomes Abraham, and The Binding of Isaac)

OVERVIEW

This story is the official launching of the Abram saga. It sets the patterns for his whole adventure: a preoccupation with the vision of God, the two-part promise, a life of blessing, and a permanent connection to the land.

Throughout **Being Torah** we have looked at stories and tried to isolate the patterns and devices used in their construction. Nothing has fit perfectly. We have seen lots of places where things come close. The story of creation is evenly divided yet refuses to be a pattern. The story of Noah is perfectly symmetric while lost in an inner chaos of conflicting detail. The Tower of Babel is an exacting construction without a basic foundation of purpose. They are each haunting and intriguing memories. In no story we've yet considered have theme-words and number-patterns, repetitions, echoes, and x-patterns led us to a single unquestionable conclusion.

In contrast, the story of Abram's first call seems perfect. The pieces seem to fit together exactly. Both the overt message of the story and the literary inner workings point to the same understanding. It is a frozen instance, a crystal-clear vision of the birth of the relationship that created the Jewish people.

Rashi, the dean of biblical commentators, opens his commentary with a surprising reaction. He says that the story of creation seems like the wrong way to begin the Torah. He suggests that because the Torah is really a book of laws, it should have begun with the first legal passage, Exodus 12.1. Faced with explaining the presence of fifty chapters in Genesis and another eleven in Exodus that tell stories rather than teaching laws, Rashi says: "They are there so that the nations of the world cannot say that the people of Israel stole the land of Canaan, taking it by force from the seven nations who lived there."

His comment is not the superimposition of an outside ideology onto the biblical text, but rather the underscoring of one of its key and central themes. The evolution of a special relationship between God and Abram's family, their growth into the nation Israel, and their movement toward a homeland in Israel is the overt thrust of the Torah's story. This is also revealed in a hidden clue. The last word of each of the five books of the Torah reveals this message: (Genesis) Egypt, (Exodus) their journeys, (Leviticus) Sinai, (Numbers) Jericho, and (Deuteronomy) Israel.

What exists on the macro level also is clearly "proved" in the seven-verse microcosm of this story. At the climax of this story, when Abram has followed God and gone to the land which was to be shown, God tells him, "To your future-family I will give this land." On a literary level, the same is true. The theme-word "land" is used seven times in this story. In a Hebrew mind-set, *eretz*/land always carries a connotation of "Land of Israel." Finally, the blessing given to Abram is made up of seven verse-clauses. There is a structural formula: Abram = Land = Blessing. The conclusion here seems obvious. We learn, "When Abram and his future-family are on the land, both will be blessed."

Just as "created" serves as a set of bookends for the first story of creation, the word "see" serves a similar function here. The story opens: "Adonai said to ABRAM: "Take yourself from your land, from your birthplace, from your father's house, to the Land—there I will let you see." It ends, "ABRAM built an altar to Adonai who is seen by him."

Cassuto suggests this connection: "The real promise made to Abram is not that a land will be shown to him, but that in that land God may be seen." As soon as Abram reaches the land, God appears. To establish a pattern, the first promise made to the Jewish people is immediately fulfilled.

Out of a history that emerged from chaos, and into a history that has not yet fully clarified itself, we can be empowered by the vision of a single pure perfect vision of our destiny.

TEACHING TOOLS

OBJECTIVES

After discovering three items, each of which is used seven times in this story—ABRAM, land and (lines of) BLESSING—the learner will develop an explanation of their interconnection.

The learner will explore the image of "being a blessing" through extrapolating how previously studied biblical heroes were blessings, and by listing ways in which people today should act in order to be a blessing.

SLIDE-IN VOCABULARY

birthplace—place where a person was born
curse—a wish that evil things happen to someone
blessing—a wish that good things happen to someone

KEY HEBREW VOCABULARY

lekh-lekha—take yourself (or go you forth)
me-artzekha—from your land
mi-molad-tkha—from your birthplace
mi-bet avikha—from your father's house

ACTIVITIES

A MATH CONNECTION
Student Commentary, page 23

This first close reading of the chapter will enable the student to discover the three NUMBER-WORD items, each found seven times: ABRAM, land and (lines of) BLESSING. This will also be the first time that students are introduced to a theme that will recur frequently throughout the Abraham saga: the two-part blessing that Abraham will receive at various times for many descendants and a connection to the land.

1. **SET INDUCTION:** ASSIGN the students to BRING to class three items they would take with them if they learned they were going to leave home/move and would not be returning. They can only bring three, and they will have to explain to the class their choices and reasons for them.

   When each student speaks, s/he should concentrate on the following: (1) why the items were chosen; (2) what kinds of things he or she had to leave behind in order to bring only three; and (3) how he or she felt having to leave items behind, knowing there would be no return to the old home.

   Have students WRITE a short description of what Abram would take as his three objects and what he would say about them. DO the same for Sarai.

2. **READING THE TEXT:** As teacher, READ the part of the narrator; ASSIGN a majority of the class to READ the words in red. ASSIGN a large minority to READ the words in green.

READ the entire text (in one reading) with the above divisions.

3. **FINDING THE CLUES:** ASK: "What did you hear/notice?" EXPECT to have the prompted words presented as answers: land, see, ABRAM and BLESS. ASK: "What do you know about each of these words?" ACCEPT all answers. This is just an open-ended asking, seeing that students have locked into the notions of THEME-WORD and NUMBER-WORD. If so, reinforce their insight; if not, just move on.

4. **MAKING MEANING:** In small groups, *hevruta*, have students READ instructions on page 28 of the **Student Commentary** and complete the exercise, COUNTING the number of times the three NUMBER-WORD items are used and COMPLETING the "equation." POINT OUT that these three items do not form a true equivalency but rather an equal worth or importance.

Have students WRITE their own comments on the message of this story.

5. **NETWORKING COMMENTS:** SHARE comments and FIND the common insights students included. EMPHASIZE the fact that Israel's blessing is tied up in the relationship with the land, and this is the relationship the text is emphasizing.

HOW TO BE A BLESSING
Student Commentary, page 24

The concept of "being a blessing" is new and potentially tough. Rachel's comment from the student text, which is reproduced in the **Student Commentary**, helps students start the process of exploration. In addition to tracing the actions of other biblical characters who could be considered "blessings," it allows students to understand that being a blessing can be an active process—one does things that create blessing.

1. **SET INDUCTION:** READ Rachel's comment on page 24 of the **Student Commentary**. ASK: "What is a blessing?" ACCEPT all answers. Then ask students to LIST as

---

Being Torah Student Commentary page 23

CHAPTER 7: ABRAM—LEAVING HOME
A Math Connection

A Number-Word Pattern

Open **Being Torah** to pages 56-57 and count:

The number of times Abram's name is used.

7

The number of times the word land is used.

7

The number of (lines of) blessings God gave Abram.

7

When we put these three things together we find out that:

$$\underline{\quad 7 \quad} = \underline{\quad 7 \quad} = \underline{\quad 7 \quad}$$

My Comment: By using three different things ___7___ times, I think that the Torah is teaching us that *there is a connection between Abram, the land and blessings. When Abram was in the land, ① he was blessed, ② the land was blessed, ③ everyone/everything was blessed.*

Choose someone else's comment and write it here.

_____'s Comment

_____ thought that the Torah used **Abram**, **land** and (the number of) **blessings** the same number of times in order to teach _____

23

many different blessings as they can. Also LIST ways of being a blessing.

2. **FINDING THE CLUES:** As a group, WORK through the top half of this exercise. GO OVER ways that ADAM, EVE, ABEL and NOAH were blessings. LIST ideas on the board so that students can COPY them into their commentaries.

3. **MAKING MEANING:** DIVIDE the class into dyads. DIRECT each group to LIST seven things a person can do to be a blessing. HAVE both members WRITE their list in the **Student Commentary**. MAKE SURE that both names are at the top of each list.

4. **NETWORKING COMMENTS:** Have groups SHARE their lists with the class. MAKE UP a master list. WRITE it directly on a ditto master or in good handwriting. Duplicate or photocopy the list of your class's ways of being a blessing and pass it out to the entire class.

ADDITIONAL LESSON SEEDS

COMMENTS

David's comment about Abraham being a "pioneer" suggests a historic look at this material. Go to a biblical atlas and find the Kings Highway and the Via Maris—The Way of the Sea. These were the two express routes from Babylon to Egypt. Many works in your congregational library will help you to establish day-to-day life in this time. A mapping exercise and some social studies work on caravans are suggested.

MIDRASH *T'MUNAH*

The photograph on page 64 shows Abram making a gift-offering to the LORD. This may be a good time to talk about sacrifice as a way of sharing your success with God, who made it possible.

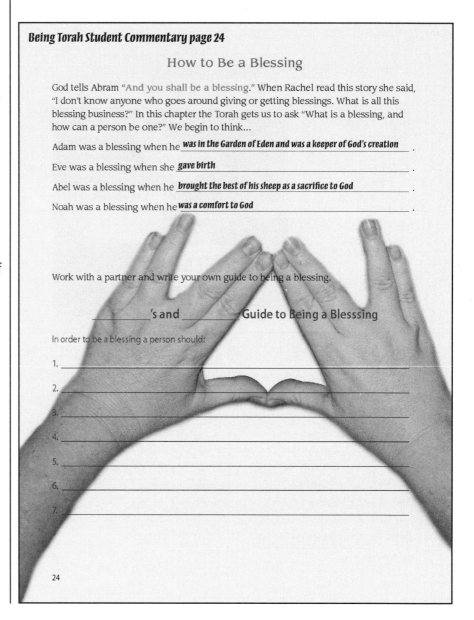

Being Torah Student Commentary page 24

How to Be a Blessing

God tells Abram "And you shall be a blessing." When Rachel read this story she said, "I don't know anyone who goes around giving or getting blessings. What is all this blessing business?" In this chapter the Torah gets us to ask "What is a blessing, and how can a person be one?" We begin to think...

Adam was a blessing when he _was in the Garden of Eden and was a keeper of God's creation_ .

Eve was a blessing when she _gave birth_ .

Abel was a blessing when he _brought the best of his sheep as a sacrifice to God_ .

Noah was a blessing when he _was a comfort to God_ .

Work with a partner and write your own guide to being a blessing.

_____'s and _____ Guide to Being a Blesssing

In order to be a blessing a person should:

1. _____
2. _____
3. _____
4. _____
5. _____
6. _____
7. _____

24

CHAPTER 8—ABRAM: LOT LEAVES

Being Torah, pages 50–62
Student Commentary, pages 25–26

ABSTRACT
FOLLOWING A WORD

Abram and Lot were not brothers. They were uncle and nephew. Examine the use of the THEME-WORD "brothers." Findings: Abram says they should make peace "because we are men who are like brothers." When the two split, the Torah says, they were divided, each man from his brother.

Find the **ECHO** of the story of Cain and Abel. Answer: There "brother" was a **number-word**. We learned that the ideal relationship was to be our brother's keeper. Here "brother" is also a THEME-WORD emphasizing an ideal relationship that can no longer continue.

Draw a conclusion: While Abram and Lot had to split up to keep the peace, it was sad, because families should "keep" each other.

OVERVIEW

When the family returns from Egypt, conflict breaks out in the camp and Abram must find a solution. He chooses to split his camp. God rewards that choice with a renewed statement of blessing.

To understand this story, one needs to begin with the second story in Genesis 12. In it, Abram and family go down to Egypt to escape a famine. When they return, they have been enriched by gifts from Pharaoh. This chapter (13) begins by listing as if in order of march the family as they return. This description will be one of the clues for unlocking the full meaning of this story. The Torah tells us:

> ABRAM went up front Egypt.
> He and his wife, and all that was his.
> And LOT went with him,
> (he) also owned sheep, oxen and tents.

As soon as they return to Canaan, a feud breaks out between the herdsmen of Abram and those of Lot. The feud results in the splitting of the family (for the sake of peace). Lot goes in one direction, Abram goes in the other. In looking for meaning in this story, our first question must be: "Why was it necessary for the family to divide?" A surface reading of the text presents a simple answer. "'The land would not support both of them SETTLING together. They had so many belongings that they were not able to SETTLE together." From this it seems clear that the separation of the tribe was a necessity— the natural extension of the growth that had taken place. This feuding between the herdsmen seemed to be unavoidable. The land had reached its limit.

However, a second explanation of this separation can be found through a careful close reading. The order of march that begins this chapter is a repetition of a list

that appeared in Genesis 12 (Abram: Leaving Home). A comparison of the two lists reveals a family secret.

ABRAM took SARAI his wife,

and LOT his nephew,

and all they owned.

When the family first came to Canaan, they collectively owned their wealth. It belonged to everyone. Now, after the return from Egypt, Abram and Lot have divided the possessions. In other words, a psychological split has already taken place. The feud between the herdsmen seems to be a product of that division, not the cause. Before the trip down to Egypt there was no sense of separate herds or herdsmen. The feud would have been impossible.

This leads us to the story's second question: Was it necessary for Abram and Lot to split? Was it good for Abram and Lot to split? To answer these question we must deal with ambivalent sets of MIXED FEELINGS that are found in the Torah.

Ono pointer is the theme-word "brother." Abram and Lot are uncle and nephew. Twice in this text the Torah describes there as relating like brothers. The word "brother" is an echo both of the story of Cain and Abel and of the famous song about brothers settling in unity found in Psalms. There is a hope and an expectation that brothers should be able to live together and to keep each other. When they part, the Torah doesn't comment positively on how the peace was kept; rather there is a sadness to the story coda: "So they were divided each man from his brother."

However, two other indicators in the story suggest that the separation was necessary. First the Torah warns us that Lot made a bad move in choosing the richness of the Sodom plain. While the land was very fertile, we are warned: "The men of Sodom were evil and sinned on purpose." Lot makes a bad choice, taking potential wealth despite an unethical environment. Twice Lot will suffer from this choice. Once he is kidnapped, and Abram must rescue him (Gen. 14). Then the city of Sodom is destroyed, and his family flees for their lives (Gen. 19).

The second indicator comes at the beginning of the extended statement of the two-part promise God gives to Abram at the end of this story. The Torah emphasizes the connection between the separation and the blessing by telling us: "Adonai said to ABRAM after LOT was divided from him." It is as if this separation was a necessary condition for God giving a full promise.

The Torah has MIXED FEELINGS. It was not good that Abram and Lot separated—it is never good for families to break up. It was necessary that they split. We can put together three factors: (1) that an emphasis on ownership caused the feud; (2) that Lot chose potential wealth over an ethical community; and (3) that God only extended the promise to Abram once he had become separate.

The last part of this chapter is a restatement of the two-part promise God made to Abram in chapter 12 (Abram: Leaving Home). Now that ABRAM has acted, gone to the land and begun to SETTLE, God's promise is more concrete. This time God provides a size to the promise. "Like the dust covering the land, your future-family will be impossible to count." Likewise, the one-sentence promise in chapter 12, "To your future family I will give this land," now contains an expanded vision of the whole land and the command to "Get up and walk the land."

As modern Jews we must ask a fourth question. In the text of **Being Torah** this question is voiced by Amy's comment: "When I read this story, I wonder where Sarai is. They don't say anything about her feelings. She should have been included." While the experience of the women's movement has sensitized us to impose this question on the text, in answering it we have an opportunity to expand the mythic fabric of our heritage amid our communal resources. This is one of the places in the text that cries out for a new layer of midrash.

TEACHING TOOLS

OBJECTIVES

The learner will trace the [ECHO] of the word "brother" in this story and struggle with the question "Was it good or bad that Lot and Abram separated?"

SLIDE-IN VOCABULARY

herdsmen—shepherds
feud—argument

KEY HEBREW VOCABULARY

a*h*im—brothers

ACTIVITIES
FOLLOWING A WORD
Student Commentary, page 25

The word "brother" was the theme-word in the story of Cain and Abel. There it directed us to the understanding that despite other emotional drives, the obligation of people to care for and "keep" each other is our central responsibility. The word is echoed in this story to bring that message into this incident.

1. **SET INDUCTION** (OPTION 1): REVIEW the relationship between LOT and ABRAM. ESTABLISH that they are uncle and nephew. REVIEW their family history. ESTABLISH that they moved from Ur to Haran, from Haran to Canaan, and then went down to Egypt and came back. POINT OUT that they have been through a lot together. ASK: What kind of relationship would you ex-

pect in a family that had been through a lot of hard times together? ACCEPT all answers.

1. SET INDUCTION (OPTION 2)**:** The feud between the herdsmen is the central incident in this text. The Torah tells us little about it. We don't know the cause of the feud. We don't know if this feud was the cause of the family split or a symptom of a growing gap. We don't even know the nature of the feud (verbal, physical, pranks, violence, etc.) This role-play activity allows you to explore those questions. It may be used as a motivational activity to introduce the problems in this text or as a review and wrap-up of all that has been learned. We believe it is more fun to interview sheep and tents about the feud once some of the text's secrets have been revealed.

Before class, the teacher should MAKE up a deck of 5 x 7 cards with one of the following characters on each card: ABRAM, SARAI, ABRAM'S HERDSPERSON, ABRAM'S GOLD AND SILVER, ABRAM'S OXEN AND SHEEP, LOT, LOT'S HERDSPERSON, LOT'S SHEEP AND OXEN, LOT'S TENTS. One card should be made up

for each student. More than one card can be made up for unnamed characters.

Begin class by having students DRAW cards for their parts. The room should be DIVIDED into Abram's stuff and Lot's stuff. Abram and Lot should be asked to introduce their sides. Then each character should be asked to tell about the feud from his/her/its perspective. Since the Torah tells us little about the actual feud, students should be ENCOURAGED to improvise (within the text's limits).

SUGGESTION: At first make Abram and Lot listen (and not participate) because, after all, the feud was between the herdsmen.

Then the whole group should DISCUSS the problem, "How do we solve this feud?" The central issue should be the possibility of keeping peace without separating. INTRODUCE the value term *shalom bayit,* "family peace."

Being Torah Student Commentary page 25

CHAPTER 8: ABRAM—LOT LEAVES
Following a Word

Find the Word-Connection

One word connects two parts of this story and also connects this story to another story we have studied.

When Abram went to Lot to deal with the fighting between his herdsmen and Lot's herdsmen, he said:

Let there be no feud between me and you
between my herdsmen and your herdsmen
because we are **men** who are like brothers.

When the two of them separate the Torah says:

So they were divided—
each **man** from his brother.

This echoes the story of **Cain and Abel** where Cain asked:

Am I my **brother's** keeper?

My Comment: The word **brother** teaches us about **Abram** and **Lot**. It teaches us that *being brothers obligates us to take care of one another and be a keeper. Even Abram and Lot, really uncle and nephew, were like brothers. They could stay together, but each took care of the other by separating and stopping the hostility beween their herdspeople.*

25

To CONCLUDE, the teacher should point out that we need more information about the feud to understand how to solve it. This leads us to close reading with exercise 8.1.

2.READING THE TEXT: For this chapter, the oral reading is not the central tool of exploration. Here theme-words and other clue elements will not directly lead us to the heart of the story. They become important later in the process. To break out this story, exploring the plot and tracing the connections to other stories will be our best tools. Therefore the method of oral introduction is not critical.

READ the first part of this chapter, the story of the separation (pages 67–69) and the restatement of the promise (page 70). ASSIGN the part of Abram to one student. ASK the remainder of the class to read the bold and CAPITALIZED words.

3.FINDING THE CLUES:

ASK "Why did Abram and Lot separate? Was this separation good or bad?" ACCEPT all answers.

OPEN **Being Torah** to page 63. Read Owen's comment. The question: "Was it good or bad that LOT and ABRAM divided into two camps?" ASK: "When is it good to stay together and work things out? When is it better to split up because of *shalom bayit* (family peace)?"

EXTENSION: *shalom bayit*—FAMILY PEACE. *Shalom bayit* is an important value. In this story Abram divides the family and gives Lot first choice of territory. It is clear that Abram is acting with *shalom bayit* as his first concern. A few minutes of discussion will allow you to introduce this value concept and connect it to this biblical scene. OPEN to page 60. READ or ENACT Abram's speech to LOT. DISCUSS: Why did Abram give LOT free choice of land? DISCUSS: What do you have to give up to keep *shalom bayit* in your family? What do your parents give up to keep *shalom bayit*? etc.

4.MAKING MEANING: Have students OPEN their **Student Commentary** to page 25. WORKING alone or in small groups, have them complete the exercise. DIRECT the students not to complete the COMMENT section at this time.

ASK: "What can we learn from the word 'brother' in this story?" ANSWER: "The Torah seems sad that Abram and Lot were not able to live together and 'keep' each other like brothers."

ALLOW students time to write their own comments.

Being Torah Student Commentary page 26

Lot Leaves—A Closer Look

Find the Change: Who Owns What?

When Abram arrived in Canaan,

> Abram took Sarai his wife
> and Lot his brother's son
> and all they owned...

When the family came back from Egypt we are told:

> Abram went up from Egypt.
> He and his wife and all that was his...
> And Lot (who went with Abram)
> also owned sheep, oxen, and tents.

What about ownership changed while the family was in Egypt? _____
Abram and Lot no longer shared what they had. Each had his own stuff.

How does this change in ownership explain the fight between the herdsmen?
The herdsmen no longer shared space. Each group wanted to get the most.

A Second Explanation

In the Torah we are told:

> The land would not support both of them settling together.

How does this verse explain why the herdsmen were fighting? *Each herd wanted too much land and couldn't share the space. There was not enough land for both herds to get enough food.*

Choose someone else's comment and write it here.

My Comment: I think the real reason Abram and Lot split up was **they were no longer able to share the land they had settled on. Each had his own stuff.** _____ .

_____'s **Comment:** _____ thought that the real reason Abram and Lot split up was _____ _____ _____ .

26

5. **NETWORKING COMMENTS:** Use your usual class procedure for networking and sharing insights.

Additional Activity: The Two-part Promise
THE TWO-PART PROMISE

Count how many times the word "bless" is used in the story "Abram: Leaving Home." Answer: 5 times

Count how many times God blesses Abram/Abraham. Answer: 5 times

Compare these five blessings. All five blessings include the same two-part promise: (1) Abram will have a large family. (2) Abram's family will inherit the Land of Israel.

OBJECTIVES

The learner will identify the two parts of the promise God gives to Abram and compare them with the same two-part promise given in chapter 12 of Genesis, "Abram: Leaving Home."

What is now a two-part promise will evolve into a covenant that "cuts" the unique relationship between God and the Jewish people. The story of Abram is really the story of the expansion and development of this promise. Starting in Haran, God's twofold commitment to create a nation and give them a land has been the central issue of the Abram story. Here, after the conflict with Lot, the promise is restated for the second of five times and provides us with an opportunity to teach its nature.

1. **SET INDUCTION:** REVIEW the meaning of the word "covenant." REVIEW the covenant between God and NOAH. ASK students if they can recall the two-part covenant God made with ABRAM in the story "Abram: Leaving Home." ESTABLISH: (1) large family, (2) Land of Canaan. WRITE these on the board. EXPLAIN: In this next portion of the story God repeats those two promises.

2. **READING THE TEXT:** READ or REREAD page 62 of **Being Torah.** ASK: "What is this page all about?" ANSWER: "God is making a promise to Abram." ASK: "What is God promising?" WRITE the two parts of the promise on the blackboard: people and land.

3. MAKING MEANING: GO OVER answers and ASK: "Why did God have to give this promise a second time?" ACCEPT all answers.

ADDITIONAL LESSON SEEDS

MIDRASH T'MUNAH

The chess board. On pages 67 and 68 Abram and Lot are shown sitting around the tent playing chess with sheep and cattle. Have students explain these pictures. Have students compare a feud to chess game (e.g., at the end of a chess game two people who have been competing shake hands and remain friends).

Chapter 8 *Abram: Lot Leaves* Genesis 13.1–18

Abram went up from Egypt.
He and his wife, and all that was his.
And Lot went with him.
Abram was very rich in herds, in silver and in gold.
And Lot (who went with Abram)
also owned sheep, oxen and tents.

59

STUDENT COMMENTARY, page 71

Owen's comment provides an opportunity to relate this story to the need for families to split and merge.

Joey's comment allows a discussion of peer pressure and how people choose the places they live.

CHAPTER 9— ABRAM: A COVENANT

Being Torah, pages 64–66

Student Commentary, page 27

ABSTRACT

A LETTER TO MY FUTURE-FAMILY

Find the two THEME-WORDS. Answer: "inherit" and "future-family"

Find the ECHO between this story and both "Abram: Leaving Home" and "Abram: Lot Leaves." Answer: The same two-part covenant is restated for a third time.

Draw a conclusion: As Abram grows older and the covenant is still not fulfilled, he needs additional reassurances that these promises will come true. While he doesn't realize it, things are moving in the right direction. His future family history will be fulfilled.

OVERVIEW

The Torah centers around two major themes, Creation and the Exodus. Each of these expresses the core of a relationship between God and people. It is in the midst of this story of a divided sacrifice that the universal relationship with a God of creation is culminated and the particular relationship with a God of history is begun.

This story is built around the two promises God has made twice before to Abram. This is emphasized by the presence of the two theme-words "future-family" (the promise of posterity) and "inherit" (the promise of the land). Here Abram doubts each commitment, and God renews the promise with both literal and symbolic proofs.

The first promise is a promise of family, "And I will make you a great nation." When God promises him a great reward, Abram doubts it, asking, "My Master Adonai, what could You give me? I have no children." God provides two answers. The first is a verbal commitment, "Only your own children will inherit from you." It is a restatement of the existing promise. The second assurance is more symbolic. God takes him outside and says, "Look toward the sky. Count the stars, if you can count them. This is the number of your future-family." The passage is rich in echoes. Just a blessing-statement before, just after he has divided himself from Lot, Abram has been told, "Like the dust of the land, your future-family will be impossible to count." The two images overlap. They say the same thing differently. Each has a purpose. Together they represent a great whole.

For the Greeks, earth, air, fire, and water were the essential elements in reality. For the Torah, these elements were heavens and earth. The stories of creation are bracketed within their reality. When God brought the flood, it had two sources: one in heaven—the rains—and one in earth—the wellsprings. Both were needed. Later in the Torah, two dreams will reveal Joseph's future. One is of the sky—stars that circle and bow; the second is in the field—sheaves that circle and bow. Heaven and earth both testify to his destiny. Here we find the same double proof—the dust of the land and the stars of the sky. With the addition of the second metaphor comes a sense of completion.

Each of these words also brings its own echoes. Dust brings us back to our common root in ADAM. He was made from "the dust of the soil." God's first promise connects Abram's family to the destiny of all people. Being like "the dust of the earth" makes them fully HUMAN. On the fourth day of creation the Torah reveals the purpose of the stars. They are to be "signs" and "lights." Such is the destiny of the Jewish people—signs and lights to the nations. With the echoes comes a renewed sense of Abram's destiny (and God's investment in his future family's success).

This first promise, the promise of a future-family, is really an expression of' God's original blessing to humankind, "Be fruitful, become many, and fill the earth." When Abram "retrusts" God, the Torah notes, "ABRAM trusted Adonai and Adonai gave him credit for being righteous. "Righteous" was the introductory word for Noah. At the end of the first half of this story the two new beginners have reached the same level of human prosperity.

The second half of the text is more confused. The Torah explains that "a deep sleep fell on ABRAM," and the text indeed reads like a dream, emerging with rich images that call for interpretation. Unlike the first half of this sequence, all the images here feed toward foreshadowing events that will come to be. God begins, "I am Adonai who brought you out from Ur of the Chaldeans to give you this land." Listening with an ear to the future, we hear "I am the LORD your God, who brought you out of the land of Egypt, out of slavery." God commands, "Take a three-year old calf, a three-year-old goat, a three-year-old ram, and a clove and a baby pigeon, and divide them for Me as a sacrifice." The midrash points out that these are all animals who will form the core of the daily sacrifices in Temple days. Another taste of the future. God then reveals a piece of history. "Know for a fact that your future-family will be strangers in a land that is not theirs. They shall be slaves and suffer for four hundred years; but I will punish the nation they serve, and after that they will exit with riches." For the first time in the Torah, God reveals that the future is carefully planned. The promise of the Land is tied to the process of history.

The specific dream is a sacrifice of halves. What in reality is divided is not just the future sacrificial animals, but Abram's universal past from his particular future. Up to this moment the focus has been on the promise of procreation—a blessing granted to all humanity. It ends with the introduction of a particular Jewish history. Their destiny will actualize in slavery, escape to freedom, revelation of the Torah and establishment of Israel. This unique experience, this tangible expression of the covenant, divides them from the rest of humankind.

The chapter ends with the introduction of the word "covenant." This, too, is a foreshadowing of a relationship that will culminate in the next chapter. This story is a story of doubts. It teaches that a person of faith can have doubts, that s/he can then find an even deeper faith.

TEACHING TOOLS

OBJECTIVES

Through comparing texts the learner will establish that the promises God made to Abram previously are repeated in this chapter. Using the THEME-WORDs "future-family" and "inherit," the learner will identify the restatement of the two-fold promise.

SLIDE-IN VOCABULARY

vision—like a seeing, but not exactly

inherit—get something from a relative who has died

inheritance—the things handed down from generation to generation in your family

nomads—people who do not live in one spot, but wander from place to place.

HEBREW VOCABULARY

magen —shield

zera—seed or offspring. We have translated it as "future-family."

ACTIVITIES

A LETTER TO MY FUTURE-FAMILY
Student Commentary, page 32

This exercise is built out of two elements: an introduction and a Mad Libs–style fill-in-the-blanks letter. The first provides the needed background for the second, which establishes that the two proofs given to Abram were rooted in the future.

1. **SET INDUCTION:** ASK "Who here has lots of patience?" ALLOW a few of those who raise their hands to SHARE a proof that they have patience. ASK: "Who has had to wait a long time for a promise to come true?" AGAIN, allow those who volunteer to SHARE a few stories. ASK: "Why did Abram and Sarah need patience?" ESTABLISH that they have had to wait a long time for the two-part promise to come true. POINT OUT: In this story we are going to see how Abram reacted after a long wait.

2. **READING THE TEXT:** In reading this story we want to highlight two things— (1) the questions that reveal Abram's doubts that these promises will come true, and (2) the new assurances God gives him.

   ASSIGN one student to read the part of ABRAM and one to read the part of Adonai.

READ the whole chapter through. STOP at the following places for the following short questions.

At the bottom of page 64, ASK: "What was ABRAM afraid of?" EXPECT: "He was afraid he would have no future-family (as God had been promising) to inherit the land (as God had been promising)."

At the bottom of page 65, ASK: "What was ABRAM afraid of here?" EXPECT: "That God would never give him the promised land."

At the conclusion, ASK: "Did God say anything that would make ABRAM feel better?" EXPECT: "The promise that the family would be as many as the stars, and the story of how in the future they would come to inherit the land."

3. FINDING THE CLUES:

DIRECT students to WORK ALONE to complete the **Student Commentary**. This exercise looks at the assurances God gives Abram that the promises will come true.

REVIEW the answers to the first section as a CLASS. ASK: "Why do you think that Abram felt better after these answers?" ACCEPT all answers. The Torah doesn't give us any clues here. It is, in many ways, just like the story of Job, where Job feels better just being answered (even though God's answer was that Job had no right to

ask). We know that Abram was comforted (somewhat), but we don't expressly know why.

4. MAKING MEANING: REVIEW directions for writing the letter to the not-yet-born future-family. ESTABLISH that the letter will review history as the students know it so far, as well as directions for the future. Allow the students to continue ON THEIR OWN.

5. NETWORKING COMMENTS: SHARE letters in _hevruta_.

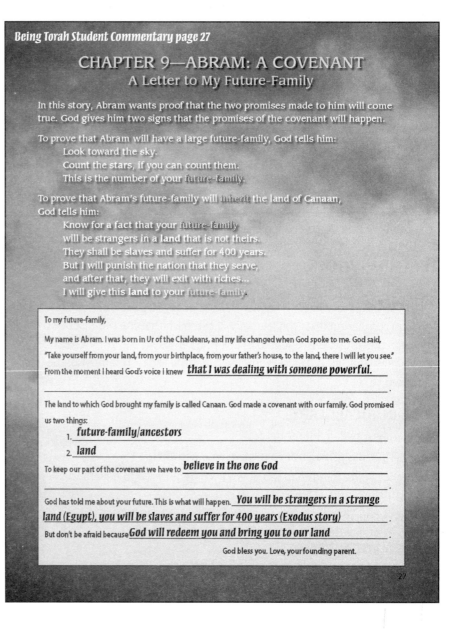

Being Torah Student Commentary page 27

CHAPTER 9—ABRAM: A COVENANT
A Letter to My Future-Family

In this story, Abram wants proof that the two promises made to him will come true. God gives him two signs that the promises of the covenant will happen.

To prove that Abram will have a large future-family, God tells him:
Look toward the sky.
Count the stars, if you can count them.
This is the number of your future-family.

To prove that Abram's future-family will inherit the land of Canaan, God tells him:
Know for a fact that your future-family
will be strangers in a land that is not theirs.
They shall be slaves and suffer for 400 years.
But I will punish the nation that they serve,
and after that, they will exit with riches...
I will give this land to your future-family.

To my future-family,

My name is Abram. I was born in Ur of the Chaldeans, and my life changed when God spoke to me. God said, "Take yourself from your land, from your birthplace, from your father's house, to the land, there I will let you see." From the moment I heard God's voice I knew _that I was dealing with someone powerful._

The land to which God brought my family is called Canaan. God made a covenant with our family. God promised us two things:
1. _future-family/ancestors_
2. _land_

To keep our part of the covenant we have to _believe in the one God_

God has told me about your future. This is what will happen. _You will be strangers in a strange land (Egypt), you will be slaves and suffer for 400 years (Exodus story)_ But don't be afraid because _God will redeem you and bring you to our land_

God bless you. Love, your founding parent.

27

ADDITIONAL LESSON SEEDS

MIDRASH *T'MUNAH*

On page 68 of **Being Torah**, the Hebrew word zera (meaning "seed") is written, entwined by the growth that comes from seeds.

EXTENSION: Have students collect family photos of parents and grandparents as young children to see if future-family resemblances can be established and traced from earlier generations to their own. Were there any other things passed down from generation to generation within the family (e.g., candlesticks, tallit, books, etc.) as part of an inheritance?

MAGEN AVRAHAM: Our prayerbook often refers to God as "the shield of Abraham." Have students list ways in which they feel God has been a *magen*/shield for Abraham up to this point, or how God might act so for Abraham's future family. Is this a good title for God?

COMMENTARY

Sachi's comment talks about the connection of faith and patience. It provides a good opportunity to talk about the things/people in which we trust.

CHAPTER 10— ABRAM BECOMES ABRAHAM

Chapter 10 *Abram Becomes Abraham* Genesis 17.1–27

When Abram was 99 years old
Adonai appeared to Abram and said to him:
"I am God shaddai,
Walk before me and be the best.

I put my covenant between Me and you,
I will make you very, very many."

Being Torah, pages 69–73
Student Commentary, page 28

OVERVIEW

After much preparation, Abram and God cut the perfect everlasting covenant, establishing the two-part promise as the beginning of a new nation.

In the previous chapter, "Abram: A Covenant," we saw the first evidence of an emerging covenant between God and Abram. That first presentation was wrapped in the mystery of a dream revelation. Here those first roots manifest themselves as the full eternal covenant. This time the Torah takes great care in setting its presentation.

God begins the process, saying: "Walk before me and be the best. I put my covenant between Me and you." In the last chapter, the Torah applied the word "righteous" to Abram. Together these words form an unmistakable echo of Noah's introduction, "NOAH was a righteous person. He was the best in his generation. NOAH walked with God." (The order is even in perfect chiastic [x-pattern] sequence). Just as ten generations of development have linked each of these two progenitors, the same word clusters introduce their qualifications to receive a covenant.

The word "covenant" is a theme-word here (disappointingly, it is only used nine times). In the full Torah text the word "circumcised" appears as a theme-word, being used eight times. The covenant process begins with God changing Abram's name to Abraham. The new name is a statement of promise, a contraction of *av hamon goyyim* (father of many nations). The midrash notes that this renaming fulfills one of the seven promises made in the first blessing, "I will make your name great" (Abram's name is now bigger). The text itself underlines its importance as the essential new beginning by using it ten times in this text. Here the two-part promise is restated as a covenant, and the concept "eternal" (forever/everlasting) is added.

One other element is added to this covenant, the mitzvah of circumcision. The midrash and commentators note that now Abraham must take action to actualize the two-part promise. This echoes the memory of Noah, who was required to build his own ark, even though "Adonai shut him in." Others have noted the conjunction of locus of circumcision with production of progeny and have suggested both spiritual and physical connections.

Within **Being Torah**, this is the first usage of the word *mitzvah*. *Mitzvah* is traditionally understood to be a commandment, a full obligation. It is something a Jew has to do. Folk Judaism has mutated its meaning, and in Yiddish (and Jewish English) *mitzvah* has come to mean "good deed" (as in "Boy Scout"). *Mitzvah* is also a boundary word in the Jewish community. The Reform movement has slowly redefined the process and tends to view *mitzvot* as Gunther Plaut has defined them: opportunities for meaningful Jewish involvement. The Orthodox movement has retained a traditional sense of obligation, and both the Reconstructionist and Conservative movements offer a blending of somewhat selective practice within a traditional rhetorical frame. *Mitzvah* is a word that must be used carefully, but which must be used. Probably a good talk with an educator or rabbi would be helpful. For our purpose, we talk about mitzvot as "Jewish behaviors we learn from Torah." It is a safe middle ground.

Unlike previous covenant statements, this one extends literally, and not symbolically, to the whole family. SARAI receives her own (unexplained) name change to SARAH and her own blessing. At this point, in a foreshadowing of an expanded announcement sequence that we will find in the next chapter, God rejects Ishmael as Abraham's heir, announcing the future birth of Isaac. Just as Sarah will do in the next chapter, Abraham laughs. This becomes the dual source of Isaac's name (which means "he laughs"). Ishmael then receives his own blessing.

There is a wonderful closure to the story. In the previous chapter Abram trusts God's promise that a son will be born. He assumes that Ishmael is that son (and is disappointed). Here, in a single revelation, God establishes that two nations will emerge from Abram (fulfilling many blessings) and shows both to be twelve tribes, full units. It is a perfect application of "separate but equal".

TEACHING TOOLS

OBJECTIVES

Students will trace the tenfold use of THEME-WORDs "covenant" and (the new name) "Abraham" to uncover the new beginning in Abraham's relationship with God.

SLIDE-IN VOCABULARY

everlasting—forever

circumcise—cut off a piece of skin from the end of the penis

HEBREW VOCABULARY

brit—covenant. Shorthand for *brit milah*, literally "the covenant of circumcision"

shomer—keeper

av hamon goyyim—father of many nations

Being Torah Student Commentary page 28

CHAPTER 10: ABRAM BECOMES ABRAHAM
Counting the Covenant

Finding a Number-Word Connection

(Open your **Being Torah** to pages 69-73)

Count the number of times that the new name Abraham is used. ___**10**___

Count the number of times that the word covenant is used. ___**10**___

My Comment: The Torah uses both **Abraham** (the new name) and the word **covenant** ___**10**___ times in order to teach us *God made a covenant with Abraham that Abraham's future-family would be very many and inherit then land (Israel).*

Choose someone else's comment and write it here.

_____'s Comment:

_____ thought that the Torah linked Abraham and covenant in order to teach _____ .

28

ACTIVITIES

ABRAM BECOMES ABRAHAM

Student Commentary, page 28

The purpose for reading this small section is to focus the students on the four bold words that form a clear ECHO connecting Abram directly to Noah.

1. **SET INDUCTION:** REVIEW the concept of an ECHO. EXPLAIN that this portion contains a major ECHO. DIRECT students to listen for this connection as they read the opening portion of this chapter.

2. **READING THE TEXT:** Section One, page 69. READ the majority of the text yourself. DIRECT the class to READ the rose words. ASK: "Where have we heard those words before?" EXPECT: "Noah." ASK: "What else do we remember about him?" ACCEPT all accurate answers. ASK: "Why does the Torah use the words used for Noah to describe Abraham" ACCEPT all answers, but FOCUS on the idea that the Torah wants us to know that the two of them were alike. ASK: "How was Abram like Noah?" ACCEPT all answers, but EMPHASIZE the ten generations.

They will find that both ABRAHAM's name and the word "covenant" are used ten times. At the same time they will have to deal with the red herring, "future-family," which is a THEME-WORD but has no numeric value. Finally, prompted by the number ten, they will find the new beginning of the covenant in the name changes and in the mitzvah of circumcision. This is the first time that the human partners in the covenant have to do something to hold up their end of the bargain.

1. **SET INDUCTION:** READ Sacha's comment on page 74 of **Being Torah**. ASK: "What do you think of his comment?" PROMPT students to express their agreement or disagreement. EXPLAIN: We are going to spend today's lesson understanding and reacting to Sacha's comment.

   Then ASK: "How do you find the hidden meaning in a story in **Being Torah**?" COLLECT ANSWERS. Expect such answers as "counting THEME-WORDs." SAY: "In the **Student Commentary** we will find how Sacha worked out his comment, but first let's read the text."

2. **READING THE TEXT:** Section Two, page 70. Limiting the size of the section read will help students to focus on these important features: the name change; the title *av hamon goyyim*; reiterations of "covenant" and "future-family"; and the new aspect of the covenant's length (everlasting, forever). Again the teacher should READ all of Section 2 while the class choruses on all

words in CAPITAL and bold letters. ASK: "What did you hear?" LIST answers on the board. ASK: "What have we heard before, and what is new?" CHECK OFF the items listed appropriately. Old: covenant (we remember Noah again), future-family, and promises; new: A BRAHAM's name change, his title *av hamon goyim*, and the new aspect of the covenant (EVERLASTING, FOREVER).

Section Three, page 71. Again, a very small section for close reading, isolated to focus on circumcision, the first time the human partners of the covenant have a specific act to perform. Teacher READS: class shouts out CAPITAL and bold words. Again, check for comprehension by ASKING students to distinguish between old and new dimensions. NOTE: Students will undoubtedly giggle at the word "circumcision," or if that confuses them, at "penis" when the former is defined. Don't worry too much. It does dissipate quickly if you don't give the giggling too much attention.

Section Four, pages 72–73 (including section labeled "5"). A fairly straight reading through to the end can now be effected. This is the second time we have heard the promise to Abraham and Sarah of a child, but now he is named specifically. Sarah receives her new name, with no explanation as to a new meaning. The EVERLASTING covenant is remembered, including its symbol of circumcision. Teacher READS both sections through, with students in chorus on all CAPITAL and bold words.

3. **FINDING THE CLUES:** OPEN the Student Commentary to page 28. As a class, WORK through the material. ASSIGN three groups, one to COUNT each of the three THEME-WORDs. SHARE results.

   ASK students to make meaning from these clues. LISTEN to all suggestions. Then ESTABLISH that the number 10 connects "covenant" and "ABRAHAM." REVIEW the idea that the number 10 represents new beginnings.

   ESTABLISH the things that have been added to the covenant: circumcision and the expansion of Abram's name into Abraham.

4. MAKING MEANING: BREAK into groups. Have each group DEVISE a list of other Jewish things to do that connect Jews to the covenant. Hope for answers like: "Hebrew school, bar mitzvah, naming a child Jewishly, commitment to active Jewish life."

ADDITIONAL LESSON SEEDS

David's and Shawna's comments on page 74 allow the introduction of the ritual of circumcision. Here is a moment where the study of life cycle and Torah overlap. It may be a good time to invite your rabbi or a local doctor into your classroom.

The WORDPLAY on page 75 looks at the name change, an issue not covered in the **Student Commentary**.

In this story Ishmael, Sarah and Hagar are standing on the sidelines. It would be an interesting extension to explore all their feelings about these changes.

CHAPTER 11—SARAH LAUGHED

Being Torah, pages 86–91
Student Commentary, pages 35–36

ABSTRACT
WHAT CAN WE LEARN FROM ABRAHAM?

Examine the language Abraham uses to address the visitors. Answer: Three times he says "please."

Examine the description of the way he provides hospitality. Answer: He "runs" twice and "hurries" three times.

Draw a conclusion: The Torah makes a big deal out of Abraham's acts of hospitality. It is an important factor/model.

WHAT KIND OF LAUGH DID SARAH LAUGH?

Explain the reason that Sarah laughed. Answer: The text provides no specific explanation. It could be embarrassment, joy, anger, disbelief, etc. We are left to fill in our own understanding. It is a question that needs a midrashic answer.

OVERVIEW

Like a Steven Spielberg film, this chapter merges the magical with the fine details of everyday life. The miracle of Isaac's birth gracefully emerges from the hospitality Sarah and Abraham provide to strangers.

The secret to *ET, Poltergeist, Gremlins, Goonies, Back to the Future,* and even *Jaws* is that the everyday is the best setting for the magical. It is the careful attention to small realistic details that allows the magic to be so potent and makes the terror so horrifying. The Torah uses this same set of contrasts in telling the story of Isaac's annunciation.

The core of the story involves a slice of daily life in Abraham's camp. Strangers are spotted and conscripted to be visitors. The camp goes into overdrive providing hospitality. Twice the Torah describes Abraham's running, we are told three times that he hurries, and three times we hear him use "please" to coerce the acceptance of his hospitality. The whole scene is a flurry of activity: Feet are washed, bread is made, a calf is prepared, and Abraham personally serves his guests. This is the key scene the Torah uses for developing Abraham's character. It is the first time we have seen him in his natural state, away from tests and revelations, and he is a wonderful, kind man, passionately invested in doing what is right. The midrash will root its entire development of Abraham in this scene, telling that his tent had four doors, one on each side, so that it would always present itself to passersby. There is a whole collection of "how Abraham gave hospitality" stories because, based on this account, the mitzvah of *"hakhnasat ora<u>h</u>im,"* welcoming visitors, was Abraham' s self-chosen passion.

Even while we develop Abraham's character, we are also painting a portrait of normal camp life. It feels real. In contrast, the story is framed with mystical encounters. We begin with a strange opening vision. The story begins: "Now Adonai appeared to ABRAHAM." This is not so unusual an occurrence for Abraham, the Seer; but God's silence is. Up to now, God only manifests presence when something is to be accomplished. The details are expanded: "He was sitting at the entrance of the tent during the heat of the day." The insertion raises the question: Vision or mirage? The text goes on: "He lifted up his eyes and saw. And SUDDENLY three men were standing over him". What has been seen? We are unsure. Who are these visitors—men or God's messengers? We are unsure. Then in the onslaught of practical details the question is all but forgotten. We become interested in the commitment Abraham makes to welcome his guests.

In the "second act" the confusion returns. The men ask, "Where is SARAH, your wife?" Abraham answers. The text then continues *"Va-yomer,"* literally "He said" (though we have rendered it as "One said" in **Being Torah**, in order to leave the image as nonsexist). As we listen, this new single voice seems to be God's voice. It says, "I (singular) will definitely return at the time of birth when SARAH your wife will have a son." It is a perfect confusion, a wonderful aesthetic bending of reality. No matter who is speaking here, the next response we hear does come from Adonai, who comments on Sarah's laughter. It is a wonderful micro-lesson, one that sets the pattern for all the "beggar is really Elijah" stories that will follow; we can encounter the Divine at any moment. God is always possible.

The third element in this story is Sarah's big moment. A chapter earlier, Abraham is told of Sarah's great expectation. He laughs, thinking, "How is a one hundred-year-old man going to father a son? How is ninety-year-old SARAH going to give birth?" His comment is two clauses long, one doubting his own virility and one questioning Sarah's fertility. Sarah, in a wonderful parallel reaction, repeats the two-clause mutual reality. "Now that my time is past, how can my old husband and I have a child?"

God then repeats Sarah's words. Remembering that every repetition is a prompt to look for a change, we notice that God has omitted one phrase clause: "Will I really give birth, now that I am old?" Rashi (drawing from the midrash) explains the change in just a few words. "God changed the words for the

sake of peace." It is a lovely expression of "family peace." God then comes down on Sarah's laughter, asking, "Is any miracle too great for Adonai?" As with many speeches in Torah, we are left to imagine the tone. Is God being loving and playful or seriously invested in Divine dignity? The answer remains in the ear of the beholder.

Somehow, without ever having to state it overtly, the story ties God's investment in Abraham and Sarah to the private family as well as the public people of ceremony. We'd all like to be visitors to their camp.

TEACHING TOOLS

OBJECTIVES

Through reading the text, the learner will discover that Abraham worked very hard to make his guests comfortable. In writing a comment, the learner will apply a value learned from this model to his/her own experience

The learner will participate in a class discussion about the different possible meanings of a laugh and then write a comment explaining his/her understanding of why Sarah laughed.

SLIDE-IN VOCABULARY
time has passed—being too old

HEBREW VOCABULARY
Yitzhak —He will laugh

ACTIVITIES

WHAT CAN WE LEARN FROM ABRAHAM?
Student Commentary, page 29

The words "hurry," "run," and "please" cue us to the importance of hospitality to Abraham.

1. **SET INDUCTION:** ASK "What kind of person is Abraham?" ESTABLISH that he is brave (going to a new land), patient (waiting on God's promises), etc. EXPLAIN: "In this chapter we are going to learn about a whole new side of Abraham."

2. **READING THE TEXT:** The chapter is really made up of two linked scenes. The first (pages 76–77) tells of the hospitality provided to the visitors; the second (pages 78–79) involves the announcement of Isaac's birth. Our purpose in the first scene is to recognize the intensity of activity that goes on in the camp. Our purpose in the second scene is to both hear the use of the THEME-WORD "laugh" and note the change in God's reporting of Sarah's words.

Because we want to see the action in this story, ASSIGN students to play the parts of ABRAHAM, SARAI, a SERVANT, and the three VISITORS. DIRECT them to MIME the parts as you, the NARRATOR, read them.

REHEARSE the students in all the movements. READ a line. DISCUSS the action implied. HAVE the students perform that action. WORK your way line by line through pages 86 and 87. Students SHOULD NOT read any of the dialogue out loud. It is not important for them to follow along in the book.

AFTER the rehearsal, PERFORM the passage. READ the text straight through. HAVE students act out the entire thing.

3. **FINDING THE CLUES:** ASK "What does this story teach us about Abraham?" ANSWER: "That he was a good host." ASK: "What did you learn about him from all the action you see in the story?" ANSWER: "That he worked very hard to be a good host." DISCUSS the value of hospitality (to strangers).

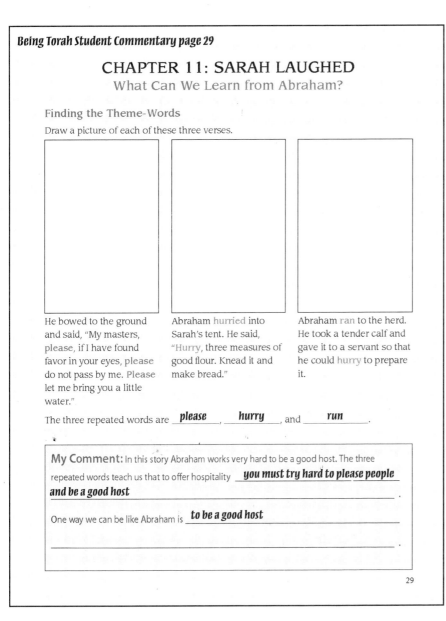

Being Torah Student Commentary page 29

CHAPTER 11: SARAH LAUGHED
What Can We Learn from Abraham?

Finding the Theme-Words
Draw a picture of each of these three verses.

He bowed to the ground and said, "My masters, please, if I have found favor in your eyes, please do not pass by me. Please let me bring you a little water."

Abraham hurried into Sarah's tent. He said, "Hurry, three measures of good flour. Knead it and make bread."

Abraham ran to the herd. He took a tender calf and gave it to a servant so that he could hurry to prepare it.

The three repeated words are ___*please*___, ___*hurry*___, and ___*run*___.

My Comment: In this story Abraham works very hard to be a good host. The three repeated words teach us that to offer hospitality ___*you must try hard to please people and be a good host*___.

One way we can be like Abraham is ___*to be a good host*___.

29

4. **MAKING MEANING:** Have students complete page 35 of the **Student Commentary** and move on to WRITING their comments without coming back together as a group.

5. **NETWORKING COMMENTS:** Follow usual procedure.

DID GOD LIE?
Student Commentary, page 30

Sarah originally says, "Abraham is too old to give me a child." God changes her words when reporting to Abraham, saying, "Sarah said, 'I am too old to have a child.'"

1. **SET INDUCTION:** DISCUSS "Does God lie? "Hear opinions and do not reach a conclusion.

2. **READING THE TEXT:** OPEN up the **Student Commentary** to page 30. Be the narrator yourself. Assign a few students to read the light blue type in the biblical texts. Have the whole class read the dark blue type.

3. **FINDING THE CLUES:** DISCUSS what they heard. ESTABLISH that God changed Sarah's words from "my husband is old" to "I am old."

4. **MAKING MEANING:** DISCUSS two things. (1) Was God telling a lie when changing Sarah's words? (Technically yes.) (2) Was there a good reason to for God to tell a lie? (Yes, to protect Abraham's feelings.) Have students FILL IN their own answers in the comment area.

5. **NETWORKING COMMENTS:** Follow usual procedure.

Additional Activity
WHAT KIND OF LAUGH DID SARAH LAUGH?

Here we are taking a close look at feelings that are treated very sparingly in the text. What does Sarah's laugh mean? The Torah doesn't provide any explanation. In this exercise we not only teach the students about the way the Torah "works" and about its characters, but we also give them an opportunity to fine-tune their perception of other people's feelings.

1. **SET INDUCTION:** REVIEW the first half of this chapter. Then MAKE a list of the different reasons people laugh. DIRECT the class: "As we read this half of the story, look for the reason why Sarah laughed."

2. **READING THE TEXT:** OPEN **Being Torah** to page 78.

DIVIDE the class in half. ASSIGN half the class to READ all of Sarah's speeches. ASSIGN the other half to read all of God's speeches. RESERVE the part of narrator for yourself.

READ the text with the assigned parts. PROMPT the class to repeat the speech Sarah gives and God's repetition.

It is to be hoped that some student (after hearing this material read a second time) will immediately jump to apply what they have learned about TEXT REPETITION up to this instance.

ESTABLISH the change and DISCUSS the possible interpretations.

ADDITIONAL LESSON SEEDS

The comments on page 90 trigger a number of insights. Shawna directs us to look at the Bedouin way of life. Angelica suggests a parallel story in the last chapter that we didn't have time to compare in the **Student Commentary**.

Being Torah Student Commentary page 30

Did God Lie?

Find the Change

When Sarah overheard God telling Abraham about having a child, she said:
"Now that my time has passed,
how can **my old husband and I** have a child?"

When God told Abraham about Sarah's words, God said:
"Why is Sarah laughing and saying:
'Will I really give birth, now that **I am old**?'"

How did God change Sarah's words? **by changing "my old husband" to "I"**
_____ .

My Comment: I think the reason that God changed Sarah's words was _____ **save Abraham's feelings. God wanted Sarah to be the focus of the birth since Abraham already had a son.** .

_____ **'s Comment:** _____ thought God changed Sarah's words in order to _____
_____
_____ .

30

CHAPTER 12—THE SODOM DEBATE

Being Torah, pages 81–83
Student Commentary, pages 31–32

ABSTRACT
BEING LIKE ABRAHAM

Draw a conclusion: Like "creation being GOOD," "brotherhood" being a constant responsibility, and "Abraham" being connected to "the land," "righteousness" is an eternal truth.

THE "KEEP" ECHO

Find the ECHO of the word "keeper." In the Garden Adam and Eve were asked to "keep" the Garden; in "Cain and Abel" Cain learned that he should have been his "brother's keeper." In this story, we learn that God wants Abraham's future-family to "keep" the mitzvot.

Draw a conclusion: Jews have a special responsibility to be keepers.

OVERVIEW

The Sodom debate provides us to with an opportunity to eavesdrop on a moment of Divine reflection and then witness a confrontation between God and Abraham. Both experiences teach us much about the process of justice.

The story begins with a prologue. God reflects: "Should I hide what I am going to do from ABRAHAM?" We are drawn in. For the first time we are allowed behind the heavenly scenes. We not only learn that God makes decisions (and hasn't planned everything), but we get to watch that decision-making process.

God plans to destroy Sodom and debates telling Abraham. Why the question? Up to this point God has only informed people of Divine intervention when it demands their response. Here we have three possibilities. One midrashic suggestion connects it to the promise of the Land to Abraham's future family. If God is changing the real estate, God then has an obligation to inform the tenant. Alternatively, the process was intended to model the process of justice. God is trying to prove to Abraham that the evil are punished. Or God is trying to evoke a sense of justice. God is really debating whether or not to test Abraham's righteousness. This theory suggests that God wanted him to argue back. As in most questions of motivation, one can gather lots of evidence but no sure proof.

The opening monologue provides two reasons for telling Abraham. The first is Abraham's political destiny, that Abraham's family will become great, powerful and influential. The second is much more revealing. "I have become close to him so that he will command his children and his future-family to keep the way of Adonai, to do what is right and just." We have learned previously that the Torah divides human evolution into three periods: Before the Flood, Before Abraham, and the History of the Jewish People. Each represents a stage of development. In the first era, humankind was abandoned to "master" the earth; in the second, a "covenant" was added; and in this monologue, God reveals that the essence of the third era of the Jewish experience was "being close." It is through the words of Isaiah (41.8) that we learn that God thought of Abraham as "My friend." This closeness is designed to teach humanity (via Abraham and family) how to act justly. Through the two halves of this monologue, God connects "all the nations of the world will be blessed through him" with "to do what is right and just".

We have often pointed out that the Torah evolves the meaning of words by slowly adding contexts. Here the word "keep," which has previously referred to "the Garden" and "brothers," now makes its first Jewish appearance in a sentence that includes *mitzvah* (command), *tzedek* (righteousness), *mishpat* (justice) and "the way of Adonai." God walking has gotten much more defined!

The essence of this story is the bargaining session over Sodom. Abraham makes a series of deals with God using the argument "Should not the Judge of all the earth do what is just?" In six steps(50, 45, 40, 30, 20 and

10) ABRAHAM bargains for the survival of the city. Each time God accedes. The key to the story: The word righteous, the central theme-word, is used seven times. It is centrally the theme-message.

Should Abraham have stopped at ten? Would God have agreed to a seventh round? Why did He stop there? Did God expect this response? All these and more remain unanswered. They all cry out for the making of midrash. What the story does make clear is that God appreciated Abraham's reaction, and that observable behavior manifests that which was being taught.

TEACHING TOOLS

OBJECTIVES

12.2a The learner will trace the further development of the "keeper" [ECHO].

12.2b The learner will isolate and define the THEME-WORD "righteous."

12.2c The learner will apply the theme concept of "righteous" to his/her actions.

SLIDE-IN VOCABULARY

numerous—very many
just righteous— according to law, correct
righteous—doing what is right

HEBREW VOCABULARY

tzadik—righteous person
tzedakah—that which is right, money shared to help others
mishpat—that which is just
shofet—judge

ACTIVITIES

BEING LIKE ABRAHAM
Student Commentary, page 31

RIGHTEOUSNESS [THEME-WORD] —"Righteous" is the core [THEME-WORD] of this chapter. In the focusing on this one word, students discover a central Jewish value.

1. **SET INDUCTION:** Have students LOOK at pages 81–83 of **Being Torah.** ASK them to look through the pages and guess the clues that we will be looking at. They should figure out the word "righteous" and the phrase that includes "keep".

2. **READING THE TEXT:** Let the students figure out the way the text is read. This shows their mastery of the learning process.

Being Torah Student Commentary page 31

CHAPTER 12: THE SODOM DEBATE
Being Like Abraham

Count the Number-Word

other answers:
· days of the week
· the word "brother" in Cain and Abel story

The words right and righteous are used ___7___ times in this story.

This is the same number of times as the word "good" in the creation story the word "covenant" in the Noah story and the number of blessing-lines Abraham received when he got to Canaan

A righteous person is someone who does the right thing

Choose someone else's comment and write it here.

My Comment: Abraham was righteous. He stood up for justice. He argued to save the people of Sodom and Gomorrah. If Abraham were alive today, he would stand up and argue for _____

_____'s Comment:
_____ would be like Abraham by _____

To be like Abraham, I should _____

3. **Finding CLUES:** DIRECT the class to COUNT the appearances of the THEME-WORD "righteous." ASK them to draw meaning from its sevenfold use. PROMPT: How is righteous here like "good" in the story of creation, and "brother" in the story of Cain and Abel? ESTABLISH that they are all absolute truths. By using it seven times, the Torah allows us to understand that it is important.

4. **MAKING MEANING:** WORK together to define "righteous." The WORDPLAY page on 85 of **Being Torah** will help. EXPLORE the connection between *tzedek, tzadik* and *tzedakah*.

   BEFORE allowing students to write their comments, DISCUSS possible answers. ENCOURAGE students to LIST as many items as possible in their COMMENTS. Then have them WRITE their comments in the **Student Commentary**.

5. **NETWORKING COMMENTS**: Follow the usual procedure with both comments.

THE "KEEPER ECHO"

In this exercise students are being asked to identify two distinct literary elements: the "Keeper" ECHO.

THE "KEEPER" [ECHO] —By now students should be very familiar with the "KEEPER" [ECHO].The first exercise forces the student to discern the pattern and immediately apply it to him/herself.

1. **SET INDUCTION:** WRITE the word "keeper" on the blackboard. ASK the class to define it. ASK: "Where in the Torah have we seen this word before?" ACCEPT no answers. Instead, DIRECT students to WORK IN SMALL GROUPS to complete the exercise on page 31 of the **Student Commentary**.

2. **READING THE TEXT:** Use page 32 of the **Student Commentary**. Students can read these texts quietly.

3. **FINDING THE CLUES:** GO OVER the answers. ESTABLISH that the word "keeper" now has a specifically Jewish application: the mitzvot.

Being Torah Student Commentary page 32

The Keeper Echo

Find the Echo in These Three Stories

In the story of The Garden we learn:
> Adonai God put the Human in the Garden of Eden to **work** it and to **keep** it.

We find an echo of this in the story of Cain and Abel:
> He said: "I don't know. Am I my brother's **keeper**?"

Now in this story of the Sodom Debate, God again echoes the Garden:
> "...he (Abraham) will command his children and his future-family to **keep** the way of Adonai."

My Comment. The echo in this story is the word _____**keep**_____. As we read the Torah we can watch this word grow. God told Adam and Eve to keep _____**the garden**_____. God wanted Cain to keep _____**his brother Abel**_____. Now God tells Abraham to have his family keep _____**the way of Adonai/God**_____.
Being a Jew means being a keeper. I think that keeping the way of Adonai means _____
_____
_____

CHECK for comprehension of the word mitzvot.

4. **MAKING MEANING:** Have students write their comments at the bottom of the page.

5. **NETWORKING COMMENTS:** Follow the usual procedure with both comments.

EXTENSION: Each group should DESIGN A POSTER listing and/or illustrating "keeping the way of Adonai," incorporating all the groups' individual answers.

Additional Activity

WHY DID GOD TELL ABRAHAM THAT SODOM WOULD BE DESTROYED?

Establish why God told Abraham about Sodom. **Missing Information**: The Torah gives no clear reason. We are left to speculate and to make midrash.

The learner will investigate the question: "Why did God tell Abraham?"

This exercise will focus attention on the question that God asks at the start of this chapter, allowing us to follow part of an internal God-conversation. We are still left with part of the question unanswered: Did God tell Abraham because of "truth-in-promising" laws regarding a bit of land, OR was the question posed as parent-to-child "teaching moment"? Both options are explored here.

NOTE: The Rashi who is quoted here, and whose picture you can find on page 121 of **Being**

Torah, was a third-grade student at one of our test schools. Rashi is his Hebrew school name.

1. **SET INDUCTION:** ASK: "How is studying Torah like riding on a train?" ACCEPT all answers. ENJOY and play with the images. Use some of them to set up this debate between God and Abraham.

2. **READING THE TEXT:** This text is one of the Torah's best dialogues. Here we want the students to hear Abraham's persistent but gracious challenge and God's polite acceptance. This is a story to read as drama.

ASSIGN one student to read the part of Adonai, one student to read ABRAHAM, and the remaining students to read the THEME-WORD "righteous". RESERVE the part of narrator for the teacher.

READ page 92. ASK: "What is really going on here?" ELICIT: "We are 'overhearing' God thinking out loud."

CONTINUE through the end of the chapter. ASK: "What attitude did Abraham have in his discussion with God?" EXPECT something along the lines of "humility."

3. **FINDING THE CLUES:** READ the two comments made by RASHI. DISCUSS possible reasons why God chose to tell Abraham about Sodom and Gomorrah. ACCEPT all answers, but help students to clarify them.

4. **MAKING MEANING:** ASK students to CREATE their comments.

5. **NETWORKING COMMENTS:** SHARE first comments within the _hevruta_. Diversity should reign supreme. Consensus is not necessary.

ADDITIONAL LESSON SEEDS

WORDPLAY: DIRECT students to page 97 of **Being Torah**. GUIDE them to understand the language building on the root TZ•D•K. TEACH them the Hebrew phrase from Deuteronomy 16:20, _tzedek tzedek tirdof_ (Justice, justice you shall pursue.) Possible EXTENSIONS: MAKE _tzedek_ posters depicting acts or issues of righteousness. LIST as many _tzadikim_ (righteous people) as possible. DESIGN a major project of _tzedek/tzedakah_ for the rest of the school year.

EXTENSION: LIST other instances in which justice/_tzedek_ is worth arguing for.

CHAPTER 13—ISAAC IS BORN

Being Torah, page 87

Student Commentary, page 33

ABSTRACT

SARAH'S DIARY

Count how many times the THEME-WORD "son" is used. Answer: 7 times

Draw a conclusion: Like the other "absolute truths" identified with seven-fold repetitions, God's first promise to Abraham is really coming true.

OVERVIEW

The central feature of this story is the assurances it gives that God keeps all promises. The long wait that Sarah and Abraham had for the fulfillment of their blessing prepares us for the longer wait Israel will have in Egyptian slavery. Ours is a God who remembers.

Abraham and Sarah each have an experience where God informs them that Isaac will be born, and each reacts with laughter. The opening of this chapter recaptures both moments.

> Adonai remembered SARAH as Adonai promised.
> Adonai did for SARAH as Adonai had spoken.

The midrash looks at this intentionally doubled statement and seeks explanation. It suggests that this double iteration was designed to recall the two instances of promise. The real secret here is revealed in the Joseph story. There, in explaining the two dreams Pharaoh had dreamed, Joseph says: "PHARAOH's dreams, they are one. God has told PHARAOH what will happen." What is suggested is that the doubling of a prophecy enhances its veracity. The same thing happens here.

Since chapter 9, "Abram: A Covenant," a new dynamic has entered the biblical narrative. While the image of remembering echoes back to Noah on the ark (see page 49 of **Being Torah**), it also serves another function. Starting with the prediction of the Exodus, symbols have begun to echo forward in anticipation. Here the doubled statement "Adonai remembered" anticipates chapter 26, where after the four hundred years of slaving and suffering, the Torah tells us: "God heard them. God remembered the covenant with ABRAHAM. God saw the Children of Israel. God knew." From that breakthrough revelation in God's first covenant with Abram, a process of preparation for the Exodus experience has begun.

Isaac, however, is still the central feature of this account. The theme-word "son" is used seven times to establish its centrality. Likewise, the democracy of parental involvement is continued, providing a moment of "naming" for each parent. Wonderfully, in Sarah's statement "God has made laughter for me. Everyone who hears will laugh for me," we get a sense of her joy, and an indicator of the meaning of her earlier laughter.

This is a short text, but one that truly celebrates life.

TEACHING TOOLS

OBJECTIVES

Through completing a short exercise and writing an entry in Sarah's diary, the learner will identify the [THEME-WORD] "son" and explore Sarah's feelings about the birth of her son.

SLIDE-IN VOCABULARY

nurse—feed a baby from its mother's breast

HEBREW VOCABULARY

yitzhak—he will laugh, ISAAC

ACTIVITIES

SARAH'S DIARY

Student Commentary, page 33

We are given relatively few textual clues as to exactly how Sarah was feeling once ISAAC was born. Sarah's particular brand of laughter is described, but very little else. The student now gets another chance to BE TORAH, putting him/herself into the story events and feelings of SARAH.

1. **SET INDUCTION:** REVIEW the two-part promise given to Abraham. ANSWER: (1) a large family and (2) ownership of the land of Canaan. ASK: "How long has Abraham had to wait for this to happen?" ANSWER: Many years. POINT OUT: In this story, the first part of the promise is coming true.

2. **READING THE TEXT:** This brief episode should be read as one unit. Our interest is in seeing both Abraham's and Sarah's individual investments in this shared moment. Let the girls in class READ the lines about SARAH, the boys READ the lines about ABRAHAM, and the teacher READ the remainder.

3. **FINDING THE CLUES:** DISCUSS (1) the special sense of joy that Abraham and Sarah felt; (2) the [ECHO] of the word "laughter." ASK: "Where did we hear about laughter in the Torah?" ACCEPT the answer of the story of the visitors, but don't

make a big deal out of it; (3) the differing roles of Abraham and Sarah. This may be a good place to talk about the fact that once the Jewish people saw the difference between men and women very differently than we do today.

4. **MAKING MEANING:** DIRECT students to work alone to COMPLETE page 33 in the **Student Commentary**. ASK students to SHARE the lesson they learned from the use of the NUMBER-WORD "son."

5. **NETWORKING COMMENTS:** Have students WRITE their diary entries individually and then SHARE them with the whole class. DISCUSS the range of emotions evidenced at different times in SARAH's life, as well as the different descriptions of various students.

ADDITIONAL LESSON SEEDS

This story deals with the practice of celebrating *simhas* (moments of joy). It may be a good time to teach that word, talk about when Jews celebrate and even throw a good classroom party.

Being Torah Student Commentary page 33

CHAPTER 13: ISAAC IS BORN
Sarah's Diary

Count the Number-Word

How many times is son used in this story? _____

I think that the Torah repeated the word son in order to point out that _____
_____ .

Dear Diary,

Today was the best day of my life. My son, Isaac, is now eating solid food. We gave a party. Abraham invited everyone.

Just a year ago, Abraham was sad. The thing we wanted most in life was **a child** _____ .

When I asked Abraham to have a child with my maid Hagar I had mixed feelings. I **very happy for Abraham to have a child** _____ but I **very jealous of Hagar** _____ .

After Hagar gave birth to a son she began to make fun of me.

When God told me that I was going to have a son, I laughed. I couldn't believe it. When Isaac was born, I was so glad. When they slapped his bottom and he cried for the first time, I felt **complete joy** _____
_____ .

Now, today we had this party and showed our son Isaac off to the whole world. All day I kept thinking **how wonderful Adonai is** _____
_____ .

Love, _____

33

CHAPTER 14—THE BINDING OF ISAAC

Being Torah, pages 90–93
Student Commentary, pages 34–35

ABSTRACT
WHY DID GOD TEST ABRAHAM?

Compare Bible stories and fairy tales. Establish that fairy tales have happy endings, are for kids, always teach one moral, make us happy, and contain their central meaning within the plot of the story. Bible stories are confusing, contain mixed messages and don't always end happily, and we must be just as concerned with the words used to tell the story as with the plot.

Explain some of the different things a test can accomplish. Answers: Tests can show a teacher how much a student has learned, show a student how much he or she has learned, let the school know what else must be taught, allow a teacher to reward a student who has learned, teach you something new, etc.

Extrapolate the purpose of the test of the binding of Isaac. Answer: **[Missing Information].** The text gives no clear explanation. We are left to find our own understanding. This is another place where we must make midrash.

OVERVIEW

The binding of Isaac is a biblical text we will never resolve and never fully understand. However, as a puzzle it does drive us to deeply consider the nature of our own faith.

This is the story of a test. We don't easily accept a God who tests us. The test involves child sacrifice. That idea seems unthinkable; somehow that idea must have been easier for earlier generations. Faith to the extreme is the story's apparent intent. We would be much more comfortable with a well-tempered faith.

Most elementary Bible curricula omit this story. It is a choice we understand. In our experience, many students have felt enriched through their struggle with this story. There is a feeling of power and pride that comes from wrestling with a difficult and important piece of Torah. Also within our experience are nightmares and fears caused by the motif of child sacrifice. Many teachers will rightly choose to skip this section. They do it with our blessings.

We considered eliminating this story as well. Two factors dissuaded us. First and foremost was an awareness that students would be exposed to this story whether or not we gave them a chance to explore its meaning. The motif of the High Holidays, the Torah reading for Rosh ha-Shanah, and the larger Christian culture give this story substantive exposure and much airplay. Whether or not they are allowed to study this text, our students will know about it. Second was a profound realization that the binding of Isaac was the necessary culmination of the Abraham cycle. Within its confusion and difficulty the saga culminates and concludes.

God makes a request: the sacrifice of Abraham's long-awaited son, Isaac. Abraham, without hesitation, proceeds step by step toward the act's completion. At the last minute the ceremony is halted. God acknowledges Abraham's faith and restates the two-part blessing. Abraham heads home. For all apparent purposes the story ends happily. Isaac is safe. The test is past, and the blessing is renewed. The path toward Israel's future seems safe. All is well, and we are shattered. The story has begun and ended in nineteen sentences, but the questions remain. How could God use child sacrifice as a test of faith? How could any father, let alone the prototypical Jewish father, accede to such a demand? How could Abraham's agreement to kill a child be considered the passing of a Divine test? What is there to be learned from this biblical tale of the macabre?

Tradition records that the Abraham cycle consists of ten tests. As usual, the number 10 is a prompt. We are directed to look for culmination and new beginnings. The binding of Isaac is the tenth and final test. For us it is the most difficult to understand. The Torah, anticipating this difficultly, suggests a process of inquiry. The text that opens this last test is an echo of the first test. The suggested solution—find the meaning in the earlier tests and see if it applies here.

The First Test

Take yourself (1) from your land, (2) from your birthplace, (3) from your father's house to the land; there I will let you see (or: which I will show you).

The Last Test

(1) Take your son, (2) your only one, (3) the one that you love, Isaac, and take yourself to the land of MORIAH (meaning "seeing") and offer him there as a sacrifice upon one of the mountains which I will tell to you.

This first test is a test of priorities. Abraham is asked to separate himself from his past, to leave heritage behind, and to pursue the vision of God. Abraham begins the quest. In pursuit of blessing, fame, family, fortune and inheritance he leaves his home and heads toward the unseen land. When he arrives, God appears.

One other test stands out as different—the Sodom debate. Here Abraham is expected to argue with God (demanding that the Teacher's behavior be consistent with the values that have been taught). If we accept the Sodom story as a test, if we

believe that Abraham passed this test, then God hoped for and expected his behavior. The test itself was both proof and learning experience. To pass this test, Abraham must reject God's plan.

To reconstruct: The central issue in this story is the nature of the test. We have difficulty with both the nature of the test and Abraham's response. The Torah anticipates this difficulty and connects this last test to the first test, suggesting that we compare. That much is clear. The results of the comparison seem to be subjective. Many possibilities emerge.

The test was, as first perceived, a check on the degree of faith Abraham will demonstrate. The test was a teaching experience. It could have been designed to show Abraham the strength of his faith; to justify a restatement of the blessing and covenant; or even to teach that God rejects the concept of child sacrifice. The test may have been designed, as was the Sodom debate, to be rejected.

Being Torah Student Commentary page 34

CHAPTER 14: THE BINDING OF ISAAC
Why did God Test Abraham?

The story of the **Binding of Isaac** begins with these words:

> After these things God tested Abraham and said to him: "Abraham." He said: "Hineini."

The first sentence of this story makes us ask, "Why did God test Abraham?" "What was the purpose of this test?"

Reasons for Giving a Test

Three reasons for giving a test are:

1. *teachers need to evaluate where you are in your work*

2. *you need to show your progress*

3. *teachers need evaluate their own progress*

34

The Torah suggests that we look at the collective tests Abraham has passed in his progress toward destiny and evaluate this one. The final understanding is in our hands.

As with many biblical stories, this one has revealed itself to us and then said, "You explain what I mean, you figure out what I teach." As we close-read, the story is simple no more. We can't just leave it as a Divine test and a human response. The text constantly challenges us to fill in blanks and expand our understanding. At the end, the ethics of God's test and the spiritual nature of Abraham's response aren't resolved. We are left to wonder and wrestle.

TEACHING TOOLS

OBJECTIVES

The learner will evaluate different responses to the question "Why did God test Abraham?" Choose an answer he/she likes, and discuss his/her choices.

Being Torah Student Commentary page 35

The Binding of Isaac is one of the hardest stories in the Torah. The hardest question in the story is, "Why did God test Abraham?" For more than a thousand years, many different Jews have struggled with this question and written their own comments. Here are some of their answers.

☐ *Just as a test in school can show a teacher how much you have learned,* God wanted to know if Abraham had enough faith to follow any command given by God.

☐ *Just as a test in school can let a teacher show how well he/she has taught the class,* God wanted to show the rest of the world how much faith Abraham had.

☐ *Just as a test in school can let a teacher reward and praise a student,* God knew that Abraham could pass this test, and God gave it so that Abraham could receive a reward for showing his faith.

☐ *Just as a test in school can let a student know how much she/he has learned,* God tested Abraham so that Abraham could learn about the strength of his faith.

☐ *Just as a test in school can teach you something new,* God tested Abraham to teach him that God doesn't want children sacrificed.

Put a ✔ next to the comments you like and an ✘ next to the comments you don't like. Discuss your choices.

Isaac

Count the Number Word

Count the number of times the word son is used in this story ___**10**___ .

> **My Comment:** Even though this story is about God testing Abraham's faith, the Torah makes a point of emphasizing the word son in order to teach us _____
>
> **that this incident had a profound effect on Isaac, his son. Isaac has a more distant relationship with God than his father did.**

35

KEY HEBREW VOCABULARY

hineini—I am here

WHY DID GOD TEST ABRAHAM?

Student Commentary, pages 34–35

This exercise goes to the core of this story. It begins by asking the central question and providing a series of alternative explanations.

1. **SET INDUCTION:** ASK "Why do you think God tests people? Why do you think tests are given?" ACCEPT all answers.

2. **READING THE TEXT:** The drama of this text demands a certain kind of quiet focus. This is the one time in the year when the teacher should just read the text. It is perhaps time to have students listen without opening

their books, just trying to imagine the scenes and action.

3. **FINDING THE CLUES:** DIRECT students to open the **Student Commentary** to pages 34–35. As a class, COMPLETE the text at the top on the first page. ASK the students to fill in the general part about the reasons for giving tests. Share answers. Then move on to the second page. FILL IN the top of the second page and DISCUSS it. There is no single answer we are trying to teach here.

4. **MAKING MEANING:** Have students open **Being Torah** to pages 90–93. Have them count the number of times the word **son** is used in this story. It is printed in blue and appears eight times. There are two ways to understand the eight. Here eight is acting like a **theme**, and eight also makes **son** a number-word in this story, with Isaac being the fulfillment of the covenant. Have students write their own comments.

5. **NETWORKING COMMENTS:** Use the usual procedure.

ADDITIONAL LESSON SEEDS

There is a dialogue that goes on between Shawna, Owen and Sacha in their commentaries on page 94 of **Being Torah.** They share their feelings about this story. This may be a good hook for allowing your students to vent their feelings about this story, too.

CHAPTER 15—REBEKAH AT THE WELL

Being Torah, pages 95–97
Student Commentary, pages 36–38

ABSTRACT

WHAT WAS THE SERVANT'S TEST?

Compare the servant's projection of what he would ask the ideal woman with her projected response. Answer: It is a TEXT REPETITION [+]. He asks for water for himself. She must add the offer to water the camels.

Compare the ideal woman's projected response with Rebekah's actual answer. Answer: It is a TEXT REPETITION [+]. The ideal woman added the offer to bring the camels water. Rebekah goes beyond that, offering to fully satisfy the camels' need for water.

Draw a conclusion: To pass the servant's test and be the ideal wife, a woman must go out of her way to be hospitable by anticipating human needs. Rebekah far exceeds the exemplary behavior.

HAVEN'T WE HEARD THIS BEFORE?

Compare the way Rebekah provides hospitality in story "Rebekah at the Well" with the way Abraham provides hospitality in the story "Sarah Laughed." Answer: It is a direct [ECHO]. The three key THEME-WORDS: "drink," "hurry," and "please".

Draw a conclusion: Rebekah is the perfect bride for Abraham's son because she exemplifies the family *mitzvah*: providing hospitality. She is just like Abraham.

OVERVIEW

In retrospective given the women's movement, it is now possible to suggest that the official list of patriarchs should read Abraham, Rebekah and Jacob. On at least one level, the Torah understands this, granting Rebekah an establishing story that is unique in the Torah.

As we will learn later (in the gray matter on page 123 of **Being Torah**), Isaac is forbidden to leave the land of Israel. Abraham sends a servant back to the old country to find the right bride. The servant and Rebekah play out this scene together. Only via the midrash do we learn that the servant is Eleazer.

Two wonderful text clues establish Rebekah as the perfect continuity for Abraham's family. Prior to beginning the test, the servant sets up the standard by which the ideal woman is to be judged: Without a jar, it is difficult to draw water from a well. (We are not talking about a wishing well with a bucket). The servant waited by the well, apparently unable to drink or water his camels. To each woman who passed by, he would ask only for himself: "Please, may I drink from your jar?" To pass the test, the woman had to do more than just grant the favor. The right woman also had to perceive the animals' needs and expand her kindness, responding, "Drink, and I will also draw water for your camels." The

Torah doesn't reveal the nature of the test, but rather allows us to discover it by comparison, a TEXT REPETITION [+]. The same device is used to show that Rebekah did more than pass the test. She adds even further to the formula: "I will also draw water for your camels until they have finished drinking." We learn that the essence of *hesed* (see below) is anticipating needs and responding.

The Torah twice tells us that Rebekah hurried and once describes her running to provide this hospitality. Both the context of the actions and the word echoes tie these actions back to Abraham's act of hospitality (Chapter 11, "Sarah Laughed"). We see the coming continuity of a family tradition.

In this story the Torah introduces the word *hesed* (usually rendered as "mercy," though we translate it as "the right thing"). While the reference is to God and not Rebekah, it becomes a descriptor for the type of act of "loving kindness" she performs in this chapter. In modern contexts, the catchwords *gemilut hasadim* have become paired with *tzedakah* (another Abraham theme-word) to cover the whole spectrum of mitzvot that respond to human need. These acts are rooted in the models of Abraham and Rebekah.

TEACHING TOOLS

OBJECTIVES

Through the use of TEXT REPETITION the learner will identify what Rebekah needed to do to pass the test.

The learner will evaluate Rebekah's actions to discover that she more than passed the test.

Through the use of [ECHO] the learner will find the connection between the stories of Abraham and Rebekah.

SLIDE-IN VOCABULARY

draw water—take water from a well

drinking trough—long, thin container that holds water

HEBREW VOCABULARY

hesed—right thing, kindness

ACTIVITIES

WHAT WAS THE SERVANT'S TEST?
DID REBEKAH PASS THE TEST?
Student Commentary, pages 36–37

These two sections of the **Student Commentary** are brief and very focused. This is a classic example of repetition with a variation. Here the servant sets a standard of performance for the ideal woman, and in exact repetition (with an addition) Rebekah surpasses it. The student will first examine the exact words of the servant to determine the specific nature of the test he would pose and exactly what the woman must offer to do in order to pass.

1. **SET INDUCTION:** REVIEW the idea of a TEXT REPETITION. ESTABLISH: When we hear something repeated in the Torah, we look very closely for what has changed—TEXT REPETITION [+] or TEXT REPETITION [-].

Being Torah Student Commentary page 36

CHAPTER 15: REBEKAH AT THE WELL

What Was the Servant's Test?

The servant was sent to find the ideal woman for Isaac. The servant invented a test that he shared in a prayer to God. He said:

> Let it be that when I say to a woman,
> "Please may I drink from your jar?"
> One will answer,
> "Drink, and I will also draw water for your camels."
> She will be the one that you have chosen for Isaac.

In this test the servant asks for *water* .

In order to pass this test the woman must do what was asked *give water*

and all go beyond it and *offer water to the camels* .

36

2.READING THE TEXT: CAST the text by assigning one person to READ the part of the servant, another to READ the part of the. ideal woman, and a third to READ the part of Rebekah. You may want to have the rest of the class READ the narration.

AFTER the first "perfect reading," have the servant REPEAT his request and the ideal woman REPEAT her response. ASK: "What has been added?" ESTABLISH: She did more than was asked. NOW COMPARE the ideal woman with Rebekah. ASK: "What has been added?" ESTABLISH: Rebekah does even more.

3.FINDING THE CLUES: OPEN the **Student Commentary** to page 36 and REVIEW the directions. Have students WORK IN PAIRS to complete both parts A and B. CHECK to make sure that the students caught the simple TEXT REPETITION [+] that the woman must offer the servant water (as requested) and offer to give water to his camels, too (beyond the request). Go OVER all answers.

4.MAKING MEANING: TALK about what this test teaches us about Rebekah. INTRODUCE the word _hesed_. DISCUSS the kinds of acts of _hesed_ needed today. DIRECT students to complete the comments on page 37 of the **Student Commentary**.

5.NETWORKING COMMENTS: Follow the usual procedures.

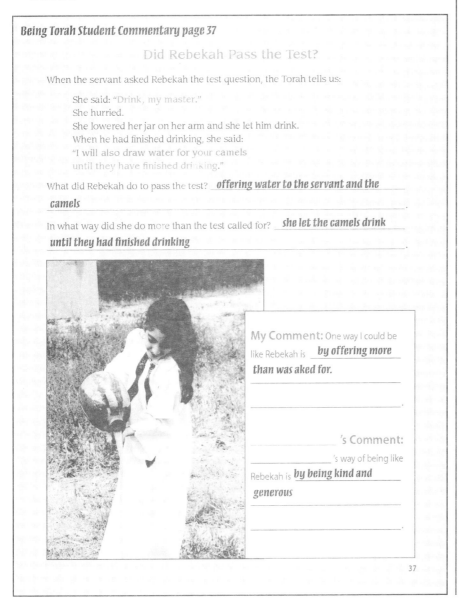

Being Torah Student Commentary page 37

Did Rebekah Pass the Test?

When the servant asked Rebekah the test question, the Torah tells us:

> She said: "Drink, my master."
> She hurried.
> She lowered her jar on her arm and she let him drink.
> When he had finished drinking, she said:
> "I will also draw water for your camels
> until they have finished drinking."

What did Rebekah do to pass the test? _offering water to the servant and the camels_.

In what way did she do more than the test called for? _she let the camels drink until they had finished drinking_.

My Comment: One way I could be like Rebekah is _by offering more than was aked for._

_____ 's Comment:
_____ 's way of being like Rebekah is _by being kind and generous_

37

HOW IS REBEKAH LIKE ABRAHAM?

Student Commentary, page 38

The clue to Rebekah's being the perfect bride for Isaac comes in the [ECHO] of the words "hurry" and "run"; her actions duplicate the hospitality Abraham showed to strangers. This exercise presents the Abraham and Rebekah texts side by side, so the students can easily compare the actions of the two characters.

1. **SET INDUCTION:** REVIEW the idea of an [ECHO]. ESTABLISH that the Torah [ECHO]s certain words when it wants to connect different stories. When we find an [ECHO] it is a clue that we are to learn something by bringing these two stories together.

2. **READING THE TEXT:** BREAK the class into small groups, DIRECT them to open to page 38 in their **Student Commentary**, read these two stories, and find the [ECHO].

3. **FINDING THE CLUES:** GO over the material. ESTABLISH that the [THEME WORD]s "run," "hurry" and "please" connect these two stories. ASK: "How is Rebekah like Abraham?" ANSWER: They both went out of their way to provide hospitality. ASK: "How does this make Rebekah the perfect bride for Isaac?" ANSWER: She would carry on the family traditions.

4. **MAKING MEANING:** ALLOW students time to write their comments.

5. **NETWORKING COMMENTS:** USE usual procedures.

Being Torah Student Commentary page 38

How Rebekah Is Like Abraham

Compare these two stories.

Abraham Welcomes Strangers

(Abraham) was sitting
at the entrance of the tent...
Suddenly three men were standing
over him.
He saw them and ran toward them.

He bowed to the ground and said,
"My Masters,
Please, if I have found favor
in your eyes,
please do not pass by me.
Please let me bring you a little water,
Wash your feet and rest under the tree.
Let me bring you some bread."

...Abraham hurried into Sarah's tent.
He said, "Hurry!"
Three measures of good flour—
Knead it and bake bread."

Abraham ran to the herd.
He took a tender calf
and gave it to a servant
so that he could hurry to prepare it.
He took yogurt and milk
and the calf that had been cooked,
and served it to them.

Rebekah at the Well

Almost before he could finish speaking
there came Rebekah, Abraham's niece.
Her jar was on her shoulder.
She was beautiful to look at.

The servant ran to meet her.
He said, "Please—
let me drink a little water from your jar."
She said, "Drink, my master."
She hurried.
She lowered her jar on her arm
and she let him drink.
When he had finished drinking, she said:
"I will also draw water for you camels
until they have finished drinking."

Hurrying, she emptied her jar in the
drinking trough.
Again she ran to the well to draw water.
She brought enough water for all the
camels.

What is alike in these two stories? **Both Abraham and Rebekkah ran, hurried and tried hard to please visitors**

How does the Torah show that Rebekah was like Abraham? What mitzvah do they share? **hakhnasat orhim—offering hospitality**

38

CHAPTER 16—REBEKAH MEETS ISAAC

Being Torah, page 99
Student Commentary, page 39

ABSTRACT
WHAT MAKES A GOOD MARRIAGE?

Compare the description of the relationship between Adam and Eve with that of the relationship between Rebekah and Isaac. Answer: In both, drawing together and comforting each other is a major idea.

OVERVIEW

Through matching destinies, Isaac and Rebekah are fated for each other. Isaac becomes whole again when she comes into his life. Yes, this is a love story.

Like chapter 13, "Isaac is Born," this chapter is a short closing piece that sums up the introduction of Rebekah into Abraham's family. In many ways the Isaac story is defective. Among the missing elements is a parental blessing. Within the framework of the Torah, that blessing is never voiced, and God only blesses him once (maybe twice) late in family development. This chapter opens with a blessing that Rebekah's parents give her, "May you become a thousand times many, and may your future-family inherit the gates of their enemies." It is a direct restatement of the two-part promise and a specific echo of the last blessing God gave Abraham (in chapter 14, "The Binding of Isaac"): "I will make you many, very many. Your future-family shall inherit the cities of their enemies." This blessing is added proof that Rebekah is destined to be part of Abraham's family (and in fact destined to be the one who insures their future). While cultural contexts made it impossible for the Torah to overtly acknowledge Rebekah's leadership role, by inclusion and omission, a subtle understanding is shared.

In the second half of the text Isaac and Rebekah meet. It is love at first sight. As with Abraham and Sarah's mutual involvement in Isaac's birth and naming, the Torah proves this instant love through separate but equal verses. Isaac "lifted up his eyes and saw" her coming; "REBEKAH lifted up her eyes and saw ISAAC." It is the biblical equivalent of a carved heart with initials. In closing, the Torah tells us "ISAAC took her into his mother SARAH's tent. ISAAC found comfort after his mother died." This is a real-life fulfillment of the relational definition given in the story of Adam and Eve (page 23), "a man leaves his father and mother and clings to his wife."

The midrash also has a wonderful time with this location, explaining that "entering Sarah's tent" meant providing Jewish continuity. They made Rebekah the second Jewish homemaker who reintroduced in Abraham's camp the customs of baking *hallah* and lighting Shabbat candles—the things Sarah had begun.

TEACHING TOOLS
OBJECTIVES

By comparing the descriptions of this marriage to that of Adam and Eve the learner will extrapolate his/her view of the special meaning of marriage.

SLIDE-IN VOCABULARY

lifted up eyes—looked

WHAT MAKES A GOOD MARRIAGE?

1. **SET INDUCTION:** EXPLAIN "You've done fifteen chapters in **Being Torah,** and you've learned a lot about how to figure out the clues in a story. This time you're going to have a chance to work out the whole story on your own."

2. **READING THE TEXT:** DIRECT the groups to (1) READ both the gray matter on page 114 and the story on page 115, and (2) complete the worksheets on page 46 and page 47 in the **Student Commentary**.

   ALLOW time for them to complete the process.

MONITOR their progress and provide help as necessary.

ESTABLISH that in the same way that Adam found help from a mate who "fit with him," Isaac was comforted by his marriage to Rebekah.

3. **FINDING CLUES:** NOTE that we have referenced the verse in the Garden story where the Torah says: "A man leaves his mother and father and 'clings' to his wife." For many, the word "clings" is problematic. This difficulty may be an opening to a wonderful discussion of the image of "clinging." It may be good to talk about whether "clinging" is a good descriptor for husband and wife, and if not, what would be better. More fun would be involving the parents of your students in the discussion.

5. **NETWORKING COMMENTS:** Go over the groups' work. ESTABLISH from the first part of the exercise that the matching blessings show that Rebekah was fated to be part of Abraham's family (by marrying Isaac) because they were to have the same future.

ADDITIONAL ACTIVITY [ECHO] HUNT

Find the [ECHO] that connects the blessing given to Rebekah by her parents with that given by God to Abraham. Answer: Both contain the same two-part promise: large family and

inheritance of the land. The THEME-WORDs "many" and "inherit" link the blessings.

Draw a conclusion. Rebekah and Isaac have the same blessing. They are destined to be together because they have been wished the same future.

The learner will compare the blessing given to Rebekah with the two-part blessing given to Abraham and, through identifying the [ECHO], establish that Rebekah and Abraham's family had a common future.

This particular text is simple and clear. Rebekah's family's blessing is a direct translation of Abraham's Divine blessing. This [ECHO] establishes a connected destiny that links her to the family. It is a good opportunity to allow students a sense of real ownership of the study material. Here we will have them work through the whole learning process in _hevruta_.

Being Torah Student Commentary page 39

CHAPTER 16: REBEKAH MEETS ISAAC
What Makes a Good Marriage?

In the story **Beginnings**, the Torah begins to teach us about what it means to be married. It says:

> This is why a man leaves his father and mother
> and clings to his wife and they become one.

In this story, we learn a little bit more. The Torah tells us:

> He took Rebekah to be his wife. He loved her.
> Isaac found comfort after his mother died.

My Comment: Isaac was sad and lonely after the death of his mother. Rebekah helped him feel better. In order for people to become a family, they need to be like Isaac and Rebekah and **help each other feel better, be a good comforter to their family members.**

Choose someone else's comment and write it here.

_____'s Comment:

_____ thought that becoming a family means _____

39

CHAPTER 17—
JACOB: ROUND 1—THE BIRTH, ROUND 2—THE BIRTHRIGHT

Being Torah, pages 101–103
Student Commentary, page 40

ABSTRACT
WHAT DID GOD PREDICT?

Explain what is unusual about the prediction God makes to Rebekah about the future of her two unborn sons. Answer: It is normative for the elder son to be the leader. It is ironic that while the elder son should be the dominant force, the Jewish tradition is filled with younger sons who run the family: Isaac, Jacob, Joseph, Moses, David, and Solomon, to name a few.

Count the number of times the THEME-WORD "Jacob" is used. Answer: 10 times, including one time when the root-word *ekev*, "heel," is used.

Count the number of times the THEME-WORD "Esau" is used. Answer: 10 times, including one time when his other name, Edom, is substituted.

Draw a conclusion: God promised Abraham that he would be the father of many nations. Each member of his future-family shared in his blessing, even those who would not evolve into the Jewish people. Esau is blessed just as Jacob is, though he will have a different future.

OVERVIEW

Starting in the womb, the new course for the development of Jewish history is set. Through a series of struggles, Jacob will lead our evolution to a new level.

Robert Alter, a professor of literature at the University of California in Berkeley, introduced the idea of "type-scene" into the active vocabulary of Torah learners. He teaches that certain events happen in the lives of most biblical heroes (e.g., meeting their wives at the well). Over the course of reading our way through the Torah, we build up an expectation of what should happen at these set-events (e.g., meet the girl, love at first sight, meet the family, get married). No hero ever completely fulfills the pattern; instead, his variation from that pattern reveals much of the uniqueness of his personality.

To qualify as a biblical hero, the first condition seems to be having a mother who has spent a great deal of time being barren. It is as if we specifically need the indication that, especially in our hero's case, God is a partner in his creation. Rebekah qualifies as a hero's mother by following Sarah's example.

The second qualification is a good annunciation. This is where God or one of the Divine messengers informs the parent(s) that a child will soon be born. This annunciation often comes with the roots of a name and with a prediction about the child's nature. Rebekah's prenatal examination reveals twins and the prediction. "Two families are in you. The two families inside you will be separated. One nation shall be stronger than the other. The older will serve the younger." Here the whole pattern is set for the Jacob cycle. We have struggle; we have the younger son disinheriting the older.

The norm in biblical life is for the elder son to inherit the father's wealth (birthright) and position (blessing). The Torah, however, is made up of exceptions: Abraham, Isaac, Jacob, Joseph and Moses are all younger sons. It is as if the merit or skill of each individual (or mother) must win his spot in continuity. This is what we will see in the Joseph saga. Rebekah, the self-assertive biblical woman (par excellence), will seek out the right course just as directly as she went into action at the well. Ultimately Jacob will win his right to be the continuity factor in Jewish history on two levels. First will be the assertiveness (survival) skills he demonstrates that insure his own victory; second will be the quality of the relationship he evolves with God.

The conception of children should be a moment of great joy to Rebekah. It isn't. With a wonderful vagueness, the Torah involves us in explaining her reaction. We are told, "Twins struggled in her womb, and she said: 'If it is like this, why am I living?'" We know she is unhappy. We don't know the source. Is it the pain of the children's kicking or the idea of their struggle that upsets her? Is it the present she is experiencing or the future she is imagining that rates the reaction? (Only her midrash-maker knows for sure!)

The next qualification is a good learning experience. Here Esau gets two names, "hairy" and "Red." Both make him the prototypical Roman warrior, which is exactly how the midrash sees him. Jacob gets the first of his two names, "the heel-grabber," which will personify his early (pre–Israel) years. The equality of each son having two names (ultimately) parallels the number-words in this section. Jacob's word stem is used 10 times. Esau's word stem is used 9 (plus). Edom is used once. This is a direct echo of the theme of separate-but-equal brothers we have seen before. In *Cain and Abel* Cain is used 14 times (7x2) and Abel is used 7. Ishmael's family produces 12 princes, as does Isaac's.

We have also seen the parallel involvement of Rebekah's and Isaac's love. It continues here: "Isaac loved Esau" and "Rebekah loved Jacob." The pattern "his son" and "her son" will continue in the next chapter. Meanwhile, the midrash-makers noted the uneven parallel: Isaac's love was conditional "because he ate the meat from the hunt," while Rebekah's love for Jacob needed no qualification.

The last part of the chapter shows the first fulfillment of God's prediction. Here the younger son inherits the birthright (wealth) of the elder. The same scene affirms three things: (1) Jacob's heel-grabbing cleverness; (2) Esau's lack of appreciation of family heritage; and (3) the trueness of the younger disenfranchising the elder.

Remember "Columbo"? Peter Falk was wonderful, but what made the show special was the fact that the opening teaser showed you the murder. You knew from the beginning who was guilty. You knew the ending. The fun was watching how it came to be. The same is true of the Jacob cycle. We know he will emerge as the leader of the next generation; the fun is in watching his victory.

This is but the beginning of the story.

TEACHING TOOLS

OBJECTIVES

Through close reading the learner will establish that God predicted that the younger brother, Jacob, would dominate the older, Esau.

After comparing God's prediction to the actual events, the learner will arrive at the question: "Why was Esau not the leader of the Jewish people?" and then answer it through the clues found in close reading.

SLIDE-IN VOCABULARY

predict—tell about the future

firstborn right—a custom where the oldest son becomes the next leader of the family after his father's death and inherits most of the family wealth.

HEBREW VOCABULARY

Ya'akov, ekev—heel

esav—grass

edom—red

WHAT DID GOD PREDICT?
Student Commentary, page 40

This text presents two of three conflicts that will take place between Jacob and Esau. It will contrast their personalities while showing a certain basic equality, using each of their names ten times. This exercise is designed to have students realize (1) that God is predicting the future of the Jewish people, and (2) that the younger son taking control of the family was highly unusual in that society.

1. **SET INDUCTION:** INTRODUCE the story as follows: "This is the first of a series of stories about Isaac's two sons, Jacob and Esau." WRITE the names on the blackboard. CONTINUE: "In it we will see the two of them struggling with each other. That is why the story is called Round 1 and Round 2, just like in a boxing match."

2. READING THE TEXT: ASSIGN the following parts: REBEKAH, ISAAC, ADONAI, JACOB and ESAU. Also APPOINT a scorekeeper to mark off every time that Jacob's and Esau's names are used.

3. FINDING THE CLUES: Working as a class, ESTABLISH three things:

(a) ESTABLISH the pattern of the two brothers fighting. MAKE sure that the students see both the struggle in the womb and the stolen birthright as part of the pattern of conflict.

(b) ESTABLISH that Isaac was silent. ASK the student who was assigned the part of Isaac what part he played in the story. THE ANSWER will be "I didn't have any words to say." ASK: "What does the Torah say you did?" ANSWER: "ISAAC pleaded with Adonai for his wife. "ASK: "Why doesn't the Torah tell uss what he said?" A FIRST ANSWER may be "It wasn't important." POINT OUT that all through his life Isaac doesn't get to say important things. Isaac is the most quiet of biblical characters. He doesn't have control over his family. Nothing he says makes a difference.

Chapter 17 *Jacob: Round 1 — Birth* Genesis 25.19-34
Round 2 — Birthright

This is the family history
Of Isaac, son of Abraham.
Abraham fathered Isaac.
When Isaac was 40 years old
he took Rebekah as his wife.

Isaac pleaded with Adonai
for his wife
because she had not
given birth to children.
Adonai let Isaac's plea work,
and Rebekah became pregnant.

Twins struggled in her womb,
and she said:
"If it is like this,
why am I living?"
She went to seek out Adonai.

101

Being Torah Student Commentary page 40

CHAPTER 17: JACOB: ROUND 1—BIRTH, ROUND 2—BIRTHRIGHT
What Did God Predict?

The Prediction

When the twins were fighting in Rebekah's womb, the Torah tells us:

> Adonai said:
> "Two nations are in you.
> The families inside you will be separated.
> One nation shall be stronger than the other.
> The older will serve the younger."

The two nations are ____**Esau**____ and ____**Jacob**____ .

The nation that will rule is ____**Jacob**____ .

Brothers

Count the number of times Jacob's name is used	**9**
Count the number of times heel is used (no words in parentheses)	**1**
Total	**10**
Count the number times Esau's name is used	**9**
Count the number of times that Edom is used	**1**
Total	**10**

My Comment: I think the lesson these names teach is ___*that the two names are used the same number of time, Esau and Jacob are equal*___ .

This is like the name lesson in Cain and Abel that teaches ___*it is good to be brothers*___ .

40

(c) DIRECT the class to LOOK at the numbers on the blackboard. They will be 9 and 9. ASK: "What can we learn from this?" ANSWER: "That the two brothers were equal." ASK: "Where have we seen this before?" ANSWER: "'The story of Cain and Abel; there the score was 7 to 14. "ESTABLISH that the number 9 has nothing to teach us. ASK: "Who can figure out how to make the score 10 to 10?" ALLOW them time to hunt. ANSWER: Add "heel," Jacob's root word, to his score, and Edom, Esau's other name, to his.

4. MAKING MEANING: ASK the students to COMPLETE the work page individually. This will establish the wording of God's prediction that the older will serve the younger.

ENCOURAGE questions from the class. ESTABLISH THESE QUESTIONS: God's words sound like a puzzle. What do they mean? How can any woman have nations in her? What is hinted at by "older" and "younger"?

ADDITIONAL LESSON SEEDS

THE WORDPLAY on page 104 allows you to focus on the meaning of Jacob's and Esau's names and the connection of the names to their personalities.

Role playing seems like a good way to demonstrate the difference between the two brothers. Scenes from the family life can be played out in class, either the famous birthright sale or imaginary ones based on the text.

COMMENTARIES

Harrison's comment on page 105 provides a chance to talk about the conflicts in Isaac's family. Point out to students that the names for both this and the next chapter, Round 3, imply a competition or a struggle. Why?

Paulina's comments allows a discussion of the woman's point of view, especially when we consider the silence of Isaac.

Rachel's comment asks if Jacob really should be the next Jewish leader. She provides a good overview for the next few chapters. Rashi (the child) responds directly to Josh.

CHAPTER 18—
JACOB: ROUND 3—THE BLESSING

Being Torah, pages 106–112
Student Commentary, pages 41–42

ABSTRACT
DID ISAAC KNOW?

Based on a close reading of the Torah, establish whether Isaac knew that Jacob was tricking him and stealing the blessing. Answer: [**Missing Information**]. We don't know. We can amass clues but must draw our own conclusion. The text calls for the making of midrash.

OVERVIEW

Even if you didn't know anything about number-words and theme-words or any of these fancy devices in Biblical narrative, you'd know that "blessing" was the key word in this story.

The story culminates in Isaac blessing Jacob with a perfect seven part blessing. The text of **Being Torah** has not been structured to reveal this, but seven verb clauses shape the blessing: dive, serve, bow, master, born, curse and bless. This is a direct echo of the seven-part blessing God gave to Abram (Chapter 7, "Abram: Leaving Home") and God gave to Isaac. It suggests that, regardless of Isaac's awareness, the blessing did go to the right son.

In the previous chapter we noticed the partisanship demonstrated by each parent toward a particular son. That pattern continues here: "REBEKAH heard what ISAAC said to ESAU his son." "REBEKAH said to JACOB her son." Ultimately, Rebekah has the greater force of will. As the story weaves its tangled plot, a series of theme-words echoes at us. "Blessing" (19 times) is the dominant voice; "son" is used 22 times (in the real text—only 20 times in **Being Torah**); and "brother" is used 7 times. These words shape the story's direction. We see through them the Torah's ambivalence. Jacob must emerge as the heir to the blessing, since he is indeed the next generation, but Esau must not be totally disenfranchised. While the right son must take the lead, the complete family must be preserved. We see this in **Being Torah**, where Isaac and Ishmael come together to bury Abraham. The same will be true (Chapter 22, "Births and Deaths") when Isaac is buried by Jacob and Esau.

It is in this spirit that Isaac ultimately blesses both sons. While he first protests to Esau, "What can I do for you, my son?" implying that his blessings have been used up, he soon gives him a five-part blessing that grants wealth and power, reserving the idea of "through you will others be blessed" to Jacob. Everything has been passed on except for the tradition of "being a blessing." We can note that this is the true family treasure.

The continuity of blessing and the portion each child has in the family inheritance is clearly the overt focus of this story, but it is far from the central issue. The story is really one of the great biblical mysteries. As with "The Binding of Isaac," we are totally perplexed by Isaac's actions. We do not know whether his actions here (like his actions there) are ironically informed or totally naïve. We do not know if he knows that he has been tricked, if he is cluing Jacob to his awareness, or whether he almost stumbles onto the truth but is ultimately fooled. Once more the Torah has left us to dig for an understanding in a story filled with overlapping clues.

TEACHING TOOLS

OBJECTIVES

After reading, considering and listing the evidence, learners will draw their conclusions and answer the question "Did Isaac know?" (that he was blessing Jacob, not Esau).

HEBREW VOCABULARY

kol ya'akov—the voice of Jacob
y'dai ey-sav—the hands of Esau

DID ISAAC KNOW?

Student Commentary, pages 41-42

Figuring out the motivation behind Isaac's comments is a great challenge (especially since you can't be wrong). Your class should have fun working with the evidence in the chapter and figuring out the different aspects of this question. Depending on the nature of your class, you may want to start with the evidence gathered by the students of Mrs. Midlo. Add to it or challenge your class to find the evidence on their own and then check against the material in the **Student Commentary**. In either case, a careful reading of the text is required. You get to unfold the text layer by layer.

1. **SET INDUCTION:** ASK "When you read a biblical text, what kind of clues do you look for?" LIST answers on the blackboard: THEME-WORD, NUMBER-WORD, [ECHO], TEXT REPETITION, and [MISSING INFORMATION].

2. **READING THE TEXT:** This is a long story, and a good one. While it has some dependence on the identification of theme-words, the central problem in this story involves [MISSING INFORMATION], and so a first reading can easily be done silently. Here we recommend that it be used to further involve students in ownership of the process of "unpacking" the text. BREAK the class into *hevruta*. DIRECT the groups to read the story and make a list of all the important clues they can find. EXPLAIN: "This time we are going to see what you can do with the text on your own."

3. **FINDING THE CLUES:** COLLECT on the blackboard all the clues that have been found. (HOPE that at least some of the elements in the "text clues" list will be found.) Then ASK: "What do you think are the big questions in this chapter?" Collect these on the blackboard. SECOND READING: DRAMATIZE the text (in order to focus on the details of the plot). This reading will point out the lack of clarity in the dialogue and reveal how little we are directly told about whether Isaac knew that Jacob was stealing the blessing.

ASSIGN students to read Jacob, Esau, Rebekah and Isaac. You may want (at this time) to assign student narrators. Having the class EMPHASIZE bold material will not enhance your purposes here.

The process here will be to use the teacher's role as director as well as the students' role as actors to show the open-ended nature of this text. ALLOW

Being Torah Student Commentary page 41

CHAPTER 18: JACOB: ROUND 3—THE BLESSING
Did Isaac Know?

Read this letter from Mrs. Midlo's class. Then look through this story in *Being Torah* to see what other evidence you can find. Write your own answer to their questions.

Dear Being Torah people,

We want to know what you think. Our class was studying Chapter 18 of Being Torah, the story of JACOB: ROUND 3—THE BLESSING. For two weeks we've been having this big argument over one question. Most of our class thinks that Jacob fooled his father, and Isaac really thought that he was blessing Esau. One group, Sean, Melissa, Uri and Debbie, think that Isaac knew that he was blessing Jacob. We've read the story at least twenty times and even had a debate. Here is what we found.

Kathy: Isaac loved Esau better than Jacob because of the meat he hunted. He wouldn't give his favorite son's blessing to the other son on purpose.

Uri: Isaac must have known that Esau sold his firstborn right. Even though he loved his son, he knew that Esau wouldn't make a good family leader. He could have been happy that the smarter son was going to get the blessing.

David: The Torah tells us that Isaac thought he was blessing Esau. It says, "He didn't know him because his hands were hairy like his brother Esau's hands." Isaac then says, "You are, my son Esau," and Jacob then answers, "I am." The Torah tells us he was fooled.

Melissa: David didn't look at everything. Isaac also says, "The voice is the voice of JACOB vut the hands are the hands of ESAU." Isaac recognized Jacob's voice and knew he was being fooled. That is why he asked so many questions.

Sara: All you have to do is look at how Isaac began the blessing. He said, "Seem the smell of my son is like the smell of a field which the LORD has blessed." Esau was the outdoor person who smelled like a field. Jacob should smell like a campfire.

Alvin: The Torah says, "He smelled the smell of his clothes." Rebekah had dressed Jacob in Esau's clothes so there was no problem.

Sean: When Isaac asks, "How is it that you found it so quickly, my son?" Jacob answers, "Adonai your God made it happen for me." Esau didn't care about the family tradition. He would never have thanked God. This answer gives Jacob away.

Margo: Esau wasn't stupid. He knew how to make his father happy. If his father wanted to hear about God, he would use God. The answer could have come from Esau.

over →

41

the reading to progress without interruption until page 127. Near the end of that page, at the line "You are my son ESAU," STOP the action. ASK the student reading ISAAC: "Do you really believe that this is Esau, or do you know or suspect that it is Jacob?" LISTEN carefully to his/her answer and then INVITE additions from other students.

READ the scene three times, once with Isaac knowing that it is Jacob, once with Isaac suspecting but not knowing, and once with Jacob convinced that it is Esau. ALLOW other students to play Isaac and see if they can express the difference.

POINT OUT that the text can support any of these readings. EXPLAIN that the Torah often gives us the dialogue but doesn't tell us how to read it. ASK: "How do we decide if Isaac knows?" ANSWER: (1) We gather evidence from elsewhere in the text. (2) We (individually) take our best guess.

4. **MAKING MEANING:** OPEN the **Student Commentary** to page 41. READ the letter from Mrs. Midlo's class together. ASSIGN a different student to read

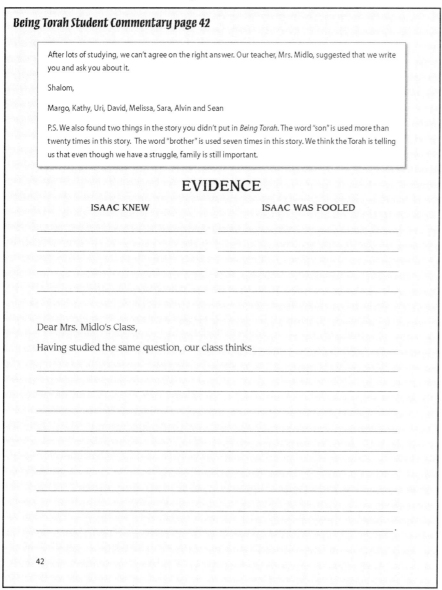

Being Torah Student Commentary page 42

After lots of studying, we can't agree on the right answer. Our teacher, Mrs. Midlo, suggested that we write you and ask you about it.

Shalom,

Margo, Kathy, Uri, David, Melissa, Sara, Alvin and Sean

P.S. We also found two things in the story you didn't put in *Being Torah*. The word "son" is used more than twenty times in this story. The word "brother" is used seven times in this story. We think the Torah is telling us that even though we have a struggle, family is still important.

EVIDENCE

ISAAC KNEW	ISAAC WAS FOOLED
_____	_____
_____	_____
_____	_____
_____	_____

Dear Mrs. Midlo's Class,

Having studied the same question, our class thinks_____

_____

_____

_____

_____

_____

_____

_____

_____

_____.

42

each of the opinions stated in it. When you have completed the letter, ASK each student (in order) to RESTATE in his/her own words the opinion s/he read.

DURING this review, TRANSCRIBE the opinions (as restated) onto the blackboard. DIVIDE the list into two columns: Isaac Knew/Isaac Was Fooled.

ASK students to COPY these lists into the columns on page 42 in the commentary.

DIVIDE the class into working groups. DIRECT them to do two things: (1) READ the story again and LOOK for additional evidence; and (2) DECIDE what they think Isaac thought and the reasons why.

5. **NETWORKING COMMENTS:** Have groups REPORT both their decisions and the reasons why.

EXTENSION: HAVE your class WRITE a letter of response to Mrs. Midlo's class. MAIL it c/o Jane Golub, Torah Aura Productions, 4423 Fruitland Avenue, Los Angeles, 90058.

Your class will get a really nice answer.

ADDITIONAL LESSON SEEDS

COMMENTARIES

Paulina's question on page 113 raises the question of Rebekah's being the real family leader. This provides a wonderful springboard for asking "Has history been fair to Rebekah?" It is another good place to raise a women's perspective.

We've talked a lot here about the motivation for speeches. Another good extension will be to record the "inner voices" of each character as they go through the actions.

The story here establishes the metaphor of Jacob's voice and Esau's hands. There is wonderful material on this in *Bible People* by Joel Lurie Grishaver (Alternatives in Religious Education, Denver, Colorado, 1980).

CHAPTER 19—JACOB'S DREAM

Being Torah, pages 114–116
Student Commentary, pages 43–44

ABSTRACT

WHAT DOES THIS DREAM MEAN?

Compare the biblical understanding of the meaning of dreams with more modern understandings. Answer: In biblical thought, a dream is a message from God; it is a kind of oracle about the future. Knowing its meaning can teach us about what will be. In more modern thought, a dream is a mirror of the inner self. Understanding its meaning teaches us about who we are.

ADDING UP JACOB'S DREAM

Count how many times the THEME-WORD God is used. Answer: 10 times

Count how many different promises God makes to Jacob. Answer: 10 promises

Find the [ECHO] in these blessings. Answer: The two-part promise is repeated.

Find the other time the number 10 is used. Answer: Jacob promises to tithe 1/10th of what God gives him.

Draw a conclusion: Even though we might have thought that Jacob didn't deserve the blessing he stole from Esau, this story shows us that God wants him to lead the family toward its future promises. The three uses of 10 show us that this is another new beginning.

OVERVIEW

Jacob's first vision establishes him as the true heir to the unique relationship that "Abraham the Seer" established with God.

Isaac is very much a middle child who gets lost in the shuffle. For a biblical hero, his life is very incomplete. His father doesn't pass on a blessing. He has no great visions of God. His name is not changed. Other than the one great moment imposed upon him by his father, his binding, the God–Isaac relationship presents no great tests. It is Jacob who continues the persona of Abraham. He is the dreamer, the visionary, the adventurer, and the spiritual entrepreneur.

Torah can never be understood when it is read for the first time. You always need to know the ending before the telling of the story can make sense. That is why Jews have always told Torah stories to their children long before they could read them on their own. We know (with hindsight) from his first introduction that Jacob will have dreams, slave for his wives, wrestle, and emerge as Israel. That much is family/national history. When we read the story, we are looking for the details of that transformation. In reading Torah, we are asking it again to recount a wonderful piece of family legend.

Religious quest is a process of transformation. Just as Abram had to manifest trust before he could undergo his metamorphosis into Abraham, so Jacob will have to outgrow the "heel grabbing" of his youth to become Israel. This story is the first step in this transformation, and it is an extension of the Abraham experience.

Before we begin the text, let us examine the situation. Jacob is functionally in exile. He is leaving "his land, his birthplace, and his parents' house." The parallel is set. He, too, goes alone. Even his journey follows Abraham's route. He goes back to the source in order to emerge as the head of a family, directed by God to a promised land. Our context is familiar.

Abraham's destiny changes in a series of dreams of future possibility and visions of present potential. With Jacob, the same process begins anew. His first independent action is a dream revelation from God. It forms a sign that he indeed merits the blessing he has received. Three sets of 10 underline the eternity of this link in the chain. We find that God's blessing/ revelation consists of 10 verb clauses; the word God is used 10 times; and Jacob promises a 10% tithe to God. Together these sets of 10 indicate that Jacob and God will have a substantive eternal relationship. Jacob was the right choice.

It takes only a few short verses of rapid action to set the stage for the dream. In the text the theme-word "place" is used three times. Then comes the dream of a ladder with angels going up and down. As in all dream images, the meaning is somewhat uncertain while the overall feeling is clear. As a symbol, the angels going up and down will elicit many things (the midrash has collected a long list); as a relationship, a clear connection is made. God is at one end of the ladder, Jacob is at the other. Angels/messengers go back and forth. Close readers and the makers of midrash build much meaning on the order of verbs used here: "going up" precedes "going down." It seems reversed. Angels should start with God and return there. The exploration of this order is yet another area in need of extrapolation and invention.

The revelation begins with a sense of history. God says, "I am Adonai, God of ABRAHAM your father and God of Isaac." The sense of history begun in Chapter 9, "Abram: A Covenant," continues here. It is important to note that the order of the two-part promise has now successfully been reversed. With Abram, questions of family size came first, then the inheritance of land. Starting with God's blessing of Isaac (gray matter, page 123), family size is more or less taken for granted, and the promise of land now becomes central. The theme-word "place" underlines the direction of this predictive history.

In blessing Isaac, God invokes the "as many as the stars" clause. With Jacob, we are back at "like the dust of the earth." The x-pattern directs us to notice that the paired promises have again been completed. The actual blessing, with its "Sea, East, North, and South," again takes us back to Abraham. As Jacob prepares to leave the land, his Divine blessing is a direct echo of the one Abraham received when he first acted (separating from Lot) to inherit the land for Jacob. This moment again assures him that he is indeed the family continuity. After the historic link, God reaffirms this with a series of five direct promises. (1) I am with you. (2) I will keep you in all your goings (a beautiful reversal of the "keeper" image). (3) And I will return you to this soil. (4) 1 will not leave you. (5) I will do all that I promised. Since the first covenant in chapter 9, all of the patriarchal experiences have become a rehearsal for the Egypt experience. Here these five promises are a direct foreshadowing of the five-part promise God will fulfill when the Jewish people are redeemed in that experience (see Exodus 6:1–9).

The morning after brings two responses from Jacob. The first is the establishment of a shrine at Beth El. Here "place" again becomes important. Note: Several scholars have pointed out that "stones" play an important part in almost every Jacob story. Here he sleeps on stones and then sets one up as a marker (a common Canaanite custom). The second is a deal-making prayer. We see it expressing both Jacob's fear and his chutzpah. This is a prayer we will later contrast with his pre-Israel prayer in chapter 21.

Jacob's odyssey has begun.

TEACHING TOOLS

OBJECTIVES

By reviewing a story from the midrash, the learner will discover that dreams are potential clues to various aspects of life and thus need interpretation.

Through tracing the three times that the number 10 is utilized in the story, the learner will determine its significance as signaling another "new beginning"— that of a new relationship between Jacob and God.

SLIDE-IN VOCABULARY

awestruck—filled with awe

interpretation—explanation

tithe—setting aside 10% of your belongings for God

holy—special

KEY HEBREW VOCABULARY

Beth El—House of God, the name of many synagogues

makom—place

Ha-makom—rabbinic name for God

ACTIVITIES

WHAT DOES THIS DREAM MEAN?
Student Commentary, page 43

This exercise is designed to point out that dreams can teach us both something about the future and something about the dreamer. The story from the midrash makes it clear that we need to interpret dreams.

1. **SET INDUCTION:** ASK students if they can recall any recent dreams. What were the people in the dream doing? What were the people in the dream feeling? How did the student feel when s/he awoke from the dream? Could the student tell right away what the dream really meant?

2. **READING THE TEXT:** ASSIGN the parts of JACOB and GOD. DIRECT the remainder of the class to READ the parts in bold.

Being Torah Student Commentary page 43

CHAPTER 19: JACOB'S DREAM

What Does This Dream Mean?

In Bible days and in the days when the Rabbis wrote the Midrash, people believed that dreams were clues to the future. Today we believe that dreams are clues to what people are thinking and feeling. Because dreams are clues they need interpretation.

My Comment: I think that Jacob's dream about the ladder may have been a clue that in the future he would **have a connection to God**.

I think that Jacob's dream about the ladder may have been a clue that Jacob was thinking/feeling **lonely, sad**.

_____'s Comment:
_____ taught us that Jacob's dream might have been a clue that _____

43

3. **FINDING THE CLUES:** As a class, CHECK for understanding of the vocabulary word INTERPRETATION and beliefs about the function of dreams.

4. **MAKING MEANING:** DIRECT each student to WRITE the comments at the conclusion of the exercise. STRESS the words "MAY BE" in the text of the interpretive questions. There is no right answer we are pushing here.

5. **NETWORKING COMMENTS:** SHARE comments one statement at a time. Allow students time to write down the comment they liked best from their classmates.

ADDING UP JACOB'S DREAM
Student Commentary, page 44

The number 10 is a significant feature of this story. The word God appears 10 times; God makes 10 statements of blessing; and Jacob promises to tithe 10 percent of his possessions to God. As we have seen with the use of tens before, we can find here a new beginning—a personal relationship between God and Jacob. For Jacob we also find the beginning of movement toward being a whole. He is beginning to move away from being the bratty grabber of the previous stories toward one who "wrestles with GOD." The move is not yet complete, but a significant step is made.

1. **SET INDUCTION:** REVIEW with your class the important tens they have encountered so far. LIST them on the board. REMIND the class of the significance of 10—being a whole, new beginnings, etc. These should INCLUDE: 10 speakings in creation; 10 generations for Noah and Abraham; 10 uses of Abraham's new name in the Covenant of Circumcision; 10 uses of the word "son" in "The Binding of Isaac"; and 10 uses of "Jacob" and "Esau" in the chapter that introduces them.

2. **READING THE TEXT:** RE-READ the text. ASK: "What did you hear?" EXPECT a repetition of the colored words. WRITE each on the blackboard. BE SURE to categorize the answers. LIST the THEME-WORDs "God" and "place" in one column. LIST the elements of the blessing in another column. Number those elements (1–10) as you write them down.

PROCESS the material that is on the blackboard. LABEL the THEME-WORDs and count each. POINT out the presence of ten elements in this blessing. SPEND a few minutes discussing the possible meaning of these clues. ACCEPT all suggestions. THERE are no particular conclusions that must be reached.

3. **FINDING THE CLUES:** Have students WORK IN PAIRS to complete the exercise on page 44 of the **Student Commentary.**

GO OVER the answers. (The first five promises have already been given to Jacob's family.) See if your students remember where they have heard other iterations of these promises. DISCUSS the meaning of these three uses of ten. ESTABLISH that Jacob is beginning his own relationship with God and that he is continuing the family tradition of being a blessing.

4. **MAKING MEANING:** Students should continue to work ALONE to complete the exercise. Hopefully, their comments will focus on the new personal relationship between God and Jacob.

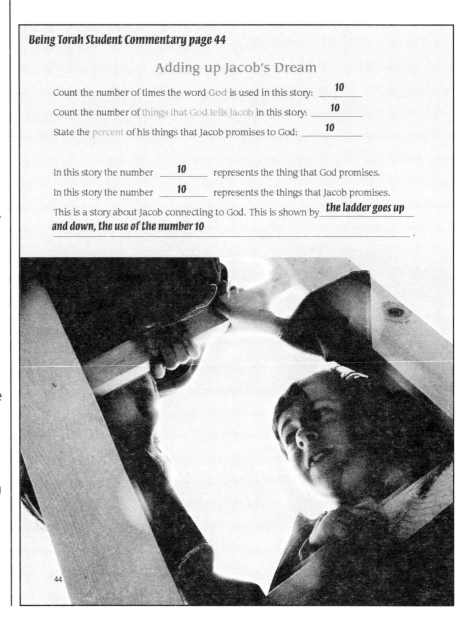

Being Torah Student Commentary page 44

Adding up Jacob's Dream

Count the number of times the word God is used in this story: ___10___

Count the number of things that God tells Jacob in this story: ___10___

State the percent of his things that Jacob promises to God: ___10___

In this story the number ___10___ represents the thing that God promises.

In this story the number ___10___ represents the things that Jacob promises.

This is a story about Jacob connecting to God. This is shown by _the ladder goes up and down, the use of the number 10_ .

44

5. NETWORKING COMMENTS: SHARE comments in class. ASK: "What changes do you see (if any) in Jacob?" ESTABLISH that he no longer merely grabs or takes. His first step on the journey of growing up is to offer, however conditionally, something to God. This is his first experience with God. The solidity of the relationship will grow.

ADDITIONAL LESSON SEEDS

On page 117 of **Being Torah**, Harrison's comment lets you talk about Jacob's chutzpa. This is an important part of his personality and story.

Sachi's comment directs us to begin noticing the evolution of Jacob from a heel-grabber into a God-wrestler.

The story on page 118 provides the rooting for a discussion of God's being in every place.

CHAPTER 20— A DOUBLE WEDDING

Being Torah, pages 119–121

Student Commentary, page 45

ABSTRACT

How many times is Rachel's name used in this story? Answer: 7

How many times is Leah's name used? Answer: 6

How many times is the word for "serve" *avad,* used in this story? Answer: 5

What does this teach us? Rachel is a foundational part of the Jewish people (like "brother", "good", etc.). Leah is also very important. Servitude/slavery is also a basic theme (like the books of the Torah).

OBJECTIVE

Through counting the words "Rachel," "Leah," and "service,"

students will evaluate the significance of this double wedding in the Jewish future.

OVERVIEW

In the Torah, history is constantly interwoven. The present both echoes the past and anticipates the future. In this complicated betrothal and marriage account, the "heel grabbing" of Jacob is relived and the years of Egyptian servitude are anticipated.

In the Passover Haggadah, the actual telling of the Exodus begins with the story of Jacob working for Laban. The rabbis intentionally misread a verse in Deuteronomy (26.5). There the verse reads, "My father (Jacob) was a wandering Aramean. He went down to Egypt. He lived there, few in number. There he became a great, mighty and populous nation." In the Haggadah the verse is retranslated, "An Aramean (Laban) sought to destroy my father. " The rabbis comment, "Pharaoh only decreed the death of the male children, but Laban tried to destroy us all." The connection of Jacob's years of labor for Laban to the Egypt experience is not fanciful. It is a connection carefully built into the Torah's use of language. Surviving Laban is another rehearsal for the great test that is soon to follow.

In chapter 31 of Genesis (in passages not covered in **Being Torah**), Jacob reports that God says (verse 12) "For I have seen all that Laban does to you. Now get up, exit from this land, and return to the land which is your birthplace," and (verse 42) "God has seen my suffering and the toil of my hand." These texts anticipate God's intervention at the burning bush. "I have seen and seen again the suffering of My people in Egypt." In our story, buried in the romantic well sequence and the resultant weddings, the word stem "a•v•d," work/serve/slave, is used seven times. It is a clear indicator. Just as Jacob could survive his servitude, so will his children be able to endure theirs.

In this chapter Jacob falls in love with his cousin Rachel, the younger of two daughters. He asks Uncle Laban for permission to marry her. A deal is set where he will work for seven years to earn her. At the end of the time her elder sister Leah is substituted. Jacob must work an additional seven years to earn Rachel. This is how a twenty-year servitude to Laban begins. The second dominant theme of this double wedding is the ironic-poetic justice of Jacob, the trickster, being outsmarted. With Jacob having stolen from his older brother both the blessing and the birthright, there is power to Laban's explanation of his fraud. "We don't do that in our place," he says, recalling the Beth El theme word. "We don't give the younger before the older." The Laban experience is clearly transformational; the Jacob who emerges twenty years later is ready to become Israel. The Torah doesn't editorialize the difference. It doesn't analyze the cause and effect. It is, however, clear that some combination of experiences—being tricked, years of servitude, and the growth of family responsibilities—has had an effect. Jacob's story has a certain wonderful work ethic. We get to watch his success as it emerges from hard work, a basic cunning and the presence of God's help.

Once again, the Torah can't resist the opportunity of dealing with the nature of family conflict. Leah and Rachel are siblings who are in conflict. Rachel's name is used ten times (the new beginning). Leah's name is used seven times (eternal connection). As with all of our pairs of conflicting brothers, the name usage implies differing but significant futures for each.

The midrash on Lamentations uses this conjunction for a wonderful inspiration. In trying to save the Jewish people, Rachel asks God not to be a jealous God. She explains that she learned how to overcome her jealousy. She tells God, "You know that Jacob, Your servant, loved me and slaved seven years for my father to earn me. When those seven years were over and the marriage was being planned, my father planned to trick Jacob and substitute my sister Leah. I was caught in the middle. I had to choose whether to betray Jacob or my sister. I told Jacob about my father's plan. We worked out a secret code so that Jacob could know whether it was me or Leah in the bridal chamber. Then I felt bad again. I told Leah about the code. I even sneaked into the bridal chamber and answered for her, so that Jacob would not hear the wrong voice answering him. I did _hesed_ for my sister and put aside all my feelings of jealousy. Being a good sister is important." (This is a paraphrase).

Being Torah Student Commentary page 45

CHAPTER 20—A DOUBLE WEDDING
Counting the Weddings

Count how many times Rachel's name is used in this story: _____8_____

Count how many times Leah's name is used in this story: _____6_____

Count how many times the word **serve** is used in this story: _____7_____

The Hebrew word for serve עָבַד *Avad*. That is a word that also means "work" or even "slave".

My Comment: The most important word in this story is_____*serve*_____.

It is teaching us about the future. It is telling us that **Abraham's future family (through Jacob) will serve as slaves in Egypt. The covenant will come through Rebekkah.**

_____

45

As we saw with the stories of Abraham the idol-smasher, the character in the Torah and the midrash's transposition of that character may emerge as substantively different people The rabbis evolve a vision of Rachel (predicated on an image in the book of Jeremiah 31:15) where she is the one who stands by the road and weeps for her future-family as they are led into exile in Babylon. She becomes the prime example of compassion—a true matriarch.

TEACHING TOOLS

SLIDE-IN VOCABULARY

serve—work for

dowry—money and other things a woman brings to her husband when they get married

KEY HEBREW VOCABULARY

avad—serve, slaving
avodah—service

ACTIVITIES
COUNTING THE WEDDING
Student Commentary, page 45

1. **SET INDUCTION:** ASK What would it be like for one man to have two wives? Would it be easy or hard? EXPECT: The girls will say it is hard and the boys will probably talk about how cool it would be. REVIEW what happened when Abraham had two wives (the family fell apart, and he had to send one wife and one son away). ESTABLISH that this is a story about Jacob taking two wives.

2.READING THE TEXT: Have one group read the orange words. Have one group read the blue words. And have one group read the purple words. You can be the narrator.

3.FINDING THE CLUES: OPEN up the **Student Commentary** to page 45. Have students do the counting of the three words.

4.MAKING MEANING: The question asks, "What is the most important word?" There are two possibilities: One is **served**, which predicts that Israel will be in slavery. The other is **Rachel**, which predicts that Joseph, Rachel's eldest son, will become most important.

5.NETWORKING: Use your usual procedure.

ADDITIONAL ACTIVITY: TRICKING THE TRICKSTER

Find the [ECHO] between Jacob's naming, the stealing of the blessings, and his weddings. Answer: Jacob's name means "heel." He got it by pulling Esau's leg. When he steals the blessing, Esau complains, "He has grabbed from me two times." This time Jacob is grabbed from and tricked. While there is no word-echo that directly links these stories, there is a strong irony. An eight-year-old can understand an echo, not irony.

ADDITIONAL ACTIVITY: A STORY FOR SABRINA

Explain the relationship between Rachel and Leah. Answer: [**Missing Information**]. We don't know. This is another place to make midrash.

OBJECTIVES

The learner will compare/contrast Jacob as a trickster to Jacob the victim of a trick to discover how the combined experience might be training for a future leader of Israel.

The learner will choose an aspect of Jacob's "training" on which to comment.

Using the midrash as a model, the learner will write comments exploring the feelings of the different characters in the story.

Additional Activity: Tricking the Trickster

This is a story of poetic justice. Jacob, the heel-grabber, the trickster, gets his just rewards. He is the one who is tricked. The ending, however, is happy. It is the working for Laban and the chance to build a large family that build the future of the Jewish people.

1.SET INDUCTION: START with this problem. IMAGINE that you are going to write a story. The hero of the story is a boy named Jack. When he was young, he used to like to play tricks on people. The first part of the story is going to show three tricks that Jack played. TAKE SUGGESTIONS as to the tricks that Jack might have played. Then ASK, "What should happen in the second half of the story?" We are looking for a response that says, "Someone plays a trick on Jack, because that way he knows what it feels like." If necessary, PROMPT that response with the question, "What might get Jack to stop playing tricks?"

EXPLAIN that Jacob, who used to trick his brother, is going to get tricked in this story.

2.READING THE TEXT: ASSIGN one student to play each of these parts: NARRATOR, JACOB, LABAN, RACHEL and LEAH. GIVE each a name tag, and have them stand at the front of the class to present their reading. ALL FIVE should read the words in bold together. READ the entire chapter as one unit. ASK: "Which characters in the story did not get a part in the reading?" EXPECT: "Rachel and Leah." Let students venture a guess as to why.

3.FINDING THE CLUES: WORKING IN GROUPS, ALLOW time to work.

4.MAKING MEANING: REMIND students of the idea that being tricked can teach a trickster what it feels like. ALLOW students time to write their comments.

5.NETWORKING COMMENTS: Follow your usual procedure.

ADDITIONAL ACTIVITY: A STORY

SET INDUCTION: REVIEW a familiar fairy tale such as SNOW WHITE or CINDERELLA—any story with enough characters to tell the same story from several points of view. Have various students RETELL the fairy tale from the points of view of the different characters, including as much detail and character emotion as they can. Ask them to PAY ATTENTION to the variations in the story as it is retold.

ADDITIONAL LESSON SEEDS

Shawna's comment on page 122 of **Being Torah** talks about the similarities between Jacob and Rachel. It can be fun both to find other similarities and to find specific examples of these similarities.

On page 123, two pieces of the close look section have not been picked up in the **Student Commentary**. One focuses on the presence Zilpah and Bilhah in this story (a kind of foreshadowing). The other plays with the image of a hard job seeming as if it took only a short time. It suggests a Horatio Alger midrash.

CHAPTER 21— JACOB: ROUND 4— WRESTLING

Being Torah,
pages 145–155

Student Commentary,
pages 46–47

ABSTRACT

HOW MANY THINGS DID JACOB CROSS?

Count how many times the THEME-WORD "cross" is used in this story. Answer: 12 times

Draw a conclusion: This story is all about crossing. Jacob leaves his servitude with Laban and becomes an independent adult. He leaves behind his taking relationship with Esau and establishes his own identity. He leaves behind his "Jacob" behaviors and becomes "Israel."

ONE THING THAT STAYED THE SAME

Find the [**ECHO**] of Jacob stealing the blessing from Esau

in this story of their reunion. Answer: Jacob's giving credit to "ADONAI" [**ECHO**]s between these two stories.

Draw a conclusion: One of the things that made Jacob the right leader for the Jewish people was his understanding that God deserves much credit.

OVERVIEW

This interwoven sequence of six experiences forms the climax of the Jacob saga. It is a story of transformation. Constructed around twelve uses of the theme-word "crossed," Jacob, the heel-grabber, completes his metamorphosis into Israel, the one who wrestles

To cross is to leave one place and come to another. To cross is to make a transition. Crossing is the essence of this story, and the Torah emphasizes this by re-using the word stem a•v•r twelve times. This is a story of transitions. The break with Laban is final; the return to the to-be-inherited land is completed; Jacob's relationship with God is changed. From bargain-making to honest petition, the great wrestling results in a new name, and the life long conflict with Esau is resolved. The Israel who emerges from these moments of transformation is indeed a fit leader for the Jewish people.

Part 1: Laban has chased Jacob. In a story not recorded in **Being Torah**, Rachel has stolen the family idols, and Laban is pursuing them. Being Jacob's perfect mate, she tricks her father. In this story, the twenty years of conflict and trickery is resolved. Jacob and Laban cut a covenant. The separation is final. Each goes his own way. Jacob's period of indenture is over.

Part 2: Angels appear. Jacob's last experience in the land of Canaan was a dream of angels. As he returns to this land, his first experience is again the appearance of angels. The midrash takes note of this, suggesting that one set of angels escorted Jacob when he was in the Land of Israel, and another set of angels escorted him when he was in the Diaspora. These appearances mark the changing of the guard. While that is a midrash, the sequence does give us one clear indicator, Jacob's response, "This is God's camp. " Even though twenty years have passed, Jacob's response echoes that of his experience at Beth El (chapter 19, "Jacob's Dream"), "This is the house of God. This is the gate to heaven." What is clear is that Jacob has the ability to recognize God's presence.

Part 3: The Hebrew word *malakh* means both "messenger" and "angel." In part 2, God sends angels to Jacob. In part 3, Jacob sends messengers to Esau. Apparently Jacob learned from God's example. As he had just done with Laban, his adversary for the past twenty years, Jacob now attempts to make peace with his original rival, Esau. The messengers come back with the ominous warning, "Esau and four hundred men are on the way to greet you." Jacob takes a defensive action. Again, the Torah apparently wants us to realize that Jacob has learned from meeting the angels. After that encounter, he called the place *Mahanaim*, a twofold (double) camp. Now, when his messengers return, he creates *mahanaim*, a two-part (divided) camp. It is a time of panic.

Part 4: Back in the story of Cain and Abel, God warned people that "when you don't do good, sin haunts your door." Two theme-words dominate this section, "hand" and "face." One is an echo of the past, the other a foreshadowing of the future. "Hand" was the key word in the theft of the blessing. Isaac had said, "The voice is the voice of JACOB, but the hands are the hands of ESAU." As Jacob thinks of ESAU, the image of a hand obsesses him. "Please save me from the hand of my brother—from the hand of ESAU" The word "brother" here echoes back to the story of Cain and Abel; we know that the rivalry between brothers can erupt in violence.

The heart of this section is a night prayer, which contrasts with the prayer Jacob spoke at Beth El. In an interview with Joel Lurie Grishaver (*CAJE Symposium on Theodicy*, September, 1986), Harold Kushner comments, "Before Jacob understands how life works, be thinks that he can bribe God. After he is grown up and matures, he knows that the only thing he can say to God is not "Help me, I'll make it worth your while". It is not "Help me or I'll take my business elsewhere." The only thing he says to God is, "Please, I need you. I can't do it alone." Here we see the first traces of the mature Israel emerging.

The word "face" also begins to manifest itself here. We will see it in the next two sections. It is the essence of the new man Israel.

Part 5: Jacob's life has been a series of wrestling matches. His name came from the first, when he pulled his brother's leg. Here his new name emerges from another wrestling match. While he is anticipating the reunion with his brother, his leg is pulled. The description of the wrestling is dreamlike. As with the visitors who announced Isaac's birth, we are unsure of the identity of the combatant-man or angel. Some psychological commentators have suggested that Jacob is actually wrestling with himself, with outgrowing his past.

The confrontation ends with his perception of God's presence. "JACOB called the name of the place PENIEL (meaning the face of God), because I have seen God face to face and my life was saved." Like his grandfather Abraham, Jacob has an experience that leads him to visions of God.

Part 6. Here the circle is closed. Jacob and Esau meet. While there is an undercurrent of tension, peace is made. On page 155 of **Being Torah** we work through the subtext of the conversation and expose the fencing between brothers. Once again, the word "cross" guides us through the transitions. We reach a resolution. Jacob tells his brother, "Please, if I have found favor in your eyes, take this gift from my hand." It is as if Esau's hands have been returned. He says, "Please take this gift-of-blessing that I brought you." To the best of his ability he has made up for the stolen blessing.

The final indicator that Jacob is indeed the right leader for the Jewish people is found in the three times he affirms God in his answers to his brother: (1) "The children with whom Adonai least favored your servant," (2) "because Adonai has favored me and I have everything," and finally, (3) "because when I see your **face** it is like seeing the **face** of God." For a second time, Jacob's encounter with the Divine has directly influenced his human relations.

TEACHING TOOLS

OBJECTIVES

The learner will the use the THEME-WORD "cross" to focus on the theme of the crossings (transitions) in Jacob's life.

The learner will discover through close reading of two sections of the text that in spite of all the changes in Jacob's life, the one thing that stayed the same was his belief in God.

SLIDE-IN VOCABULARY

messenger—one who does an errand for another, goes in place of another

selected—chose

favored—given kindly or with love

KEY HEBREW VOCABULARY

Yisrael—One who struggles with God

ACTIVITIES

HOW MANY THINGS DID JACOB CROSS?
Student Commentary, page 46

While this chapter has many THEME-WORDs, the word "crossing" (used twelve times) is the connecting theme. In this section students will concentrate on the concept of "crossing," leaving something behind and coming to something new in one's life. The work will focus their attention on the twelve crossings in this chapter and then review Jacob's life to identify additional crossings.

The final series of Jacob story events comes in an interwoven flurry of both activity and words. It is a rich text that easily offers up THEME-WORDs, NUMBER-WORDs and [ECHO]s in abundance. Because of the nature of this text, we recommend that you follow one of two patterns. Either read it through as a group, stopping after every section to collate the text-clues found in that section, or allow students to read it in small groups and make a list of all the clues they find. When we get to our actual objectives, only two clues will be important to us (the rest, while valuable, are just too much to handle). When you are done reading, we want to (1) isolate the THEME-WORD "cross" and the [ECHO] "Adonai your God made it happen for me." Rather than providing a detailed script for this extended close reading, we have chosen to manifest trust in your extended experience with twenty previous **Being Torah** texts and in the section-by-section overview in the Teacher's Guide. The two lesson plans that follow assume that this close reading has already taken place.

1. **SET INDUCTION:** After your students have read the whole chapter, WORK AS A CLASS to TELL the story without using the text. Give each student a chance to tell a continuing part of the narrative, adding or correcting details when necessary. ASK if they can list the THEME-WORDs, NUMBER-WORDs

and [ECHO]s. They will probably have partial success. ELICIT the full list. ESTABLISH that a story in the Torah doesn't always teach us the full message, and that the way it is told is also very important.

2. **FINDING THE CLUES:** ESTABLISH that "cross" was a THEME-WORD used twelve times in this story. DEFINE "cross" as "leaving one place and coming to another." ASK your students to think of one time in their lives when something important happened to them, when they "crossed" (or changed) from being one kind of person to another (even if the change was a small one).

3. **MAKING MEANING:** Have students COMPLETE the exercise on page 46 of the **Student Commentary**, including the comment.

5. **NETWORKING COMMENTS:** GO OVER the answers and share comments. A logical EXTENSION to this text is having the students draw life maps that show the course of their lives, with special attention to the crossing points.

Being Torah Student Commentary page 46

CHAPTER 21: JACOB: ROUND 4—WRESTLING
How Many Things Did Jacob Cross?

This chapter is made up of four stories: (a) Laban catching up, (b) preparing to meet Esau, (c) the night of wrestling, and (d) the family reunion. The word cross connects all four stories.

Counting the Word Cross

Cross is used __10__ times in this story. This is the same number as __10 plagues__ .

10 generations
10 commandments
10 plagues

When you cross you leave one side and come to something new. In this story Jacob crosses __10__ times and grows into a new person, Israel.

Explain how Jacob crossed each of these things in this story. What did he leave behind? To what new thing did he come?

Thing Crossed	Thing Left Behind	New Thing
Serving Laban	*living in the old country*	*living at his home as master of house*
Taking from Esau	*stealing birthright and blessing*	*reconnecting with his brother*
Acting like Jacob	*acting like a selfish child*	*becoming Israel, the next leader*

ONE THING THAT STAYED THE SAME
Student Commentary, page 47

This chapter is a study in the way Jacob changes and matures. In contrast to the evolving traits, one central factor remains constant: Jacob's acknowledgement of God's centrality. This insight is especially important to emphasize, because it is a trait we will also find in Joseph. It is one of the keys to unlocking the full meaning of the Joseph story.

1. **SET INDUCTION:** REREAD section 6 of this story, pages 130–131 of **Being Torah**. DIRECT students to listen for an important [ECHO] that connects this story with the story of the stolen blessing. Even though we are looking for the two verses that give credit to Adonai, EXPECT that they will list both "gift-of-blessing" and "hand." Acknowledge that they are good [ECHO]s, but there is a third one that teaches us an important lesson.

Being Torah Student Commentary page 47

One Thing That Stayed the Same

And **echo** between an earlier story and this story teaches us something about Jacob.

When Jacob was pretending to be Esau, he answered Isaac's question about his hunting success by saying:

"Adonai, **your God, made it happen** for me."

In this story when Esau asks about his family, Jacob answers:

"The children with whom Adonai has favored your servant."

My Comment: The word connection between these two stories is ___*Adonai*___.

It teaches us that Jacob always _____

Jacob gave God the credit for what the good things that happen

_____'s Comment:

_____ thought that Jacob always

47

2. **FINDING THE CLUES:** TURN back to page 109 in **Being Torah**, or find the same pair of verses on page 47 of the **Student Commentary**. As a class, READ the first three lines on the page. ESTABLISH that when Isaac asks Jacob how he succeeded, Jacob gives credit to Adonai. DISCUSS why giving credit to God for success is important. POINT OUT that admitting that we are not all-powerful and that we succeed with God's gifts makes all people equal and keeps us from being big egotists.

RETURN to pages 130–131 of **Being Torah**. ASK students to find the place where Jacob gives credit to God in this story. FIND the two verses.

4. **MAKING MEANING:** DIVIDE the class into small groups. DIRECT them to complete page 47 in the **Student Commentary**, including the MY COMMENT section. ALLOW them working time

5. **NETWORKING COMMENTS:** Follow your usual practices.

ADDITIONAL LESSON SEEDS

Have each student WRITE a diamante poem comparing Jacob and Israel. In this kind of poem the lines are arranged in the following way:

1 Noun

3 Two words describing first noun

5 Three "ing" action words related to the first noun

7 Phrase uniting both nouns

6 Three "ing" actions words related to the second noun

4 Two words describing second noun

2 Noun that is the opposite of the first noun

If the children have trouble, use Jacob as noun #1 and Israel as noun #2 to help them structure the poem.

We don't know much about the relationship between Isaac and God. We do know a great deal about the relationships between God and Abraham and between God and Jacob. Central to both patriarchs was the aspect of seeing God. By tracing the parallels between the two patriarchs, the student will come to an understanding of Jacob's place as a parent of the Jewish people.

ASSIGN on a previous session the following: ASK your parents and perhaps your grandparents to help with this assignment. How are you like one of your grandparents? Use photographs, or have the adults in your family help you by describ-ing things that you do that are similar to your grandparent. MAKE a poster that shows how you and your grandparent are alike. Conduct a SHOW AND TELL in class, and if the grandparents are in town, have students bring them as well as part of the presentation.

Make a chart showing the parallels between Abraham and Jacob.

Have each group CREATE a campaign poster advertising Jacob/Israel as the third father of the Jewish people. ENCOURAGE the use of a simple slogan and an illustration on the poster.

Have students REREAD Harrison's comment on page 133. He talks about who or what Jacob was wrestling. Working ALONE or IN PAIRS, have students create a CHARADE about one fear they had when they were younger but have now outgrown. Have classmates try to guess what fear it was. In addition, have the students tell HOW they were able to overcome this fear. EMPHASIZE that this is part of growing up and struggling with fears. As Harrison points out, it is one of the growing-up crossings Jacob had to go through.

CHAPTER 22—BIRTHS AND DEATHS

Being Torah, pages 134–136
Student Commentary, page 48

ABSTRACT

THE JACOB PATTERN

Many things in the Jacob saga happen two times. Find the pattern. Answer:

a. Jacob fights with Esau, pulls a leg and is named the "heel-grabber."

b. Jacob steals a blessing and birthright from Esau.

c. Jacob has a night dream of angels. He names the place Beth El and sets up a rock. He then leaves the Land of Canaan.

d. Jacob builds a family and works for Laban.

c. Jacob returns to the Land of Canaan, sees angels and has a night encounter. His leg is pulled, and his name is changed to Israel.

b. Jacob gives Esau a gift-of-blessing.

a. Jacob and Esau part in peace.

x. Jacob's name is again changed. God again gives the two-part promise. Jacob again sets up a rock and names the place Beth El.

Draw a conclusion: The Jacob story is a story of growth. Many of the best parts of Jacob grow and develop. Many of the worst traits are outgrown and made up for. Everything seems to happen twice.

OVERVIEW

This is a chapter of second times. Jacob returns to Beth El. His new name Israel is given again. The two-part promise is restated. The restatement gives a sense of completion to earlier promises and blessings.

Like the Tower of Babel and the story of Noah, the Jacob saga is built around a reflexive pattern. In parallel stages we see Jacob transformed into Israel.

a. Jacob and Esau fight (in the womb).
 Jacob is named "heel grabber" because he pulls a leg.
 Esau is named twice.

b. Jacob steals the blessing from Esau.

c. Jacob flees from Canaan.
 He has a dream and sees angels.
 He has a nighttime God experience.
 God makes a two-part promise.
 Jacob sets up a rock.
 He gives the place a God name.
 Jacob prays (and makes a deal).

d. Jacob works twenty years for Laban.
 He marries Rachel and Leah.
 Twelve children are born.

c. Jacob returns to Canaan.
 Angels meet him.
 He prays to God (asking help).
 He has a nighttime God experience.
 A second name, ISRAEL, is given when his leg is pulled.
 Jacob gives the place a God name.

b. Jacob gives a gift-of-blessing to Esau.
 Jacob and Esau part after making peace.

As we have noticed with each of the other examples of a mirror pattern, things are not in perfect parallel. The single naming of Jacob (in contrast to Esau's double naming) and the two-part promise (now given to Abraham, Isaac and Jacob) stand out.

In this chapter (the functional climax to the story) the restatement of the two-part promise is accompanied by a second naming of Beth El and a second giving of the new name Israel. In the story "Jacob's Dream" we realized that God in essence repeals the blessing that Isaac had given Jacob to assure him that his fate was real (and not stolen). Here the second name change matched with the restatement of the family covenant assures the transformation. The journey that began long ago when a boy slept on a rock pillow at Beth El has reached its culmination.

The second half of the story brings a return to family details. Benjamin is born and Rachel dies. The twelve sons are listed. Then, in a final tribute to family unity, Jacob and Esau come together to bury their father Isaac, just as Isaac and Ishmael had done for Abraham.

TEACHING TOOLS
OBJECTIVES

The learner will review events in Jacob's life before he left home and after he returned.

The learner will identify and make meaning out of the "fruitful" echo.

SLIDE-IN VOCABULARY

labor—the hard work and pain of giving birth to a child
escape—running away

KEY HEBREW VOCABULARY

Beth El—House of God
Binyamin—right-hand son

ACTIVITIES

TRACING THE "FRUITFUL" ECHO

1. **SET INDUCTION:** ASK students to identify and define the phrase "be fruitful and multiply." ANSWER: It is first used in the first chapter in Genesis for both animals and people. It is also used to bless Noah's family. It means that you should have a family that grows and becomes big.

2. **READING THE TEXT:** READ the text on **Being Torah** pages 134–136. Ask students why the things in color were highlighted. There is only one line in red and one set of lines in blue. ANSWER: Both are echoes of things we have seen before.

3. **FINDING CLUES:** TURN to page 48 in the **Student Commentary**. TRACE the two echoes. First, this is another time when we are told to be fruitful. Second, this is the second time that Jacob's name was changed to Israel.

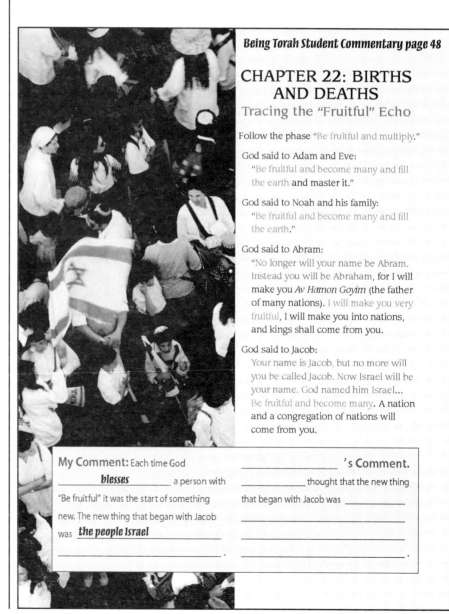

Being Torah Student Commentary page 48

CHAPTER 22: BIRTHS AND DEATHS
Tracing the "Fruitful" Echo

Follow the phase "Be fruitful and multiply."

God said to Adam and Eve:
"Be fruitful and become many and fill the earth and master it."

God said to Noah and his family:
"Be fruitful and become many and fill the earth."

God said to Abram:
"No longer will your name be Abram. Instead you will be Abraham, for I will make you *Av Hamon Goyim* (the father of many nations). I will make you very fruitful, I will make you into nations, and kings shall come from you.

God said to Jacob:
Your name is Jacob, but no more will you be called Jacob. Now Israel will be your name. God named him Israel... Be fruitful and become many. A nation and a congregation of nations will come from you.

My Comment: Each time God _____ 's Comment.
_____ blesses _____ a person with _____ thought that the new thing
"Be fruitful" it was the start of something that began with Jacob was _____
new. The new thing that began with Jacob _____
was the people Israel _____ _____
_____ . _____ .

4. **MAKING MEANING:** DISCUSS the commentary and have students suggest answers. Then give them time to write.

5. **NETWORKING COMMENTS:** Follow your usual pattern.

Additional Activity: The Jacob Pattern

Like the Noah story and the Tower of Babel, the Jacob story is built with a reflexive structure. There is a symmetry to the events in Jacob's life that emphasizes the transformation into Israel.

1. **SET INDUCTION:** Have the class LIST the things that have happened two times in Jacob's life. Include two names, stealing two things from Esau, seeing angels twice, two wives, two seven years of working for Laban, two night encounters with God, two big prayers to God, etc. POINT OUT that in this chapter we are going to find a lot more things happening for the second time. The importance of things happening two times will become very clear and important in the Joseph story.

2. **READING THE TEXT:** To best highlight the three main concerns of this story, we will read it in three sections.

   SECTION ONE: The focus of this section is JACOB'S return to BETH EL and the reiteration of his name change to ISRAEL. The auditory cues are not crucial for full understanding of the story.

   ASK: What two items are familiar to you in this story? ESTABLISH: We have learned of the place BETH EL (from Chapter 19, "Jacob's Dream") as the location of JACOB'S first encounter with God; and just last chapter we read of JACOB'S name change to ISRAEL. ASK: Which word tells you what might he the main idea of this section? EXPECT "name," which appears three times, but so does BETH EL. SUGGEST the possibility that both BETH EL and ISRAEL are important names.

   SECTION TWO: Here we hear the [ECHO] of the first divine command.

   The section on page 134 should be read by two students: one playing God, and the other reading the part of the narrator.

   Your focus will be on helping the students hear the [ECHO] of familiar words and phrases: "Be fruitful and become many." ASK: "What parts of this section leave you heard before?" LIST on the board all the correct answers, including mention of BETH EL, if it occurs.

   SECTION THREE: In this section, page 135, we are immersed in the life transitions of Jacob's family. Rachel dies giving birth to Jacob's last child, a new baby, Benjamin, is born; Isaac dies, and Esau and Jacob unite to bury him.

   CHOOSE three students to be the narrator/readers, and DIRECT the class to read together the words in CAPITAL letters. All but two of these words are family member's names, thus directing the students' attention to the PEOPLE who are the primary focus of this last section.

3. FINDING THE CLUES: LIST the things that happened for a second time in this chapter. This should include: naming Beth El, changing Jacob's name to Israel,

and receiving a repetition of the two-part promise.

4. MAKING MEANING: Make a chart of the pattern on the board. Have students help you fill in details.

ADDITIONAL LESSON SEEDS

Harrison's comment on page 137 provides a wonderful [ECHO] of the parallel between Abraham's sons and Jacob's sons. It is both good Torah and a good insight into how families work.

CHAPTER 23—THE DREAMS COME TRUE

Being Torah, pages 138–162

Student Commentary, pages 49–55

OVERVIEW

The Joseph story is a story of transitions. On a literal level, it is the tale of how the Jewish people came to live in Egypt. On a literary level, the story forms a series of proofs that God will remember the Jewish people (and rescue them). Finally, on a religious level, it provides the paradigm of a man who has proud faith without the direct experience of revelation.

The Joseph epic needs to be read on a number of levels. As a story, it is one of two great biblical adventures. It has drama, tension, irony and all those necessary elements. The other great adventure is the David cycle. Beneath the surface of the plot are a number of important symbolic lessons.

Joseph represents a new kind of Jew. He is the first post-patriarchal family leader. He isn't privileged to have a Divine birth announcement. He doesn't talk to God; no one blesses him; he receives no personal confirmation of the two-part contract. He is the first existential Jew, one for whom the experience of God is a matter of history, not direct encounter. Yet, in spite of a lack of visions and personal revelations of Divine presence, he is a Jew whose life is both guided and enriched by his trust in Adonai. It is an important example, because one of the underlying concerns of this story is the preparation of the Jewish people for their predestined four hundred-year stay in Egypt. Joseph's series of enslavements and imprisonments—over all of which he triumphs—forms the guarantee that the Jewish people will also triumph over their future trials. The text of the "Perils of Joseph" is studded with two kinds of allusions.

One type of word echo roots Joseph's life and actions in the experiences of his predecessors. The story opens around the theme-word "brother." As in both Isaac's experience and Jacob's experience, the use is ironic, underlining a conflict rather than a bonding. Joseph's first dramatic action is the recounting of his dreams. These dreams, like Abram's visions at the covenant between the pieces (chapter 9, pages 64–66) and Jacob's dream at the ladder, are symbolic foreshadows of the future. As the story continues, the theme-words "eyes" (connected to Abraham's obsession with vision) and "hands" (connected to Jacob's encounters with Esau) guide the story's flow. When called to difficult family service, Joseph's "Hineini" response echoes Abraham's response to his great call and foreshadows those of Moses at the burning bush and Samuel in the sanctuary. When the Torah describes Jacob's appearance in Potiphar's house, it tells us "Joseph was nicely shaped and nice to look at." This makes him the perfect image of his mother, Rachel, who is described with exactly those words. The most important echo, however, is the Torah's repeated explanation that "the LORD was with Joseph." This is a direct fulfillment of the promise God made individually to Abraham, Isaac and Jacob: "I will be with you."

The other kind of allusion foreshadows the coming enslavement. While the word "slave" makes an appearance early in the story, it manifests itself as a theme-word (translated as "servant") with six appearances in Judah's dramatic defense of Benjamin. It announces the forthcoming enslavement of the family.

The central message of the story is, however, revealed in Joseph's explanation of the formula of two-time happenings. The story is built around things that happen twice. Joseph has two dreams. In jail, Joseph interprets two dreams. Pharaoh has two dreams. Twice Joseph is thrown in a pit (one pit = jail). And twice Joseph rises from slave/prisoner to head of the household/jail because God was with him and helped him succeed. The brothers come down to Egypt twice, are twice imprisoned and released. When Joseph comes to interpret Pharaoh's dreams he says, "Pharaoh had two dreams because the thing is true." When we read that line, the story's full purpose becomes clear. Events that happen twice are indicators of truth, just like Joseph, who was twice imprisoned and released, just like his brothers who share this two-timed fate. We know that it is true that the Jewish people will emerge from their enslavement in Egypt. Retroactively, we learn that the repetitive promises God made to each of the patriarchs are warranties that we will not be forgotten. Just like Abraham, who left the promised land to go down to Egypt, just like Jacob, who was in exile in Laban's house, we will fulfill God's promise to return to our homeland with great wealth. Therefore, Joseph's final revelation to his brothers is: "God sent me before you to save life."

The theme-word "recognize" also plays a kind of bookend role in this story. In the first act the word "recognize" is used to indicate Jacob's reaction to the faked murder evidence—the bloody robe of many colors. In the story's climax, the word reflects the brothers' lack of awareness that Egypt's second-in-command is their brother Joseph. These two failures to perceive the true nature of what is happening are important. Joseph represents the first biblical experience where God is silent. It will lead to four hundred years of silence and slavery. Recognizing that the promise will be fulfilled is the secret to survival.

TEACHING TOOLS

In the Torah, the Joseph story fills thirteen chapters, almost a third of the book of Genesis. Because of the demands of classroom pacing, we have heavily edited the material and reduced it to one extra long twelve-part chapter. It should take three or more class sessions to complete. To allow for individual pacing, the material in this chapter will all be organized by the twelve section headings.

SLIDE-IN VOCABULARY

tending—watching

plotted—planned

caravan—group of people traveling together

shekel—a unit of money

mourned—showed sadness when someone died

overseer—boss, head person

famine—period when there is very little, if any, food

signet—special design or initial for a ruler to use

KEY HEBREW VOCABULARY

k'tonet passim—robe of many colors

vay'hee adonai et yosef—Adonai was with Joseph

ACTIVITIES

JOSEPH BEGINS A NEW CHAPTER IN THE STORY OF THE JEWISH PEOPLE
Student Commentary, page 49

Count the number of family histories in the Torah from Creation to Joseph. Answer: 10

Draw a conclusion: Joseph represents a new beginning. With him, the two-part promise begins to come true.

Family histories have been a part of the Torah's constant rhythm. Two of them—those leading to NOAH and to ABRAHAM—each contained ten generations. We took each ten as a sign of a new beginning. The Joseph story begins with the tenth family history in the Torah (though only eight are found in **Being Torah).** We use this sign of new beginnings to introduce this chapter and its significance.

1. **SET INDUCTION:** Before class, CREATE a poster of the family trees listed in **BEING TORAH**, noting where the two not recorded in our text belong. LEAVE GAPS, and DIRECT your students to fill in the missing names. The students may use the text for help. Design the family tree chart to show Jacob's as the TENTH family history.

   WORKING CLUE: The format of this chapter differs from previous **Student Commentary** material. Here the comments don't begin as a fill-in-the-blank exercise; instead, students are expected to respond to the introductory prompt statement, such as "JACOB BEGINS A NEW CHAPTER IN THE STORY OF THE JEWISH PEOPLE." The data gathered from the exercises that follow allow them to elucidate the theme sentence.

WORK AS A CLASS to complete the exercise on page 49 of the **Student Commentary**. REVIEW the importance of the number ten (from ten sayings in creation to ten generations for Abraham and for Noah, we have learned that ten means new beginnings).

This text begins with a TEXT REPETITION. We would expect the family history of JACOB to list all twelve sons. Instead, only Joseph is mentioned. HELP students to (1) understand how this repetition of a pattern with a change is a clue, and (2) recognize this clue to Joseph's importance (such that he alone will fulfill the family history).

2. **MAKING MEANING:** Have each student WRITE his/her comment and then SHARE with the class. SUMMARIZE their comments into notes and LIST them on a poster.

JOSEPH IS A LOT LIKE HIS FATHER JACOB
Student Commentary, page 50

Find the [ECHO]s that connect Jacob and Joseph. Answer: "brothers" and "dreams."

Draw a conclusion: Both have childhoods centered in sibling rivalry. Both are dreamers.

In this section the words "brothers" and "dreams" serve both as THEME-WORDs and as connecting [ECHO]s. In particular, they suggest a consistency of Joseph's experience with Jacob, his father, who struggled with his brother and who learned through dreams. The tradition records a large number of similarities between father and son. Both had mothers who were initially barren and then had two sons; both mothers had troubles in pregnancy and childbirth; both had brothers who hated them and wanted to kill them; both lived in exile from their homeland.

Being Torah Student Commentary page 49

CHAPTER 23: THE DREAMS COME TRUE
Joseph Begins a New Chapter
in the Story of the Jewish People

Clue 1: In the book of Genesis we find:

1. This is the family history of the heavens and the earth.
2. This is the family history of Adam.
3. This is the family history of Noah.
4. This is the family history of Noah's sons.
5. This is the family history of Shem.
6. This is the family history of Terah.
7. This is the family history of Ishmael.*
8. This is the family history of Isaac.
9. This is the family history of Esau.*
10. This is the family history of Jacob.

*These two family histories are in the Torah but not in *Being Torah*.

Clue 2: At the beginning of the Joseph story we find:

This is the family history of **Jacob**.
Joseph was 17 years old.
He was a shepherd with his **brothers**.

My Comment: *Even though we are talking about Joseph, the Torah is setting up the family history of Jacob or B'nai Israel, the children of Israel (Jacob).*

49

1. **SET INDUCTION:** HAVE students begin a DREAM NOTEBOOK. This should be an illustrated record of each of the dreams in this chapter. The first entries will be Joseph's two dreams in this section. Each illustration should be captioned with a statement of interpretation (taken from the text when possible). ELICIT from the students the connection between these two dreams, stars (heaven) and bundles of grain (earth), and the two promises God made to Abraham about his future-family, "like the stars in the sky and the dust of the earth."

2. **READING THE TEXT:** ASSIGN the class to read the colored words. READ or ASSIGN the part of narrator. This will establish the THEME-WORDs "brothers" and "dreams."

3. **FINDING THE CLUES:** AFTER the reading, ESTABLISH the two THEME-WORDs and the [ECHO]s they suggest. "Brother" connects us to a series of conflicts: Cain and Abel, Lot and Abram, and Jacob and Esau. "Dream" is a link to both Abram (Chapter 9, "Abram: A Covenant") and Jacob.

Chapter 23 *The Dream Comes True* Genesis 37:1ff

This is the family history of Jacob.

Joseph (meaning the *added one*) was seventeen years old. He was a shepherd with his brothers. Joseph made bad reports about them to his father. Israel loved Joseph best of all his sons. He made him a robe of many colors. When his brothers saw that his father loved him more than all his brothers, they hated him and could not speak peacefully to him.

וְיִשְׂרָאֵל אָהַב אֶת־יוֹסֵף
מִכָּל־בָּנָיו כִּי־בֶן־זְקֻנִים הוּא לוֹ
וְעָשָׂה לוֹ
כְּתֹנֶת פַּסִּים

138

Being Torah Student Commentary page 50

Joseph Is a Lot Like His Father Jacob
Pages 138–142

Two theme words in the beginning of this story are brothers and dreams.

Brothers: In most stories where brothers is a theme word we learn that brothers should be "keepers." In those stories, the brothers usually wind up feuding or fighting. Two examples are:
Cain and Abel, Jacob and Esau

_____ .

Dreams: Jacob had a dream of a ladder. When we studied that dream we learned that dreams in the Torah can teach us both about what the dreamer was like and about that person's future.

Joseph's dream showed us that Joseph _____
he thought he was the greatest
_____ .

Joseph's dream shows us that in the future Joseph_____
he will be an important person
_____ .

50

4. **MAKING MEANING:** Students are to WORK IN PAIRS to complete the exercise on page 50 of the **Student Commentary**, amending their DREAM NOTEBOOK captions if necessary after their discussions.

5. **NETWORKING COMMENTS:** DISCUSS the two interpretations of Joseph's dreams. From a psychological point of view, the dreams could show us that Joseph was self-centered. From the point of view of biblical prophecy, the dream suggests (as we know will happen) that Joseph will come to rule over his family.

ADDITIONAL ACTIVITY— JOSEPH WAS LIKE ABRAHAM
Part 2—Being Torah, page 141

Find the [ECHO] that connects Joseph and Abraham. Answer: When both were tested, they each answered "*Hineini.*"

Draw a conclusion: While Joseph looks like a self-centered

brat, he has the basic resources (being like Jacob and Abraham) to be a great Jewish leader.

More word [ECHO]s appear—*hineini* and "blood." They lead us back through Joseph's family history. The *hineini* response shows us a side of Joseph we may not have recognized before, that he is a dutiful and responsive son (in the same tradition as Abraham, Moses and Samuel). "Blood" reminds us of the responsibility to protect human life (and the penalty for shedding blood). It is a theme we saw in both the story of CAIN and ABEL and the story of NOAH. The stories of CAIN and ABEL and NOAH are part of the family's collective history. Reuben's statement about spilling no blood, without further explanation, suggests that all the brothers implicitly understood.

1. **SET INDUCTION:** SAY This section contains a clue, a very important [ECHO].

2. **READING THE TEXT:** ASSIGN students to play the parts of ISRAEL, JOSEPH, and REUBEN. ASK the class to play the chorus of brothers.

DRAMATIZE this section. You can decide if you want to add body movement to active reading.

3. **FINDING THE CLUES:** ASK "What words call attention to themselves? What words stand out as clues?" LIST and EXPLORE these words. INCLUDE "brothers," a continuing THEME-WORD that ironically [ECHO]s conflict, and "dreams", a THEME-WORD

that connects Joseph to Jacob. In the Bible, dreams are moments of communicating with God. *Hineini* is the willingness to answer and respond, the sign of a righteous person. It is a link with Abraham, Moses and Samuel. "Blood" is a link to Cain and to Noah. This word triggers a legal responsibility. "Hand," another Jacob [ECHO], is a word that (because of its link to Esau) focuses on power.

WAS JOSEPH JUST LUCKY?

Find the [ECHO] that connects Joseph's success in Potiphar's house with Joseph's success in the dungeon. Answer: Both passages tell us "Adonai was with Joseph," "everything was placed in Joseph's hands," "Joseph found favor in his master's eyes and "everything was placed in Joseph's hands."

Draw a conclusion: Joseph's success came because Adonai was with him. Because the same exact thing happened twice, we know it was no accident.

In the Joseph story, many things happened twice. The parallels point to something beneficial and important. In this section we get our first close look at this pattern. In Potiphar's house and in the dungeon, the same things happen to Joseph. In another interesting parallel, we discover the same words depict the relationship between God and Jacob and God and Joseph.

1. **SET INDUCTION:** SAY "In this section we are going to see the same thing happen twice, just like in the Jacob story."

2. **READING THE TEXT:** RETURN to our traditional reading format. ASSIGN the class the bold type and SERVE as narrator.

3. **FINDING THE CLUES:** EXPLAIN to the class that it is now their turn to unpack the meaning of this section. ALLOW students to WORK in small groups. HAVE them find the key phrases and their meaning. LIST all theories on the blackboard. If students need HELP, prompt them to use the CLOSE LOOK section on pages 147–150 of **Being Torah**.

LIST prompt words, theories and creators on the blackboard. REFER to it as you work through the material in the Student Commentary. UTILIZE every opportunity to praise students on the quality of their insights.

ADDITIONAL ACTIVITY: WHY WAS ADONAI WITH JACOB AND JOSEPH?

Find the [ECHO] that connects Jacob and Joseph. Answer: At critical points in their lives, each of them gives God credit for the help that has been given to him. Draw a conclusion: Crediting God is a basic Jewish leadership skill.

The drama continues. As a matter of fact, it picks up momentum and leads toward the happy ending, emphasizing the lesson learned in the former section, that God is really in control. The essence of the interchange with the BUTLER and the BAKER, found in this gray-matter section, is Jacob's act of *k'dushat ha shem*—public acknowledgment of God's rulership over the universe. This is a behavior he shares with his father Jacob. This show of faith, even in the dire circumstances, suggests that God chose a good person to be with.

1. **READING THE TEXT:** READ pages 151–152 as a whole story. It has a beginning, a buildup of tension, a climax, a resolution and an afterthought/anticlimax from our hero's point of view: Joseph was forgotten. All we know is that in the beginning he said God can give meanings to dreams. We don't know whether he now feels that God is still with him. In the Torah's next literary cycle, the entire Jewish people will share the anguish of a similar captivity. They, too, will wonder if the God who promised to be with them has forsaken them.

2. **MAKING MEANING:** DISCUSS the message. HAVE students write the comment, based on the exercise and the class discussion.

FINDING THE JOSEPH PATTERN, PART I

Review the Jacob pattern. The basics: Many things in Jacob's life happen twice. If something happens two times, it is highly likely that it is true (and not just an accident). Find the things that happen two times in the Joseph story. Answer: Joseph has two dreams. In the dungeon Jacob interprets two dreams. Pharaoh has two dreams. Joseph is thrown into two pit/jails. Joseph rises to success two times.

Draw a conclusion (see Part II).

Even though the objectives of sections 6 and 7 have been combined and we guide the students to see by the titles of the sections in the **Student Commentary** (Finding the Joseph Pattern, Parts I and II), we can still teach them as separate sections. The first, Section 6, which sets the groundwork for Joseph's reappearance, is shorter than Section 7, in which the role of God becomes clear. Joseph actually speaks the words we are looking for in the exercise on page 178: "Pharaoh

---

Being Torah Student Commentary page 51

Was Joseph Just Lucky?
Pages 147-150

The Torah twice tells the story of Joseph's rise from failure to success, first when he came into Potiphar's house and then later when he is thrown into jail. Read both versions, compare them, and see what you can learn. Write the number of the parallel text in the **In the Dungeon** text.

Potiphar's House (pages 147-48)

[1] Adonai was with Joseph.
  He was a man who succeeded.
  He lived in the house of his Egyptian master.

[2] His master discovered that Adonai was with Joseph
  when everything placed in Joseph's hands succeeded.

[3] Joseph found favor in his eyes.
  Joseph served him personally.

[4] Everything that was his, he put in Joseph's hands.
  Adonai blessed this Egyptian's house
  because of Joseph.

In the Dungeon (pages 149-50)

[**1**] Even in the dungeon
  Adonai was with Joseph

[**3**] Joseph found favor in the eyes of the dungeon-master.

[**4**] The dungeon-master put in Joseph's hands
  all the prisoners and all that was done there.

[**2**] The dungeon-master didn't need to check on
  anything Joseph did, because Adonai was with him.
  Everything he did, Adonai made succeed.

51

had two dreams because this thing is true. It came from God, and God will quickly do it."

1. **READING THE TEXT:** READ Section 6 with the class. Any old way will do. It is short.

2. **FINDING THE CLUES:** TALK about the images. Try to SOLVE the dreams. What do they tell, what is their meaning, what are the elements in each one (the Nile, the fat cows and ears of corn, the skinny cows and dry ears of corn)? COLLECT all possible interpretations. Even if the class already knows the right outcome, have fun constructing other possibilities.

3. **MAKING MEANING:** ASK students to complete the exercise on page 52 of the **Student Commentary**. HAVE them WRITE their comments. SHARE the answers and the comments here. We have really allowed them to discover the patterns of "twice happenings" on their own.

FINDING THE JOSEPH PATTERN, PART II

Find the [ECHO] between the dreams Joseph interpreted in the dungeon and the dreams he interpreted for Pharaoh. Answer: Both times he says "Meanings come from God."

Find the TEXT REPETITION. ANSWER: Joseph tells Pharaoh, "Pharaoh had two dreams because this thing is true."

Draw a conclusion: Things that happen twice (with God's help) are true. That means that all the promises God has repeated two or more times will come true. Specifically, even though the Joseph story leads Abraham's family into slavery in Egypt, we know that they will emerge as a great nation who will inherit the land of Israel. In this section the heart of the Joseph story is revealed, showing clearly that God keeps promises and rescues chosen people from difficult circumstances. When a promise is repeated and when an oracle comes with two witnesses, we know that it will be true. The Joseph story serves to guarantee the Exodus from Egypt.

Being Torah Student Commentary page 52

Finding the Joseph Pattern—Part I
Pages 150-151

1. Joseph has __2__ dreams, one about __stars__ and one about __wheat__.

2. In the dungeon, Joseph is asked to interpret __2__ dreams, one for __butcher__ and one for __baker__.

3. Pharaoh has __2__ dreams, one about __cows__ and one about __corn__.

4. When Joseph asks the Butler and the Baker to remember him, he calls the dungeon a (page 150) __pit__. His brothers also put him in a __pit__. Joseph got out of a __pit 2__ times.

5. Joseph went from failure to success __2__ times, once in __jail__ and one in __Potiphar's house__.

My Comment: ____
_____
_____
_____
_____
_____
_____
_____
_____

52

1. **SET INDUCTION:** REVIEW the notion of "two times" from the previous section. ASK students to INTERRUPT your reading any time you report about an event happening for a second time.

2. **READING THE TEXT:** The reading should stop at the following points. (1) Pharaoh's comment "I have dreamed a dream, and there is no one to tell me what it means." This is an [ECHO] of the butler and the baker. (2) Joseph's answer, "God will answer for Pharaoh's peace." This again is an [ECHO] of Joseph's previous answer. (3) The repeating of Pharaoh's two dreams.

When you reach the verse "PHARAOH had two dreams because this thing is true," hands should shoot up. Students should see immediately the connection between this idea of "twice means true" to the two-times events we have been collecting. LET the discussion flow.

Finish the reading. Pay attention to the two times that Pharaoh shows that Joseph has taught him about God's power.

4. **MAKING MEANING:** Have students COMPLETE the exercise on page 64 of the **Student Commentary** and NETWORK their comments.

ADDITIONAL ACTIVITY: WHY DID JOSEPH MAKE SURE THAT EGYPT FED THE WHOLE WORLD?

MISSING INFORMATION. Another place for midrash.

ADDITIONAL ACTIVITY: DID THE DREAMS COME TRUE?

Find the [ECHO] of Jacob's dreams in his meeting his brothers in Egypt. Answer: The brothers did bow down to Joseph, and he was a lord over them.

Draw a conclusion: Dreams, promises, and predictions (from God) do come true.

Part 9 brings a series of revelations. We see Joseph do _hesed_ and feed the world, we witness the dream of the family bowing to Joseph come true, and we see the beginning of his test/revenge.

Being Torah Student Commentary page 53

Finding the Joseph Pattern—Part II
Pages 152-153

Compare these passages:

1. (With the Butler and the Baker) They told him: "We dreamed dreams and there is no one to tell us what they mean." Joseph said to them, "Don't meanings come from God?"

2. Pharaoh said to Joseph, "I have dreamed a dream and there is no one to tell me what it means." Joseph answered Pharaoh, "God will answer for Pharaoh's dream."

3. "Pharaoh had two dreams because this thing is true. It came from God and God will do it quickly."

My Comment: What I see when I connect these passages is _____ _everybody dreams and Joseph tells what the dreams mean with God's help_ .

When things happen twice in the Torah we are supposed to learn _____ _these things will come true_ .

53

1. **SET INDUCTION:** ASK "Was Jacob a good person or a self-serving, selfish kid?" ALLOW for open discussion. ASK students to bring facts from the text. EXPLAIN: We'll see the truth in this section of the text.

2. **READING THE TEXT:** READ the section in **Being Torah**. ASSIGN the section to narrator (or narrators), JACOB, the brothers, and JOSEPH.

3. **FINDING THE CLUES:** DISCUSS two questions. "Why did Joseph arrange for Egypt to feed the world?" and "Why did Joseph trick his brothers?" ACCEPT all answers.

ADDITIONAL ACTIVITY: WHY DID JOSEPH GIVE HIS BROTHER A HARD TIME?

Find the [ECHO] in the meeting of Joseph and his brothers. Answer: Joseph treats his brothers as strangers. This is an [ECHO] of the prediction that God made to Abraham, "Your future-family will be strangers in a land which is not theirs."

Draw a conclusion: The Joseph story is proof that the promises made to Abraham will come true.

This section explains why Joseph tested his brothers, while 23.11 focuses on what he tested.

READING THE TEXT: Because this is gray matter (**Being Torah**, page 160), it can be quickly glossed. READ the section with the class. TALK about the events, their significance, and their impact on the participants. ASK: "What could be Joseph's reason for giving the brothers such a hard time?" ACCEPT all answers. ELUCIDATE the two possible answers found above.

HOW DID JOSEPH LEARN THAT HIS BROTHERS HAD CHANGED?

Find the THEME-WORD. Answer: "Slave/servant"

Draw a conclusion: Judah's speech shows that he has changed. Given the chance to better himself by hurting a younger brother, he risks his own life. The THEME-WORD "slave" foreshadows the future. What did Joseph mean?

Joseph tells his brothers, "God sent me before you to save life." Explain. Answer: (1) Joseph saved many lives by giving out food. (2) Joseph saved his family by bringing them to Egypt. (3) Joseph saved the Jewish people by helping God's prediction come true.

Being Torah Student Commentary page 54

How Did Joseph Learn That His Brothers Had Changed?
Pages 161–162

Theme Words

What two words are used over and over in this part of the story?

_____ **servant** _____ and _____ **brother** _____

My Comment: *The brothers did not recognize their brother Joseph. They behaved like servants to the great lord.*

54

The Joseph story climaxes in the dramatic speech given by Judah, which is filled with the word stem [עבד] (servant/slave) and Joseph's revelation to his brothers. The connection to the forthcoming Exodus is doubly underlined as we realize that "Gad sent Joseph…ahead to save life."

1. **SET INDUCTION:** REVIEW the whole Joseph story up to this point. On the BOARD, LIST everything that has happened so far.

2. **READING THE TEXT:** We recommend that you READ the entire section to the class YOURSELF. It should be a slow and dramatic reading; this is one of the Torah's best third acts. DIRECT the class to listen to Judah's words. Guide the class to realizing the changes that the brothers have gone through: humility, consideration of their father's feelings, caring for their brother Benjamin.

   READ pages 161–162 in **Being Torah**, where Joseph makes himself known to the brothers. TALK about the excitement of the moment. (How does the text talk about it?) What are Joseph's concerns? His father's well-being and his brothers' feelings.

3. **MAKING MEANING:** ASK the students to FILL IN, DISCUSS in small groups and WRITE their comments about "What did Joseph mean?" NETWORKING COMMENTS: There are many aspects or focal points by which you could put the pieces of the Joseph saga together and help the students construct a whole out of the sections you have dealt with. The important thing is to leave this chapter only after some form of closure has taken place. Listen to students' questions about the events, guide them to answer each other and make meaning of the whole through their own efforts.

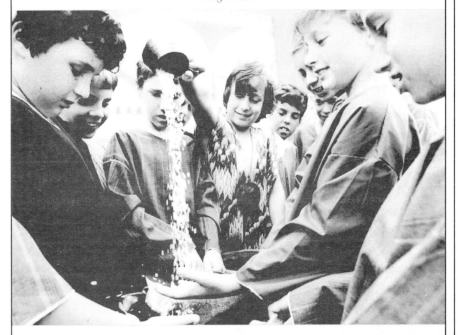

Being Torah Student Commentary page 55

What Did Joseph Mean?
Page 162

Now do not be pained. Do not feel guilt that you sold me. God sent me before you to save life.

My Comment: I think Joseph was trying to tell his brothers that *he was not angry with them for selling him. God had a plan for Joseph to be in Egypt and to save the life of his family.*

55

CHAPTER 24—
THE NEW KING

**Being Torah,
pages 164–165
Student Commentary,
page 56**

ABSTRACT
5 + 5 = PHARAOH'S PLAN AND GOD'S PROTECTION

Count the number of ways the Torah describes that the Jewish people grew. Answer: 5

Count the number of ways that Pharoah tried to hurt the Jewish people. Answer: 5

Find the verse that connects these. Answer: "The more they made them suffer, the more they multiplied and the more they spread out."

Find the [ECHO] suggested by the phrase "spread out." Answer: In God's first promise to Abram inside the land of Israel (Chapter 8 "Abram: Lot Leaves"), God promises that his future-family will (spread out and) cover the land like dust.

Draw a conclusion: God is fulfilling the promises made to Abraham. Also, the suffering seems to be part of the plan.

OVERVIEW

In introducing the Exodus, the Torah shows us that oppression can emerge from hatred and fear, and that it can be overcome by human courage.

The story of the Exodus is a women's story. The midrash dwells upon this, elaborating the ways women sustained and saved the Jewish people, forcing their husbands to risk fathering children, hiding and saving their babies, nurturing their families through the suffering, and providing the strength and courage for the people's survival. While these midrashim are among the tradition's most wonderful portraits of women's unique strengths, they are nothing more than the creative extension of the Torah's narrative revelations.

The book of Exodus begins with a recounting of Jacob's family. It is listed as being seventy people. When their children leave Egypt, they will number 600,000. To show us the rapid growth, the Torah employs five adjective phrases for their growth: (1) fruitful, (2) increased, (3) became many, (4) became very strong, and (5) filled the land. Humankind's three-part blessing— "Be fruitful, become many and fill the land/earth"— is more than fulfilled. The first two parts of Abraham's family's unique covenant are on their way to fulfillment. The family has become a nation.

The new king of Egypt reacts to this change. "The nation of the Children of Israel is many. Let's outsmart them." A five-part plan of attrition emerges: (1) assigning tasks and taskmasters; (2) state slavery; (3) bitterness through hard slavery; (4) genocide via the midwives; (5) national genocide. While there is an obvious connection between the size of the growth and Pharaoh's panic, the Torah also testifies to Divine involvement (at least in the people's willpower) with "The more they made them suffer, the more they multiplied."

In the second half of this story the word "midwives" appears seven times. It is a theme-word/number-word. Like the seven goods of creation and the seven brothers in the story of Cain and Abel, the midwives represent an absolute essential human quality. While in contemporary (secular) language this would be described as "the courage to do what is right," the Torah explains it in different terms: "The midwives were in awe of God." Their moral character was tied to an absolute conviction.

In the Torah the Hebrew reads *mi'yeldot ivriot,* and its meaning is ambivalent. It can be understood to mean "the Hebrew (Jewish) women who served as midwives" or as "the (Egyptian) women who served as midwives to the Hebrews." Evidence exists for both of these intriguing possibilities—Jewish women who revolted against Pharaoh's authority and Egyptians who rejected their own national connection to stand for what was right. The midrash explores both options. In the end, it doesn't matter. The example of these women's courage and faith stands as the single source of tremendous hope in the onslaught of human oppression. These women are the essence of this story.

TEACHING TOOLS

OBJECTIVES

The learner will find the five word groups describing the growth of the Jewish people, the five steps in Pharaoh's plan and the verse that connects the two.

SLIDE-IN VOCABULARY

taskmasters—bosses

midwives—people who work like doctors, helping women give birth

HEBREW VOCABULARY

am Yisrael—the nation Israel

avadim—slaves

mi'yeldot—midwives

Being Torah Student Commentary page 56

CHAPTER 24: THE NEW KING
5 + 5 = Pharaoh's Plan and God's Protection

We are at the beginning of the book of Exodus. It begins by telling us these things about the Jewish people.

1. The Children of Israel were fruitful.
2. They increased.
3. They became many.
4. They became very strong.
5. They filled the land.

Next the Torah describes a plan of Pharaoh's.

1. They put taskmasters over them...
2. The Egyptians made slaves of the Children of Israel.
3. They made their life bitter with hard slavery.
4. The King of Egypt spoke to the Hebrew midwives..."When you help the Hebrew women deliver a baby and you see that it is a boy, kill it."
5. Pharaoh commanded his whole people: "Every Hebrew son that is born you will throw in the river."

Connecting these two lists, we are told:

The more they made them suffer, the more they multiplied and the more they spread out.

My Comment: ___*No matter what Pharoah tried to do, the Israelites were*___
fruitful and became many because God was with them.

56

ACTIVITIES

5 + 5 = PHARAOH'S PLAN AND GOD'S PROTECTION

Student Commentary, page 56

This exercise exposes the 5 + 5 structure of this chapter.

1. **SET INDUCTION:** AGAIN, start by encouraging the students to develop their independent study skills. Introduce the exercise in the **Student Commentary** and ask for ideas how best to complete it. ALLOW your students to determine the working process (groups, individually, etc.).

2. **READING THE TEXT:** ACCEPT students' ideas regarding reading the text again together; having a student leader lead the class in working together, doing parts together and the rest individually or working in small groups. The process of deciding how to approach the task is important but should be concluded after a short time, and the work should start.

3. **MAKING MEANING:** SUM up the content and the form of the exercise. What did the students learn? How did they learn it? How does the text MAKE SURE we get its special message here (the 5 + 5 and the sentence "the more...the more")?

ADDITIONAL ACTIVITY: THE BIG CHANGE IN THE FAMILY

Find the ECHO of the promises made to Abraham in the beginning of the Exodus story. Answer: God promised that Abraham's future-family would grow to be many. In this story, Jacob's family have grown to be many—a "nation." Draw a conclusion: The promises are coming true. One down and one to go.

OBJECTIVE

Through listing Jacob's sons and identifying the first use of the term "the nation of Israel," the learner will identify the growth in the nation of Israel.

ABSTRACT

The chapter marks the transformation from Genesis to Exodus. We will also use it as a transition, moving the students toward more independence in their close reading. Up to now we expected them to find answers and write questions; from now on we guide them to choose their method of investigation.

In this chapter we will note the transformation of the word "family" into the word "nation."

1. **SET INDUCTION:** LET students KNOW that they are expected to work more independently from here on. Because of the skill they have shown thus far, we expect them to now direct their own study.

2. **READING THE TEXT:** There is much we want to emerge from the reading of this story: an awareness of the two series of five, the presence of the THEME-WORD "slave" and the use of the NUMBER-WORD "midwives."

   DIRECT students that in this reading we want them to figure out the important elements in this story. ASK them to try to think of the reason that each of the key cues is in color.

   BREAK the class into three parts. ASSIGN each part the reading of one type of cued text. READ the part of narrator yourself.

3. **FINDING THE CLUES:** WRITE the following elements on the blackboard. ASK students what kind of clue each of these is, and/or what message they teach. The five terms for the growth are fruitful, increased, became many, became very strong, and filled the land. Students may identify this as TEXT REPETITION, the blessings given to Abraham corning true. That is a good insight. However, PROMPT them, if necessary to count the elements.

   ASK them to look for another string of five elements. HELP them to find the five stages Pharaoh went through in trying to destroy the Jews.

   IDENTIFY the word SLAVE as a THEME-WORD. ACCEPT any other connections they want to make. IDENTIFY the word "midwives" as a THEME-WORD and HELP them to find that it is also a NUMBER-WORD. DO NOT go into its importance.

4. **MAKING MEANING:** In small Torah circles, ASK students to create comments.

5. **NETWORKING COMMENTS:** ASK every group to SHARE their answer to "what was the change" and "my comment" with the whole class. TALK about the discovery of being able to work more independently. How does it feel? How is it different than the more guided steps before?

ADDITIONAL LESSON SEEDS

On page 188 Angelica's comments talk about the senselessness of prejudice. The theme is an important one.

A large number of exercises and materials focus on the slave experience. Any of these would make for a good extension.

CHAPTER 25—
AND INTRODUCING MOSES

Being Torah, pages 167–170
Student Commentary, pages 57–58

ABSTRACT
WHAT MADE MOSES THE PERFECT LEADER? PART I

FIND the [ECHO] that connects Moses' birth to the creation of the world. ANSWER: In both stories, the creation is seen as "good."

FIND the [ECHO] that connects Moses' birth to the second creation of the world, the story of Noah. ANSWER: In both, the word "ARK" saves life.

DRAW A CONCLUSION: Moses' birth is a major event in the history of the world, like Creation and like the flood.

WHAT MADE MOSES THE PERFECT LEADER? PART II

FIND the [ECHO] that connects Moses to the story of Cain and Abel. ANSWER: "He went out to his brothers."

DRAW A CONCLUSION: While Cain needed to learn that he was supposed to be his brother's keeper, Moses instinctively knew and understood that.

OVERVIEW

Moses is to be the ultimate leader of the Jewish people. His birth and development stories are keys to understanding his nature and qualifications. They set his experience as unique but connected to patterns we have seen before.

The Jewish people have traditionally been dynastic. The story of Abraham's future-family represents the first major thrust. The Davidic monarchy forms the second expression of familial leadership. The Aaronite Priesthood is the third expression of this dynastic tendency. One model of individual charismatic leadership stands in contrast to this cast of familiar leaders: the prophets. Moses is the archetype of prophetic leadership, emerging from anonymous parentage and leaving no related heir to assume his role. In setting the story of Moses' origins, we will see him as heir to the best we have seen about humankind and Abraham's family in the book of Genesis, yet totally original in his essence.

Family history has been the essence of every previous birthing story. Usually the pattern has been barrenness, a divine announcement, and a parental/divine naming experience. Moses has none of these. He never even spends time rivaling his sibling. His parents are described as "a man from the tribe of Levi" and "a daughter of the tribe of Levi." The Torah, however, knows better. In a genealogy presented later in the book of Exodus they are introduced as Amram and Yocheved. Here, however, it is important that he could be any Jew. Nothing exceptional marks his birth.

Beneath the surface of the plot, however, word echoes reveal the coming destiny. Right after his birth the Torah speaks of his mother's reaction: "She saw that

he was GOOD." This is a direct echo of God's reaction to each stage of creation, "God saw… that it was GOOD." There is something primordial about his birth. When his mother needs to do something with the child, he is placed in a *teva,* commonly translated as a basket of bulrushes. The word has only one other usage in the Bible: It is the ark Noah built. To complete the echo, both are pitched with the same tar. While the specific meaning is in the eye of the interpreter, the Torah wants us to know that Moses is like Noah.

In the last story the midwives served as the role-model saviors of the Jewish people. In this story, the same role is served by a different series of women. They are linked by a sevenfold use of the word **daughter.** Moses' mother and sister violate Pharoah's laws to save and protect him. Pharaoh's daughter violates her father's orders when she saves Moses. Jethro's daughters provide the next nexus of support and sustenance for Moses. Guided by the theme-word **daughter,** we are again directed toward women's role in insuring the survival of the Jewish people.

Moses is established as a man locked between cultures. Raised by Hebrew women and by Pharaoh's daughter, his identity is in constant confusion. The Hebrews whom he helps resist his involvement. While he sees them as brothers, the feeling is not mutual. They doubt the sincerity of his involvement. Echoing the brothers' ironic question at the beginning of Joseph's story, the Hebrews sarcastically ask, "Who made you our boss and our judge?" The answer will soon be known. For now, Moses, the privileged Hebrew, is driven into exile because of his misunderstood humanity and commitment to his brothers. When he comes to Midian he again encounters oppression and fights to save Jethro's daughters. Fulfilling the twofold Joseph pattern, Moses has now twice stood up for the underdog and freed them from their persecutors. A life truth has been demonstrated. The daughters, however, still confuse his identity, explaining to their father, "An Egyptian man saved us from the hand of the shepherds." Echoing the Abraham/Rebekah paradigm of hospitality, he "draws water many times" for their sheep. The essence of this identity confusion is revealed when Moses names his son Gershom, explaining, "I have been a **stranger** in a **strange** land."

Unlike our previous experiences with naming formulae, this one reveals more about the father than the son. The word **stranger** connects us to one of the Torah's major themes. **Stranger** was the key word in God's revelation to Abram about the future history of his future-family (Chapter 9: "Abram: A Covenant"). It is the essence of Abraham's experience in Canaan, revealed when he purchases a cave in which to bury his wife (a story only glossed over in **Being Torah**): "I am a resident stranger among you." While the exact word form (גֵר) doesn't appear in the Joseph story, the word (נֵכָר), also *stranger*, is used when the Torah tells us, "When JOSEPH saw his brothers, he **recognized** them, but treated them as **strangers**."

Gershom's naming formula does more than just lock Moses into the essence of Abraham's family destiny. It also prepares us for the essence of a coming law code. Moses will teach the Jewish people God's ethics, which are rooted in the experience of the stranger. He will teach us, "Make one law both for the citizen and for the **stranger**" (Ex. 12.4-9). "Do not treat a stranger badly, nor make a **stranger** suffer, for you were **strangers** in the land of Egypt" (Ex 20:20). And "Do not make a **stranger** suffer, because you understand the heart of a **stranger**— you were **strangers** in the land of Egypt."

Moses has lived the isolation and suffering of the Jewish experience to the maximum, and his double alienation allows him to become the prime interpreter of that experience. In the story of his origins we see Moses three times reach out to help, just because "he understands the heart of a **stranger**." Being good, understanding the "ark type" and feeling a deep connection to his brothers, Moses represents the essence of the Genesis experience as he begins to resolve four hundred years of suffering as **strangers**.

In the early portion of the twentieth century two Jewish immigrant kids felt a connection to this story of the good-doing savior, the stranger in a stranger land. They transformed it through their imagination into a "strange visitor from another planet" who was exiled by his parents in order to insure his survival. An Egyptian prince's perception of his Hebrew brothers was the foundation of "truth, justice and the American way." When you look into Superman's heart, you find the teaching of the Jewish tradition as rooted in the first Super Teacher, Moses.

TEACHING TOOLS
OBJECTIVES

The learner will find two [ECHO]s that connect Moses to CREATION ("saw" and "GOOD") and NOAH ("ARK" covered with "tar") and then explain how these connections highlight characteristics that make Moses the right leader.

The learner will isolate and identify the word "brothers" as an [ECHO], associate it with "brother's keeper," and add this to Moses' qualifications as the perfect leader for the Jewish people.

HEBREW VOCABULARY
bat—daughter
ivri—Hebrew (person)
ger—stranger

ACTIVITIES

WHAT MADE MOSES THE RIGHT LEADER, PART I
Student Commentary, page 57

With this exercise the work gets hard. We do not refer the students to specific pages. We do not tell them overtly what to look for. We believe that with general guidance from you (don't be too easy and give them the answers!) they will not only come up with the right stuff but will also feel great for being able to do it on their own.

1. **SET INDUCTION**: RESTATE the introduction to this exercise. SAY: "This chapter tells three different stories about Moses. One word connects those stories. Find that word and look for the lesson it teaches."

2. **READING THE TEXT**: GROUP the class into Torah circles or DIVIDE them into two groups. APPOINT a student leader to conduct the work on the exercise. GIVE THEM THIS CLUE: "Reading the text will help find the title/description of

each story." INSTRUCT the groups to COMPLETE the whole exercise. MONITOR the work.

3. **FINDING THE CLUES**: GO OVER the answers. ESTABLISH the connection between Moses' mother "seeing" that he was "GOOD" and God "seeing" that the world was "GOOD," AS WELL AS that the word "ark" is what the Hebrew really says, even though we usually call it a basket. These two places are the only places in the Torah where this word is used. The Torah is forcing the connection that both water vessels carry the person who will save the human race.

APPLY these clues: TALK about the new beginnings in the Creation and Noah stories. How does our story connect to them? Why is there a new beginning now? How is Moses like Noah? *This is a good review of previous studies. It should help the students achieve a sense of bonding all of the Torah. Here are themes that span the whole cycle.*

CHAPTER 25: AND INTRODUCING MOSES
What Made Moses the Perfect Leader? Part I

In this paragraph are two clues that Moses was fated to be a great leader. Find them.

A maN from the tribe of Levi
married a daughter of the tribe of Levi.
The woman became pregnant
and gave birth to a son.
She saw that he was good.
She hid him for three months.
When she was no longer able to hide him
she took an ark of bulrushes,
covered it with slime and tar, put him in it,
and put it in the reeds
on the bank of the Nile.
His sister watched from a distance
to know what would happen to him.

What words connect this story to the story of creation? ___*saw that he was good*___

What words connect this story to the Noah story? ___*an ark*___

What did Moses and creation have in common? ___*it was good*___

_____.

How was Moses like Noah? *he was in an ark and would save the Jewish people*

_____.

MY COMMENT: _____	_____ 'S COMMENT:
_____	_____
_____	_____
_____ .	_____ .

57

SUM up with the title question: "How does the Torah tell us that Moses is the right leader for the people?"

WHAT MADE MOSES THE RIGHT LEADER, PART II
Student Commentary, page 58

The ECHO "brother" will probably need very little prompting from you.

1. **SET INDUCTION**: SAY "**Student Commentary**, page 56. Do it." TRUST US, this is all the set induction you'll need.

2. **FINDING THE CLUES**: ASK "What did you find?" LISTEN FOR ANSWERS. *In case you haven't figured it out, we are particularly confident of success.* OPEN the discussion up.

   "Why is it important? What's special about Moses referring to the Hebrews as his brothers? Where did he grow up? Who was his nurse when he was very young?" (His mother!) You may want to mention that even though he grew up in the palace, he might have felt like a stranger even then (this sets the tone for the next exercise regarding Moses' son's name and its meaning).

3. **MAKING MEANING**: Write and share comments.

ADDITIONAL ACTIVITY: WHAT'S IN A NAME?

Explain the meaning of the name Moses gave to his son. Answer: "Stranger."

Find the ECHO that connects "stranger" to Abram. Answer: God told Abram, "Know for a fact that your future-family will be strangers."

Find the ECHO that connects "stranger" to Joseph. Answer: The Torah tells us that Joseph recognized his brothers but treated them like strangers.

Find the ECHO that connects "stranger" to the laws that Moses will teach to the Jewish people. Answer: In Exodus 12.49, 20.20, 21.9 and a number of other passages, the word "stranger."

Draw a conclusion: Being a "stranger in a strange land" was the essence of Abraham's experience; it also characterized the Jewish experience in Egypt. Memories of these experiences will form the core of Jewish ethics.

Being Torah Student Commentary page 58

What made Moses the Perfect Leader? Part II

In this paragraph we find another word clue that shows that Moses was the perfect leader for the Jewish people. Find that clue and write a comment on the lesson it teaches.

> When Moses grew up he went out to his brothers. He saw their suffering. He saw an Egyptian man beating a Hebrew man— one of his brothers. No one was around. He killed the Egyptian and hid him in the sand.

MY COMMENT: _____   'S COMMENT:

Even though Moses grew up in the palace, he felt a connection to his suffering brothers and sisters.

58

OBJECTIVES

The learner will explain the meaning of Gershom's name as "stranger," trace the **[ECHO]** of this word through the Torah, and connect Moses' teachings about strangers to his qualities as a leader.

This exercise is devoted to introducing the Torah's "stranger" theme and connecting it to Moses' leadership role. Here again we read of Moses giving his son a name that reflects his feelings now (and probably throughout his life so far). The name Gershom, "the stranger," serves as a reminder of the status of the Hebrews, echoes God's prediction to Abraham about this time, and leads us into looking at the major importance of the concept of strangers in Moses' teachings. So you still wonder what's in a name?

1. **SET INDUCTION**: REVIEW the importance of naming and the meaning of names in the Torah. Last time we discussed it was in regard to Joseph giving his sons names that reflected his special position, away from his family but very successful in Egypt.

2. **FINDING THE CLUES**: The class should have no trouble following the **[ECHO]** of "stranger." Their only problem will come in the drawing of conclusions. You can help them with this retroactively.

3. **MAKING MEANING**: ASK "What can we learn from the word **stranger**?" LISTEN to all the theories. REFLECT on the contemporary ways of dealing with strangers, the reasons for them, the pros and cons of the situation. EXPLAIN that the Jewish way of healing strangers is significantly different from what the students are normally taught as survival skills for daily life. We must emphasize the ethics involved in treating strangers with special concern because of the very fact that they are strangers and we should know how it feels.

NOTE: We are in a day and age when the word "stranger" is a loaded word. We teach kids to be afraid of strangers. Kids are exposed to a lot of anti-stranger (anti-accepting candy) training. We are not trying to undo the safe-kids lessons; instead, we want to give strangers another dimension. It may be important in your context to draw a distinction between helping people who are in need and putting yourself at risk. We have a responsibility to help strangers (but that doesn't mean to do it all by yourself).

CHAPTER 26— THE BURNING BUSH

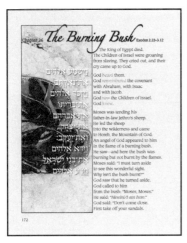

Being Torah, pages 172–173

Student Commentary, page 59

ABSTRACT
THE PROOF IS IN THE ECHO

Find the ECHOs that connect God's actions described at the beginning of "The Burning Bush" with those God shares with Moses later in the chapter. ANSWER: God "sees," "hears," and "knows." Also, not repeated in both places, but an important ECHO, there is "remember."

Find the ECHO for the word "see." ANSWER: God saw the suffering of both Leah and Jacob.

Find the ECHO for the word "hear." ANSWER: God heard the suffering of Hagar, the voice of Ishmael, and the cries of Leah and Rachel.

Find the ECHO for the word "remember." ANSWER: God remembered Noah and those in the ark, Abraham and Sarah, and Rachel.

Draw a conclusion: Based on the "two time" lesson learned in the Joseph story, we know that God is going to keep his promises. These ECHOs reassure us that God remembers and cares for us.

OVERVIEW

Just as the story of the covenant between the pieces (chapter 9, pages 64–66) brought us to a new age that divided a universal history of a God of creation from the particular (Exodus) history of the Jewish people, so the story of the burning bush brings us into a new age by dividing between familial history and a national future.

God has been silent for more than four hundred years. Not since the days of Jacob has a human been in somewhat regular communication with the Divine. The vector of an earlier direction of history has long been running; Abraham's family is nearing the end of the promised years of suffering as strangers. The awaited course change toward a promised land is but a mythic memory. We can imagine that faith is at issue. So far Moses's story has been ethnic, with no mention of God.

This chapter begins with a pan of the goings on in heaven. We learn that God **heard, remembered, saw,** and **knew**. In other words, learning from our experience in Genesis, God is ready to act. In Genesis the Torah set a pattern of God responding to human need. Each of these four verbs triggers the echoes of situations to which God responded.

Next we cut to Earth. We see Moses as a shepherd (a familiar training ground for Jewish leaders). Five uses of the word **see** introduce the burning bush. In good form, Moses responds, "*Hineini.*" The echo is clear. Like Abraham, Moses is a man who can perceive the vision of the Divine; he is a man ready and willing to respond to the Divine call. The silence is broken.

God reintroduces God's self to humanity as a God of relationships. The connection to family history is made. The word "face" recalls earlier encounters. God repeats the verbs of divine perception: **seen, heard** and **know**. The repetition assures their truthfulness. The second part of the two-part promise is restated. Moses' call is much like those of the patriarchs. The first part of the two-part promise (great nation) has already come to pass.

God then reveals Moses' mission, and Moses expresses doubt. This scene is a direct echo of Abram's encounter with the covenant of the pieces. MOSES asks two questions: (1) Who am I to go to Pharaoh? and (2) Why am I the one to bring the Children of Israel out of slavery? God answers each question. The first answer is a direct continuation of the patriarchal chain, "I will be with you." The second answer, like Abram's second answer, roots itself in future history. God in essence is saying that "when My plans are complete, you will understand." The answer becomes assuring, not because it is real proof, but because the revelation has changed the nature of the universe. Moses, like Abram before him, has understood that his people's history has both purpose and possibility. It is the new window of hope that makes the difference.

TEACHING TOOLS

OBJECTIVES

The learner will trace the [ECHO] of the verbs to discover God's perception of human needs.

OBJECTIVES

The learner will recognize that the dialogue contains two questions and two answers.

HEBREW VOCABULARY

sneh—bush

Being Torah Student Commentary page 59

CHAPTER 26: THE BURNING BUSH
The Proof is in the Echo

The Torah begins the story of the Exodus from Egypt by telling us:

God **heard** them.
God **remembered** the covenant with Abraham, with Isaac, and with Jacob.
God **saw** the children of Israel.
God **knew**.

At the Burning Bush God tells Moses:

I have **seen** and **seen** again the suffering of My people in Egypt.
I have **heard** their cry—
I **know** their pain...
God said, "I will be with you."

Use a copy of the complete Torah and look up the things that God has already done for Abraham's family.

Genesis **15.1** *God heard Abram's cry for a future-family* _____

Genesis 16.11 *gave a son to Abraham because God heard his call for one* _____

Genesis 21.17 *God heard the cry of the baby and saw its pain* _____

Genesis 29.31 *God saw that Leah was unloved and gave her a baby* _____

Genesis 30.6 *God remembered Rachel and gave her a son through Bilhah* _____

Genesis 30.22 *God remembered Rachel and gave her a son* _____

Genesis 31.12 *God knew all that Laban had done to Jacob* _____

Genesis **31:42** *God saw Abraham's situation with Laban* _____

> **My Comment:** In the Joseph story we learn that things that have already happened twice continue to come true. By reminding us of things that God has already done for the people with the words "hear," "see," and "remember" _____
> **we know that God will continue to watch out for B'nai Yisrael by hearing,**
> **seeing and remembering them.** .

59

---

elohei—God of (Avraham, Yitzchak, and Ya'akov)
avot—(the) fathers.

ACTIVITIES

THE PROOF IS IN THE ECHO
Student Commentary, page 59

The Torah has been building up to this moment for a long time. In the stories of the fore-parents we have seen numerous examples of God remembering, seeing distress, hearing pleas for help, etc. While there is an anxiety that God has forgotten and abandoned the chosen people to slavery in Egypt, the introduction to the burning bush reestablishes the pattern of a helping God.

This is the first time we expect the students to use the full text of the Torah. MAKE SURE there are enough copies of the new JPS translation available.

1. **SET INDUCTION**: BREAK the class into groups and ASK the students to READ the text on their own, LOOKING for all the **ECHO**s they can find. The text literally resounds with them. Second reading should be done as a class, in which the students will share their findings.

2. **LEARNING TO USE A TORAH**: INTRODUCE students to a real Bible or Torah. SHOW them that every chapter is numbered, and so is every sentence (verse). WORK with them to find the first example, Gen. 31.42. *Note we are going to work*

this page from the bottom up, looking up the past examples and then reworking this passage.

3. **FINDING THE CLUES**: HAVE groups work to look up all of these quotations. GO OVER the answers.

4. **MAKING MEANING**: ALLOW time for students to write their own comments.

Additional Activity: Questions and Answers

Explain the structure of Moses' conversation with God at the burning bush. **Answer**: It is two questions matched with two answers.

Find the **[ECHO]** in these two questions and answers. **Answer**: These match the two questions and answers in the covenant between the pieces (chapter 9, pages 64–66).

Draw a conclusion: The proof that God's promises will come true is established by the fact that they did come true.

The conversation between God and Moses at the burning bush is in many ways consistent with God's words to Abraham in our Chapter 9 (Genesis 15). The assurances Moses receives are both personal ("I will be with you") and national ("all of you will serve Adonai at this very mountain"). Likewise, the final proof rests in an elliptical vision of history: When everything I say comes true, that will be proof.

1. **SET INDUCTION**: DISCUSS the burning bush. ASK: "Why did God need a sign in order for Moses to talk to God?" ACCEPT all answers. ASK: "Who was the last person to talk to God (that the Torah tells us about)?" ESTABLISH that it was Jacob, back more or less four hundred years before.

POINT OUT that Jews had become used to God's silence.

POINT OUT to students that most of this conversation consists of Moses doubting and God reassuring.

2. **FINDING THE CLUES**: Have students WORK through the questions in this exercise. It will be difficult. It is somewhat hard to find the answers to match the questions; it is very hard to understand how a future proof is acceptable. *You may want to compare this with Abraham's future guarantee in Chapter 9.* THE BEST single explanation is that God is showing Moses that the Jewish people's history is both monitored and preplanned. This is the assurance.

3. **MAKING MEANING**: *We suspect that the two comments will be difficult for students to write without some discussion beforehand.* ASK the two comments' questions and collect answers. The normative understanding is that Moses is humble or modest, not scared, and that God is patient. ALLOW students to WRITE and NETWORK comments.

CHAPTER 27—
THE TEN COMMANDMENTS

Being Torah, pages 176-178
Student Commentary, pages 60-61

ABSTRACT
THE TEN COMMANDMENTS PATTERN

Explain the pattern in the Ten Commandments. **Answer**: The first five commandments (which are all between God and people) match the second five commandments (which are all between people).

Draw a conclusion: Our relationship with God matches our relationship with other people.

OVERVIEW

The giving of the Ten Commandments is the dramatic culmination of the Exodus. With it, the spiritual transformation of the Jewish people is completed. It is a moment of recreation, echoing in many ways the first Creation.

In the first chapter of the Torah we found that the word **said** was used ten times, that God created the world through ten utterances. To someone who has a sense of Hebrew, the echo is automatic, because what the English mind knows as "commandments" given at Sinai are known in the Hebrew as *dibrot,* speakings. Ten acts of speaking create the world. Ten acts of speaking recreate Abraham's Jewish family by beginning the relationship known as Torah.

When we looked into the story of creation, we found that it was built in two layers, the first three days introducing raw products and the next three days completing these elements (see the overview for Chapter 1). When we look into the Ten Commandments, we can see the same two-part structure. The rabbis of the Talmud divide mitzvot into two categories, *ben Adam L'makom*, between people and God, and *ben Adam L'Havero*, between people. The distinction is one learned from the Ten Commandments.

1. I am the Lord	6. Do NOT murder
2. NO Idols	7. DO NOT commit adultery
3. NO misuse of God's name	8. Do NOT steal
4. REMEMBER Shabbat	9. Do NOT lie about your neighbor
5. HONOR father and mother	10. Do NOT wish for your neighbor's stuff

The first four items are clearly items between God and people. The last five are clearly interpersonal. It is the fifth commandment that seems to keep the text from symmetry. Honoring parents seems to be an issue between people. Rabbinic insight (and a long experience with biblical patterning) leads to a resolution. It is explained that parents are God's partners in the creation of every human life. During the child's growth and development they represent God and teach the child what s/he needs to know to grow into righteousness and happiness. Obeying parents is a tangible expression of obeying God.

When we look more closely at the structure, this parallelism seems more obvious. Each commandment has a mate. "I am Adonai" matches "Do Not murder." One who kills denies God's image in his/her victim. "No idols" is a parallel to "No adultery"; both are cheating on exclusive relationships. Not swearing falsely has a direct connection to not stealing. Swearing by God's name usually means a business oath. Lying with God's name is usually an act of cheating and stealing. Remembering Shabbat and no false witness are equally a pair. Shabbat is defined as a sign, as a witness that God created the world and brought us out of Egypt. By not observing Shabbat, we are being poor witnesses to God's importance. Honoring parents and coveting that which is your neighbor's are also connected. Coveting that which is your neighbor's is rejecting the quality of your own home and inheritance; it is a rejection of that which your parents have done.

Just as with the first creation week, the first level prepares us for the second. The raw products prepare for advanced creations. Here our relationship with our Creator becomes the basis for our interhuman relations.

In the night vision in Chapter 9 ("Abram: A Covenant"), the relationship that results in the Jewish people was first defined. Among the images Abram perceives is a smoking furnace. At the foot of Mt. Sinai, at the moment of definition of the Jewish people through their national connection with the Divine, the image recycles. The Torah tells us "The smoke rose like the smoke of a furnace." The revelation at Sinai is both beginning and culmination.

Old word-themes echo. **Listen, keep** and **commandments** appear together. God says: "NOW, if you will **listen** to my voice and **keep** my commandments, and be my treasure from among all peoples, then you shall be to Me a kingdom of priests and a holy nation." It is a moment of national chosenness. It echoes the first revelation of the unique God–Abraham nexus (Chapter 12, "The Sodom Debate"). "I have become close to him so that he will command his children and his future-family to **keep** the way of Adonai and to do what is **right** and just." It also evokes God's blessing of Isaac, where God reviews the unique relationship with Abraham. "Abraham your Father **listened** to My voice and **kept** My mitzvot, My laws, and My Torah." The relationship begun with one man who left home

and family behind has now been consummated by his entire future-family. They have left their birthplace and lifestyle behind in Egypt and have responded, "All Adonai has said we will do."

God has chosen Israel. Israel has chosen God. Now the goal is clear, "a kingdom of priests and a holy nation." In the pattern set by Abram so long ago, the people are ready to walk before God and be the best. The long–Promised Land lies ahead.

TEACHING TOOLS
OBJECTIVES

27.1 Through comparing the statements about the relationship between God and Israel in this Torah portion to statements about the relationship of God to Abraham, Isaac and Jacob, the learner will discover that Israel's national relationship to God both evolves from the patriarchal and adds new dimensions.

27.2 The learner will look at the Ten Commandments as a whole to discover these patterns: the division between God–oriented commandments and

CHAPTER 27— THE TEN COMMANDMENTS
The Ten Commandment Pattern

The Ten Commandments were carved on two tablets, five commandments on each tablet. There is a pattern to the commandments. The first five commandments are **between God and people.** The next five commandments are about the way that people should live together.

The fifth commandment looks like it is about relationships between people. Can you figure out how it is on the **between people and God** side?

God is a partner in conception of a child.

Parents are representatives of God in child rearing.

There is also a match between the first five commandments and the second five commandments. Look at this chart.

person-oriented commandments and the parallel between the first five commandments and the second five.

SLIDE-IN VOCABULARY

Adultery—a married person "cheating" on that relationship

HEBREW VOCABULARY

Esser—ten
asseret ha'dibrot—ten commandments (sayings)

ACTIVITIES—THE TEN COMMANDMENTS' PATTERN
Student Commentary, pages 60–61

The Ten Commandments are constructed around a parallel pattern very much like the first story of Creation. The first five represent God–people commandments, the second five people–people commandments. Commandments 1–5 match commandments 6–10 (linearly, not reflexively). The hardest part of this model is seeing

---

Being Torah Student Commentary page 61

Between God and People	Between People	Reason
I am Adonai your God who brought you out of the land of Egypt, out of slavery.	Do not murder.	People are created in God's image. Murdering a person is like destroying God's image.
You will not have any other gods before me. You will not make any idols. Do not bow down to idols or serve them.	Do not commit adultery.	Adultery is when you have an agreement to have a special partnership and you cheat.
Do not use the name of Adonai your God when making a false promise.	Do not steal.	God's name stands for a set of rules that we live by. When you lie and swear by God that what you say is true, you are stealing God's name.
Remember the Shabbat. Make it holy. You may labor for six days and do all your work, but the seventh day is Shabbat.	Do not lie about your neighbor in an oath.	The Torah says that the Shabbat is a witness to the fact that God created the world and took the Jews out of Egypt. When you don't keep Shabbat you are being a poor witness to God's miracles.
Honor your father and you mother.	Do not wish to take over your neighbor's house or anything that belongs to your neighbor.	When you reject your parents and dishonor them, you are saying that your home is not good enough and you want a better one.

My Comment: From the way that the _____'s Comment:
commandments were written on the two _____ that you can learn
tablets I think you can learn that _____ _____
they are related to each other. _____
_____. _____.

61

---

commandment 5 (honoring parents) as being on the God side. The tradition explains that it is because parents are God's partners and local representatives.

1. **SET INDUCTION**: EXPLAIN "Through this exercise you are going to get to 'x-ray' the Ten Commandments and see their hidden structure. The first thing you need to know is that they are made up of two sets of five commandments. The first five are between God and people; the second five are between people and people." EXPAND and EXPLAIN as necessary. For those who want hands-on versions of this process, *Bible People Books Two* (A R E) contains a card game that does this wonderfully.

2. **READING THE TEXT**: Use your discretion and read your way through this text. Take time to explain each of the commandments.

3. **MAKING MEANING**: ALLOW time to complete the exercise. GO OVER answers.

CHAPTER 28— ALMOST THE PROMISED LAND

Being Torah, pages 181–182

Student Commentary, pages 62–63

ABSTRACT—AN ENDING

Find the **ECHO**s that connect the last chapter in the Torah with the first promise made to Abraham. ANSWER: The promises made to Abraham, Isaac and Jacob are recalled. Also, the relationship that began with the promise of "seeing the land" culminates in "seeing the land."

DRAW A CONCLUSION: God keeps promises.

OVERVIEW

The Torah ends with a eulogy for Moses, a eulogy that takes us both back to the conception of the Jewish people and forward in the fulfillment of the two-part promise.

Back in Chapter 5, God first called to Abram. The word **land** was used seven times, a two-part promise was made and there was talk of vision. Much time has passed. Isaac, Jacob and Joseph expanded that relationship. Four hundred years of suffering in Egypt resulted in an Exodus with great wealth. The visions of the future experiences by Abraham at the covenant between the pieces (chapter 9) and Moses at the Burning Bush (chapter 26) have both been actualized. We stand on the edge of fulfilling the two-part promise. Already a great and numerous nation, Israel awaits the long-promised land.

As had been done with Abram, God shows Moses the land. The promise (now only the one remaining part) is restated, and the word **land** is used seven times. The circle is closing. There is even an echo of **seeing**. Moses, the LORD's servant (echoes of the Egypt experience), who knew Adonai face to face (echoes of Jacob), dies, The long-awaited goals will be fulfilled.

Joshua, son of Nun, is filled with the same spirit that hovered over the deep as the Torah began. All is well. The story is made for a sequel.

Being Torah Student Commentary page 62

CHAPTER 28: ALMOST THE PROMISED LAND
An Ending

Theme-Word
Around what **word** is this passage organized? _____ *land* _____

My Comment: The Torah ends with the death of Moses, but it points us toward *the land of Israel, the future of B'nai Yisrael—the Jewish people* _____ .

_____'s Comment: _____ thinks the Torah points us toward _____ .

62

TEACHING TOOLS

OBJECTIVES

The learner will compare the text of this portion with the beginning of the Jewish people, Abraham, to find the connection (the word land appearing seven times in each) and the use of "vision."

Through writing a diary of Moses, the learner will explore the mixed feelings of Moses the leader, whose personal mission is complete, yet he knows that the task is not over.

HEBREW VOCABULARY

Navi—prophet

ACTIVITIES—AN ENDING
Student Commentary, page 62

The Torah has come full circle. We end as the Jewish people first began, with visions of the Land that has been long promised. The story is not over, but the two-part promise has been realized. God has remembered. God has been with us. We are now God's keepers.

2. **READING THE TEXT**: The reading of this portion can be divided into two parts: p. 206 and p. 207. The teacher should do the first reading of the first part of the text in order to avoid the problems of the many names, some of which are unfamiliar to the students. A large-scale map of Eretz Israel is a helpful aid here. STUDENTS should be asked to read the words in **bold** but should be directed to do so quietly. A quiet, reflective tone should be set for this text.

The second part of the text, p. 207, sets a different tone and should also be read at first by the teacher. This is a eulogy as well as a last testament, a summing up and a promise of a new beginning all rolled into a very brief text. After reading this portion, allow the students time to ask questions and formulate answers about the text.

3. **FINDING THE CLUES**: ESTABLISH the seven-fold use of **land** as a **THEME WORD**. MAKE the CONNECTION to Chapter 7, the first story of Abram's call (the beginning of the Jewish

people), where land is also a **THEME WORD** used seven times. POINT out that "seeing" is also important in each story.

FOLLOW our standard process. ALLOW LEARNING TEAMS to work through the exercise. Then **NETWORK THE COMMENTS**.

MOSES' DIARY
Student Commentary, page 63

*This exercise is like many of the **Being Torah** pieces. It draws together pieces of the entire Torah experience in a personal form. Enjoy!*

Being Torah Student Commentary page 63

Moses' Diary

Today a family dream is finally ready to come true. I will not live to see it happen, but I can stand here *and look over the land*

As I stand here, I have mixed feelings. *I am happy that we finally reach Eretz Yisrael, but sad that I will not be able to enter it.*

Thinking back on my life, *I am proud that I was part of this important moment in our life. Freeing my people from Egypt, leading them though the wilderness, helping my people reach their new homeland*

My one big hope is that *B'nai Yisrael will continue to live by God's commandments, striving to be better people.*

Being Torah Student Commentary page 63   63

THEME-WORD

In every Torah story there are one or two ideas that are most important. The central idea in a story is called the "theme." The Torah has different ways of showing us a story's theme. One way it does this is by using a **THEME-WORD**. This is a key word that is used over and over again. Another way of doing this is by using a **THEME-WORD** at the beginning and ending of a story.

NUMBER-WORD

One special kind of **THEME-WORD** is a **NUMBER-WORD**. Sometimes the Torah uses a word a special number of times in a story. Often we find a word used **5**, **7**, **10**, or **12** times. Each of these numbers has a Jewish meaning. When we find a word used one of these numbers of times we know that the Torah wants us to see that this word teaches something important.

TEXT
REPETITION

When the Torah REPEATS a piece of text, it usually does it with a change. When the Torah says something twice, the second time we see the message there is usually a change. Something is either added or taken away. When we find the change we have a clue to the meaning the Torah is trying to teach us.

ECHOES

Another way the Torah points out lessons it wants us to learn is by making connections between two stories by using the same words in both stories. When we hear words that remind us of the words in an earlier story, we are hearing an **ECHO** of the first story in the second.

MISSING INFORMATION

Sometimes reading the Torah is like watching a television show where you leave for a while and have to figure out what you missed. Often there are "holes" or **MISSING INFORMATION** in the story. When we find that a story has **MISSING INFORMATION** we have to use the information in the Torah to try to figure out what happened in the part of the story we weren't told.